Tough Choices

PORTFOLIO

Tough Choices

| A MEMOIR |

Carly Fiorina

PORTFOLIO
Published by the Penguin Group

Penguin Group (USA) Inc., 375 Hudson Street, New York, New York 10014, U.S.A. • Penguin Group (Canada), 90 Eglinton Avenue East, Suite 700, Toronto, Ontario, Canada M4P 2Y3 (a division of Pearson Penguin Canada Inc.) • Penguin Books Ltd, 80 Strand, London WC2R 0RL, England • Penguin Ireland, 25 St. Stephen's Green, Dublin 2, Ireland (a division of Penguin Books Ltd) • Penguin Books Australia Ltd, 250 Camberwell Road, Camberwell, Victoria 3124, Australia (a division of Pearson Australia Group Pty Ltd) • Penguin Books India Pvt Ltd, 11 Community Centre, Panchsheel Park, New Delhi – 110 017, India • Penguin Group (NZ), Cnr Airborne and Rosedale Roads, Albany, Auckland 1310, New Zealand (a division of Pearson New Zealand Ltd) • Penguin Books (South Africa) (Pty) Ltd, 24 Sturdee Avenue, Rosebank, Johannesburg 2196, South Africa

Penguin Books Ltd, Registered Offices: 80 Strand, London WC2R 0RL, England

First published in 2006 by Portfolio, a member of Penguin Group (USA) Inc.

1   3   5   7   9   10   8   6   4   2

Copyright © Carly Fiorina, 2006
All rights reserved

Photograph credits: Insert page 7 (top) : Getty Images; (middle) : Corbis Corporation

LIBRARY OF CONGRESS CATALOGING IN PUBLICATION DATA
Fiorina, Carly.
Tough choices : a memoir / Carly Fiorina.
p. cm.
Includes index.
ISBN 1-59184-133-X
1. Fiorina, Carly.   2. Women executives—United States—Biography.   I. Title.
HD6054.4.U6F56 2006
338.7'61004165092—dc22
[B]   2006048336

Printed in the United States of America
Set in Fairfield • Designed by Kate Nichols

Without limiting the rights under copyright reserved above, no part of this publication may be reproduced, stored in or introduced into a retrieval system, or transmitted, in any form or by any means (electronic, mechanical, photocopying, recording, or otherwise), without the prior written permission of both the copyright owner and the above publisher of this book.

The scanning, uploading, and distribution of this book via the Internet or via any other means without the permission of the publisher is illegal and punishable by law. Please purchase only authorized electronic editions and do not participate in or encourage electronic piracy of copyrightable materials. Your support of the author's rights is appreciated.

For Frank,

a very special man who changed my life

Acknowledgments

WRITING A BOOK involves tough choices as well. One of the toughest is what, and whom, to leave out. As I thought about this book, and wrote this book, people and places and events flooded my memory. Many hours could pass in the company of these reflections and I would silently thank again the countless people who have made a difference in my life. I truly wish I could have named everyone, but a book is not a diary.

For those who are disappointed by their exclusion, I beg forgiveness and hope they take some small comfort in my struggles to edit and reedit—careful to preserve the authenticity of the memoir, while recognizing that not everything is of relevance to the reader, even when it matters deeply to the author.

I was not sure I wanted to write this book at all. So now, I want to thank those who believed in it from the beginning, who encouraged me to keep going, and who were blunt when necessary. Frank read and reread every word. My sister, Clara Sneed, the real writer in the family, offered sound advice early on in the process and read the second draft with a critical eye. My sisters-in-law, Claudia Beyer and Ursula Feldman, provided unwavering support. And Deborah Bowker, Rollins Emerson, Kathy Fitzgerald, Barbara Marcin, Dan Plunkett, Carole Spurrier and Richard Ullman all gave their time, their care and their candor to me and to this book. Finally, and especially, Adrian Zackheim has my deepest gratitude and appreciation.

Contents

Prologue

I N THE END, the Board did not have the courage to face me. They did not thank me and they did not say good-bye. They did not explain their decision or their reasoning. They did not seek my opinion or my involvement in any aspect of the transition. Having asked me to come to Chicago for a meeting, they left me waiting in my hotel room for more than three hours. As I waited, I knew whatever came next would be a turning point. After I finally received the call to rejoin the meeting, I thought about each Board member as I rode the elevator down past those twenty-four floors. I didn't know what to expect, but I assumed I would be facing them. I wasn't prepared for the empty conference room I entered. Only the two designated messengers and a lawyer remained in the room. The chair of the Nominating and Governance Committee said, "Carly, the Board has decided to make a change at the top. I'm very sorry." I knew he had opposed my ouster. And then the new chairman said they wanted my help in "positioning" the news. She said they thought I should describe this as my decision: I should say I thought it was "time to move on." I asked when they wanted to make the announcement. "Right away." The meeting lasted less than three minutes. I asked for a few hours to think and I left the room.

I believe the truth is always the best answer, whatever the consequences. Less than two hours later I sent a message to the new chairman
saying we should tell the truth: the Board had fired me. When the announcement was made, I simply said, "While I regret that the Board and I
had differences over the execution of the strategy, I respect their decision.
HP is a great company and I wish the people of HP all the best."

I had always known I might lose my job. I was playing a high-stakes
game with poweful people and powerful interests, but I had not expected
the end to come in this way. I knew we were on the verge of reaping tremendous benefits from all our hard work, and I thought the Board knew this too.
I wanted so much to be able to gather my team one last time and tell them
how proud I was of all we had accomplished together. My heart ached that I
was not give an opportunity to say good-bye to the people of HP, whom I had
grown to love.

I knew the announcement would be big news. I was a woman, and a
bold one at that, and things had always been different for me. All the criti-
cisms that had ever been leveled against me would be recycled and thrown
back in my face with new delight: "She's too flashy." "She's just marketing
fluff." "She's too controlling." "She's a publicity hound." "The merger was her
idea and it was the wrong thing to do." "She's imperious, vindictive and employees didn't like her." The coverage would go on and on, and the critiques
would not be balanced against the facts or my contributions or the positive
changes that had been made. It would be ugly and it would be personal.

I knew all this as I steeled myself for the public announcement on February 9, 2005. The reality of the coverage was even worse than I had imagined. It hurt me, but it hurt my family and friends more. I felt lonely, but no
lonelier than I'd felt for the past six years. I was deeply sad that fellow Board
members I had known and trusted would not pay me the simple respect of
looking me in the eye and telling me the truth. I felt betrayed when I considered that some Board members, having spoken outside the boardroom, had
broken their duty of confidence to one another and to me.

I felt all these things, but after a lifetime of fears I was not afraid. I had
done what I thought was right. I had given everything I had to something I
believed in. I had made mistakes, but I had made a difference. I was at
peace with my choices and their consequences. My soul was still my own.

Tough Choices

1 | A Gift from My Parents

HOW A STORY ENDS has much to do with how it begins, and so I must begin with my mother and father. My mother, Madelon Montross Juergens, was the only child of a Ford Motors assembly-line worker and a lovely woman of French descent named Clara Hall. They lived in Rossford, Ohio, a town where many European immigrants gathered. Clara Hall died of stomach cancer when my mother was only ten.

It was, according to my mother, an agonizing death and was surely a profound trauma for a young girl. Her memories were of a beautiful, loving, refined woman of imagination who spoke often of France and wanted a cultured life for her daughter. Her father had other ideas. He was a stubborn, taciturn, deeply practical man who quickly remarried. Her new stepmother, whose name my mother never shared with me, was neither affectionate nor concerned about my mother, whose childhood became unhappy and lonely. When she became a parent herself, she refused to talk about it in any way, other than to praise her mother. It seems her life began only after she ran away from home.

She did so because she wanted to go to college. She had been her high school's valedictorian, and so her guidance counselor told her father that his daughter was the one student in school who absolutely should go to college and offered to help him obtain financial assistance. Her parents quickly concluded that this was a frivolous use of money and not worth the effort. Neither of them had gone to college, and besides, she was a girl. So they decided she should stay in Rossford and work until she got married.

My mother had different plans, and she left town on a bus one night without saying good-bye. At eighteen she joined the Women's Army Corps, the WACs, as they were called during World War II, ending up at Shepherd Field, an air base in Texas. She quickly proved herself and became the secretary to the commanding officer, which was a very prestigious position. It was there that she met my father.

Eventually, when she was well into her sixties, my mother would earn both a bachelor's and a master's degree in art history. She would also take up her painting virtually full-time, ultimately completing hundreds of canvases brimming with color, energy and life. Today my home is filled with them.

My father, Joseph Tyree, was born in a tiny Texas town called Calvert. His father, Marvin Sneed, a well-respected rancher and landowner, died of congestive heart failure when my father was barely twelve years old. Mr. Sneed seems to have been an outgoing adventurer, taking the family on cross-country road trips in a Model T Ford, way back in the 1920s. His death created real financial difficulties for his family. And as devastating as the loss of his father must have been, less than nine months later, in September, my father's elder brother, Marvin, died of a virulent infection caused by a botched tooth extraction. Marvin had been athletic, charming and good-looking, and clearly his mother's favorite. My grandmother wore only black for the rest of her life and went into mourning for the entire month of September each year until her own death at eighty-four.

The burden of being the only man in the family rested very heavily on a young boy's shoulders. In contrast to his brother, my father was a small, sickly child, born with severely reduced lung capacity and one missing vertebra. His mother consulted many specialists about these physical difficulties (my father has called them "deformities" all his life). Ultimately the doctors told her that he should avoid physical exertion and that he should never play football. But football was the rite of passage for all young men in Texas, and my father was determined to measure up. And so almost by sheer force of will, he became a winning player on his high school team. His ferocity on the field was legendary and made up for his lack of physical gifts.

My father knew, however, that his future lay in the use of his mind. He knew as well that he had to escape Calvert. And so he went on to college and eventually enrolled in law school, but he jumped at the chance to join the Army Air Force during World War II. Because of his physical impairment he could not fight; he ended up at Shepherd Field.

Both my parents grew up feeling they had something to prove and something to escape. They were strong, self-reliant and deeply insecure all at the same time. They were determined to build a better life for themselves and their children. For both of them, a better life was to be found in education and hard work. They believed hard work, discipline and willpower were essential ingredients of a worthy life and an admirable character. My father wanted his children to be educated in a classical way—history, literature, Latin. He was a man of letters—he had become a professor of law—and his children should be the same. My mother wanted everything for her children that she remembered her mother talking about, and so I was taking French lessons at four, going to the opera at seven, visiting museums and taking classical piano. She wanted her children, son and daughters alike, to be cultured, refined, successful. If my father judged his success by his own career, my mother judged her success by her children.

Perhaps because I knew the stories of their childhoods, I grew up afraid that I would lose my parents. It was almost an obsession. Nothing could be more terrible than this. The death of a mother or father was like falling into an abyss. I would dream of just such a fall often—I suffered from violent nightmares and a vivid imagination from the time I was a young child until I was well into college. Several times a week I would wake out of fear and go stand silently by my parents' bed. I would stare at my mother, making sure she was breathing, willing her to wake up. When other children would delight in slumber parties with their friends, I would never go in case something terrible happened to my family while I was gone. When I finally went to my first pajama party as a teenager, I lay awake all night picturing our house in the dark and wondering if my mother and father were safe. I could imagine all sorts of tragedies that might befall them. When my parents would go out for the evening, I would stay wide awake until they returned safely home. I would say the Lord's Prayer, over and over like a chant, to calm myself. And it became almost a joke in our family that when my parents had to travel out of town, I would always fall ill just before they left. Psychologically, it seems, I was hoping to shame them into canceling their trip.

We were a modest, middle-class family. My mother was a full-time mother and homemaker, my father an academic, and there were three children to raise. Success was not, to my parents, about fame and fortune. It was ultimately about the quality of one's mind and one's character. There was never any question about whether we would go to college or graduate school. It was assumed. Character was everything, and character was defined as candor, integrity and authenticity. Candor was about speaking the truth, and about speaking up and speaking out. Integrity was about preserving your principles and acting on them. Authenticity was about knowing what you believed, being who you were, and standing up for both. For my parents, success was measured on the inside, not judged from the outside. From a very early age, I clearly understood that my mother and father would not compromise on their expectations of my mind or my character.

My parents were rigorous, disciplined, demanding and judgmental. Always they would focus on what I could do and what I should do. The fact that I was a girl made no difference to their level of expectation, and while this seemed entirely natural at the time, it was only later in life that I realized how rare this was, particularly in the 1950s and 1960s.

My sister, the eldest, was the child my parents thought they would never have. They waited eight years for a child, and when Clara Hall (named for my mother's beloved, deceased mother) was finally born in 1952, they were sure she was the last. My father always remarked on Clara's beauty and her physical resemblance to his side of the family. He loved that she was an avid reader of great books. My mother rejoiced in her creativity and artistic nature. She wasn't a painter like our mother, but she was a gifted writer from a very young age. At age eight she wrote her first award-winning poem, and she's been writing ever since. My mother said Clara had an artistic temperament to go along with her talent. She was tempestuous and frequently defiant. Perhaps because mother and daughter shared a creative passion and a willful nature, they also clashed on many issues for many years.

My brother, the youngest, was the only son, born after my mother had suffered a painful miscarriage. Named after my father, Joseph Tyree IV was tall, strong and athletic. My father was proud that his son excelled at every sport he tried. He was creative as well, becoming his elementary school's cartoonist and drawing elaborate cartoon strips every week of a fanciful world filled with "coot birds," which he published for his class. They were funny and smart, and my mother loved them. But Joseph didn't much like schoolwork, and as he grew into his teenage years, the tension between father and son became a fixture of our family life.

I was the middle child, named after my father's mother, Cara Carleton. I didn't feel particularly smart or creative in any way. One Sunday at church I received a small coaster that read "What you are is God's gift to you. What you make of yourself is your gift to God." I decided early on that my gift to God would be to please my parents. I idealized and idolized them.

To please my father, I studied hard and always got good grades. To please my mother I became the family diplomat—always intervening in every family argument, listening to every side, empathizing with everyone and trying to find a way to bridge the gaps. To please them both, I was obedient, diligent, cheerful and reliable. There were many times when I felt as though no matter what I did, it simply wasn't quite as much as they expected. To my siblings I was probably an insufferable goody two-shoes most of the time.

Both my parents pursued excellence in everything they did. My father was a gifted teacher and a true intellectual. Learning was not simply a way to make a living—learning was a goal in and of itself. My mother was a unique and talented artist, but she largely put her painting aside to raise her children, and invested all her energies in them. My parents' expectations were high and sometimes felt like a heavy burden. I grew up afraid of losing them and afraid of disappointing them.

My mother wanted each of her children to study an instrument, and so I studied the piano. Although I started because it was expected of me, I soon found that learning the music and perfecting my playing could completely absorb me. I would practice for hours on end. I enjoyed the rigor and the attention to detail that was required, but I also came to find in music something beautiful that spoke to my own fears, self-doubts and nightmares. Many years later, someone asked me who my favorite composer was. Without hesitation, I said "Beethoven," because whenever I was troubled, I would choose his music. "Why not Mozart?" I was asked. I had to think. It was a good question. Mozart's music was angelic and otherworldly in its beauty. I could imagine divine inspiration, but I couldn't hear human struggle. I could hear angst and fear in Beethoven. His music was sublime, and ultimately triumphant in its suffering and humanity.

My parents were not sympathetic to fear, insecurity or self-doubt. Perhaps it was because they had so much of their own. They were stoic and expected me to be the same. And so I never told them about my own fears or insecurities. I told them only of the things that would please them. I remember moving, for the fifth time since I had entered high school, to a new school as a senior. I missed my friends, who were all in California, and North Carolina seemed like another world. The senior class at Charles E. Jordan High School in Durham was tightly bonded and formed into various cliques as all senior classes are. It was hard breaking in, and I cried a lot. My parents did not seem to understand just how difficult this move was, but their expectations were clear: neither my piano study nor my grades were to suffer. When I came home with my first report card, which contained one B and seven As, they reminded me that I was capable of straight As. The next semester I got them.

We moved a lot because my father was working his way up the academic ladder. He taught at the University of Texas, Cornell, Yale, Stanford and Duke and took sabbaticals at the London School of Economics and the University of Ghana in Accra, West Africa. (Eventually he would become a federal judge on the United States Court of Appeals for the Ninth Circuit.) I went to elementary school in New York, Connecticut and California; to junior high in California and England; and to high school in Africa, California and North Carolina. In the course of all this moving around, I learned a lot about people and a lot about change.

I was perpetually the new kid in class, and as the new kid, I wanted desperately to fit in, to be liked, to make friends. Over the years I had watched my mother at her many famous parties (she threw great theme parties). She always asked her guests questions and was always interested in the answers. And so I did this too. (Friends from those early years recall me almost backing them into corners to "interview" them.) It turns out that people, whether they're children or adults, like to be asked about themselves. They're flattered by the attention that's paid to them, and they feel good when someone listens. I made friends quickly this way and also learned a lot about wherever I was. Much later, as I moved from job to job, I discovered that this is a great management tool as well. You not only pay others respect by asking to learn from them, but you get smart fast by listening.

I was always encountering adventures. In England, I went to an all-girls school in London. The whole experience seemed almost like a movie to me, with our uniforms, and our headmistress and our all-girls version of *Romeo and Juliet*. I was given the part of Juliet, which I played with a distinctly improper British accent. Even the name of the school seemed right out of a novel: the Channing School for Select Young Ladies. I loved that time. My newfound friends seemed high-spirited and daring. We spent so much of our time trying to break the school's rules that we didn't have any time to get into serious trouble. I learned how to roll up my skirt above regulation length and how to tear down the back staircase of school so no one would know we had been hiding in the classroom when we were supposed to be outside for break. It was all harmless and silly, but we had the excitement of being bad.

In Africa I experienced being the only white person in a room, and reflected on how the few blacks I knew back home must feel. I felt both anxiety and sympathy when children would surround us and beg for money each time we went to the city markets. I remember hearing, for the first time, Muslims pray, and how over time their sound evolved from being frightening in its strangeness to comforting in its cadence and repetition—I would feel the same peace when I listened to the sound of summer cicadas around my grandmother's house. I grew to love being awakened in the morning by the sound of the devout man who always came to pray under my bedroom window. I learned to play *owari*, a West African board game played with seed-pods, with a ten-year-old boy from a nearby village. He was bright and funny, and somehow, over this game, we bridged a world of difference.

My father was teaching the new Ghanaian constitution to law students. Ghana in 1969 was experimenting with democracy after the overthrow of Kwame Nkrumah. I listened to great debates at our dinner table when my father's Ghanaian students would visit. I saw how difficult building a nation was when smaller but more powerful tribal loyalties conflicted with the larger but more abstract idea of a nation. Much later, at HP, I would recall this experience and coin the phrase "a thousand tribes" to describe the intense turf battles waged between executives and their divisions at the expense of the company.

In North Carolina I understood for the first time what football meant to high school life in some parts of the country and the pressure my father must have felt. I taught remedial reading to several of the football players. They were about to graduate from high school, were stars on the football team, but they literally couldn't read. It was heartbreaking and frightening to witness their frustration, but together we were able to make progress. I also began teaching severely retarded children as a volunteer. I still remember one of my favorites: a boy named Kenneth. He was five, and it took me six weeks to teach him to identify and say "eye" and "ear." We were both triumphant when he finally got it—almost—and from then on, every morning when he would see me, he'd shout across the playground, "Eye! Eee!" When I came home from college on Christmas break, I went to visit him, and he remembered still. He could not say his name, but he still shouted, "Eye! Eee!" It was the first time I felt that joy and exhilaration that comes from helping someone achieve something they believed they couldn't.

Over time I learned to recognize the pattern of change and became familiar with that churning, nervous feeling that was both fear of the unknown and the excitement of something new. And whenever I met new people, I could get past the fear and move on to the excitement. I discovered that there were sometimes vast differences between people and cultures, but I also learned that those differences could usually be bridged by showing respect and developing empathy.

I wrote long entries in my diaries and long letters to the friends I made along the way. When I read those diary entries today, they are filled with facts, observations and feelings. I'm struck by what I said in writing as compared to what I could say in conversation. Later, when I went to college, I would write my mother and father voluminous letters. I said to them in those pages what I could not say face-to-face.

And now, writing about my childhood, I can say that I experienced first-hand the power of high expectations: had less been demanded, less would have been achieved. I saw my parents' fears and feelings of inadequacy propel them forward, and their example persuaded me never to allow my own fears and insecurities to stop me in my tracks. I learned that change can be both difficult and exciting: with each separation and loss came a great adventure. I discovered the impact of asking a question and listening to the answer, because people everywhere have something to teach and are eager to share. And I realized how truly fortunate I was.

My favorite memories of my mother during my childhood are from when she would wash my hair. I had very long hair, and she would wash it in the kitchen sink and then comb it out and rebraid it in front of her dresser. These were ordinary, everyday times, but our conversations were intimate— sometimes serious and sometimes funny. We were all alone together. When my hair was finally finished, she'd put me to bed and stroke my forehead with her hand. Sometimes she would sing to me. I can hear her voice and feel the touch of her hand to this day.

My favorite time with my father was when we drove across country together. We were moving again, and it was just the two of us and the dog, and a lot of boxes. We had grown-up conversations, and it felt as if we understood each other in a grown-up sort of way. He let me drive the car and took me to a restaurant every night. Today my father's memory is dimming, but he still remembers that road trip.

Later in their lives I realized how much character my parents really had. They were not perfect people, but they were truly honest and authentic. They believed in self-determination.

I did not feel gifted as a child. I know now that my parents were the most precious gift I had.

2 | The Stranger

WHEN IT CAME TIME TO GO TO COLLEGE, I chose Stanford University. California was far enough away from North Carolina (I was clear I wanted to move away for college), and yet it was also familiar, given that I'd spent time as a child in the area. I had no notion of going to college to earn a living. Because I had always assumed I'd go to graduate school, I thought of college as a time for pure learning. My parents encouraged this approach, and so I had the wonderful experience of studying the subjects that truly interested me. I took classes in chemistry, biology, physics, economics, anthropology, astronomy, music. This smorgasbord of newfound knowledge was both exhilarating and intimidating. I wrote a letter home and exulted in the fact that I had suddenly realized how little I actually knew. I also realized I loved to learn. And history and philosophy truly captured my passion.

When I was choosing my very first semester of courses as a freshman, I remembered a book I'd read in high school French class. My teacher had asked the class to read a work of fiction by a French author in the original language. I don't quite remember why I was attracted to *L'étranger*, by Albert Camus. Perhaps, given that I'd just moved again, I identified with the title:

The Stranger. Certainly it was an ambitious choice—the philosophy of existentialism was tough enough in English. I found it difficult, absorbing and rewarding work. I'm not sure how much of it I actually grasped, but the book was a revelation to me. It was about a big idea and how an idea, a philosophy, can motivate action. It was a story of a man who chose to live his life based on that idea. The power and importance of choice, the act of becoming rather than the stasis of being—these were to me profound ideas with personal meaning: ". . . what you make of yourself is your gift to God." If we cannot choose our circumstances, we can always choose our response to them. If we cannot choose who we are, we can always choose to become something more. To stop choosing is to start dying.

I decided to take as many philosophy courses as I could. Ultimately I would study philosophers from the ancient Greeks to the modern age. The power of ideas to fundamentally change how people see the world; the impact of ideas from one century on the people and ideas of many centuries later; the fact that the human race, not just individual human beings, can learn—all this was exciting.

Hegel had as profound an effect on me as Camus. The philosophy of thesis, antithesis, synthesis, the possibility of reconciliation between two seemingly opposing ideas, seemed both brilliant and practical to me. Later in life I would use this mental model over and over in business. In fact, many years later when a reporter asked me who my favorite business author was, I responded, "Hegel. You know: thesis, antithesis, synthesis. At Lucent we were trying to turn a one-hundred-year-old company into a start-up. At HP, we're trying to both celebrate our history and create the future."

I studied ethics and learned that questions of right and wrong could be nuanced and complex, requiring rigor to unravel. I would remember these courses when we were wrestling with the dilemma of ownership of our customers' information at HP. How we chose to use that information was a business opportunity, but it was also an ethics question. Ultimately we decided to forgo the business opportunity that might come from selling customer information because of the ethical considerations involved; our customers owned their information and it was our responsibility to protect it, not sell it. I studied logic and discovered that disciplined thought processes and well-structured questions are as powerful as the answers. In many ways this recognition gave me the courage to move into a number of different jobs and industries. And whenever I encouraged an employee to move out of the comfort zone of their experience into a new job for a development opportunity, I advised them: "Never underestimate the power of logic."

I decided to keep studying languages in order to read works of philosophy as originally written, so I studied ancient Greek—to read Plato and Aristotle—as well as Latin, French and German. (I took Italian classes, but that was just for the fun of it.) Because my father loved history, I studied that too. I found I liked it because it was about people, and mostly it was the story of people who chose to make things different. I learned that although history is frequently made by rich and powerful people, it's just as often made by ordinary people who, inspired by the idea of something different, choose a new course.

Among the most valuable classes I took was a graduate seminar called Christian, Islamic and Jewish Political Philosophies of the Middle Ages. Each week we had to read one of the great works of medieval philosophy: Aquinas, Bacon, Abelard. These were huge texts—sometimes we were reading a thousand pages a week. And by the end of the week we had to have distilled their philosophical discourse into two pages.

For me the process would begin with writing twenty pages. Then I'd edit to ten, then five and finally two. I finally would get to a two-page, single-spaced paper that I hoped didn't merely summarize, but rendered all the fat out of a body of ideas, boiling it down to the very essence of its meaning. Two pages were not an easy, superficial abstraction of a work; they were the distillation of all the details of a work. Certainly the philosophies and ideologies left a deep impression on me, but the rigor of the distillation process itself, the exercise of mental refinement, the ability to say clearly in two pages what previously had been said in twenty—all were important new skills. Invariably I learned that I understood the text much better when I finished this process than when I'd begun. Without knowing it at the time, I was developing an important management tool: how to understand and get from a seemingly overwhelming amount of information to the heart of the matter. And I was learning a leadership lesson: understanding and communicating the essence of things is difficult, takes a lot of thought, and has a big impact.

From the time I started learning French at four, until I took my last college course at twenty-two, I was exposed to all kinds of knowledge: important analytic skills like math and science, food for the soul in art and music, enrichment of the spirit in literature and philosophy. I was given the opportunity to educate my character as well as my intellect. I saw a bigger world that changed and broadened my perspective, and I know it has made all the difference. And so many years later, in 1989, I wrote a master's thesis at MIT entitled "The Education Crisis: Business and Government's Role in Reform." I argued that our education system is failing our nation: we are falling behind in teaching competitive skills and increasingly ignoring those subjects that are fundamental to character. The education crisis has deepened since 1989 across every dimension, but still, as a nation, we have not yet harnessed the collective will or sense of urgency to address it. Our competitiveness as a nation requires us to understand the bigger world, and prepare our children's hearts and minds to lead.

As freshman year turned to junior and senior years, the pressure to decide what to do with my life began to build. The truth is I didn't have a clue. I had spent my life until then trying to please my parents and get good grades. The success criteria for both were clear, but beyond that I had never had particular goals or obvious direction. I was interested in a multitude of things, and at one time or another I had wanted to become everything from a firefighter to a dancer. My parents had always encouraged each ambition. Anything was possible for me, but whatever I chose had to be something that I would do with excellence, dedication and discipline. Both my mother and father had taken great risks in their own lives and were not afraid for me to do the same. All they insisted upon was that I be fully engaged in a pursuit worthy of my talent and passion.

I couldn't paint like my mother. I could play the piano, though, and so I imagined that I could be a professional musician—that was as close as I could come to emulating my mother. Over time I learned that although I loved the music, I could not live with the isolation that came along with it. And who knows whether I really had the talent anyway?

My father fervently loved both the law and the classroom. And so it was entirely predictable that eventually I would decide to go to law school. If I could not follow in my mother's footsteps, I would follow in my father's. I don't think I used any imagination at all in coming to this decision. I never even really considered the alternatives. The decision would satisfy my mother and please my father immensely.

My time at Stanford wasn't particulary happy; my college years were serious ones. I was afraid I couldn't measure up because everyone seemed so much smarter. I carried a huge course load, wrote an honors thesis on medieval judicial systems and trial by ordeal, and worked three days a week to earn the money to pay for room and board. I contracted a very bad case of mononucleosis and struggled with bad health for a year. I don't remember having a lot of fun; I do remember working all the time.

The day I graduated I was afraid. I was scared to leave the protective bubble of the university, afraid of the choice I was making, afraid of squandering the incredible gift of my Stanford experience. I was afraid of making irrevocable mistakes. If I could talk to that young woman today, I'd tell her to lighten up, but at the time it all seemed like such serious business to me.

I went to UCLA Law School without enthusiasm, and from the very first day it left me cold. I found the focus on precedent confining. What about creating something new? The decisions that were hailed as brilliant frequently had, to my way of thinking, nothing to do with justice and everything to do with legal constraints predetermined by other case law. Although I could respect the law, I felt no passion for it. I had terrible headaches every day and barely slept for months. When my father came to visit, I told him I hated it. He was concerned, but he didn't want me to quit. Quitting was failure—you stuck it out, even in a tough situation. And so, although I had planned to tell him I'd decided to leave law school, I didn't. I went back and stuck it out for another month.

I came home one weekend to visit. I was in turmoil. As dramatic as it sounds, it really is the case that I had an epiphany while taking a shower on Sunday morning. My body had been trying to tell me something with all those months of headaches. I can still picture the exact tile in the shower that I was staring at when I suddenly realized I had no idea why I was in law school at all. At twenty-two, at that moment, it finally dawned on me that my life couldn't be about pleasing my parents. If I was to use all of my capabilities and all of my gifts, if I was to make something of myself, then I had to find something that challenged my mind and captured my heart. My life was my own. I could do what I wanted. My headache disappeared. I got out of the shower and prepared to disappoint my parents.

It was Albert Camus who said, "To be happy, we must not be too concerned with others." Having arrived at what was for me a momentous decision, I felt happy—afraid but happy. I grew up that day. I had made a truly difficult decision on my own. I felt lonely in that choice, afraid of its consequences, but certain that I had chosen well.

3 | Don't Think About the Next Job

THE NEXT SEVERAL HOURS were terrible. My mother said, "This is so out of character for you. I'm very worried." My father said, "I'm very disappointed. I'm not sure you'll ever amount to anything." When they asked me what my plan was, I literally had nothing to tell them. I had to make a living—I had been putting myself through law school and my parents could give me no assistance—but I did not know how.

In 1976 a history and philosophy major wasn't exactly employable unless he or she wanted to go back to school for another degree. In all the time from childhood to the day I dropped out of law school, I had never considered the world of business as a career. My parents had no experience with it, and I don't even remember hearing the term *business* until I was in college. We'd always lived on or around college campuses. We simply didn't know any businesspeople; all my parents' friends were academics or artists or homemakers. If my mother had any opinions about business, they probably had been influenced by her father's, and as an assembly-line worker, his were not positive. My father was an intellectual, and business didn't seem very intellectual to him. At the dinner table every night we had serious conversations and light ones. We talked about art, music, philosophy, history, politics, the weather, our day at school, our friends; but we never talked about companies in our area, or where the products we used came from, or economics.

The closest I had ever been to a businesswoman was on television. My parents were very strict about television. We didn't even own a TV until I was about ten or eleven, and so I had to choose the shows I would watch very carefully. For some reason I loved the world of espionage (my best friend and I used to pretend that we were CIA agents on a regular basis), so *The Man from U.N.C.L.E.* and *Mission: Impossible* were my favorites. On *Mission: Impossible* there was a woman spy. She was in business of some sort, and I thought she was wonderful. Her name was Cinnamon (played by Barbara Bain), and she was elegant and capable. Always cool, she hid neither her intellect nor her beauty. She was a full partner to the men on the team. She was frequently underestimated by the enemy and always got the last laugh. She was, I decided, how I wanted to be when I grew up.

Back in the real world, I never met anyone who was a business owner until I went to work to earn money of my own. During the school terms at Stanford I needed to pay for my room and board, so I worked at DJ's Hair Design—a local salon that's still at the same address—doing their books, answering phones, making appointments. I don't remember thinking particularly about the business aspects of the salon: the revenues, the products, the costs. I was more fascinated by the clients and their behavior and the hairdressers and their challenges. I learned a lot about how some people treat those they perceive as powerless—in this case I was the powerless receptionist who stood between a woman and her hairdresser. I saw both the best and the worst in women. I used a lot of the diplomatic skills I'd learned at home, and picked up some new ones. I loved the hairdressers— the owners, Dan and John, ran a fun, boisterous shop. I met gays for the first time. Those were the days when no one talked about sexual orientation and many monogamous gay couples would go to parties with appropriate female dates. We would have long conversations, and some great laughs, about how painful and funny this could be sometimes. I was fascinated by the people of this business, although I never thought about the profit of it.

During the summer months, when I needed to work full-time, I would sign up with a temporary agency, Kelly Girls (its name has since been changed to Kelly Temporaries). I could always get a job as a secretary, and thanks to junior high school typing lessons, which my mother had insisted upon, I could type very well. I was sent to many companies, including Hewlett-Packard. At the very bottom of the totem pole—a temporary secretary—I didn't get any sense of what a particular business, or business in general, was about. I remember typing a lot, and answering phones, and the other women in similar jobs (there were no men) who were usually kind and frequently frustrated. I remember being coached about the importance of quality in our work. This made sense to me because I had been raised to believe that quality was important in every aspect of work and life, but I don't remember having any sense of why we were typing whatever we typed.

Now, having dropped out of law school with no plan and very little money, my first real introduction to business was searching the want ads. I looked for secretarial and receptionist jobs. I took every interview I could get and accepted the very first job offer. My first apartment was a dive, but it was all I could afford. It was in a questionable part of town, and because I couldn't afford a car, I walked every day to work. I lived next door to a couple who fought continually and the walls were paper thin. All in all, it wasn't a very auspicious beginning to my new independent life. Still, every step felt like a triumph. I was scared, keenly aware of the sound of my parents' concern and disappointment every time we spoke, but exhilarated. I was doing it! I was making my own way into the great unknown world. I was a Grown-up.

Marcus & Millichap was a commercial property brokerage firm. It was, and still is, located one block from the headquarters of Hewlett-Packard in Palo Alto, California. There were two other women who worked at the firm then, one of whom hired me. One was the secretary to Messrs. Marcus and Millichap. She was, as far as I was concerned, the big boss. Her subordinate would be my immediate supervisor. My job was to sit at the front of the offices and greet all visitors, answer the telephones and direct calls, and type whatever I was asked to. I threw myself into the job, frequently arriving early and staying late. I was determined to be good at it. I didn't think about where it would lead, and I didn't think it was beneath me. I was grateful to have a job, interested in learning about what was for me a new world, and eager to prove to my bosses that they hadn't made a mistake.

I liked the people at Marcus & Millichap. I liked the hustle and bustle of the office. I saw how excited the brokers got when they made a sale, how dedicated people were to growing the business. I learned that a simple thing like how I answered the phone could say a lot about how customers viewed the business. I remember a customer coming in and saying he'd decided to do business with us, after talking to a number of other companies, because I was so friendly and helpful when he called. I started to identify with the people of Marcus & Millichap and experienced, for the first time, the feeling of being on a team. My academic studies had been reasonably solitary. I liked this newfound teamwork.

I took pride in my work and went out of my way to volunteer to do things to help out. People started to take a chance on me. I will be forever grateful to brokers like Charlie Colson and Ed Dowd, who saw more than a receptionist. They began to ask me to help them write up proposals, visit and assess property, make cold calls, and participate in strategy sessions about upcoming negotiations. I found I loved the dollars and cents of a deal. It was great fun to figure out how to make the numbers work—for us and for a client. I loved the pragmatic nature of the work. This wasn't academic and it wasn't abstract. You did something and something happened. I loved the pace of it. I always had the feeling of forward momentum.

Most of all, I loved the people of business. I loved working with them; I loved collaborating with them and negotiating with them. I learned for the first time that some people in business are driven by facts and numbers, some are driven by judgment and intuition, and most are driven by both. And some are driven by emotion and ego more than others. I loved the camaraderie of working hard and then winning, or losing, together. I even found the politics of office life interesting, because I was often asked to intervene to help people find common ground.

That receptionist's job at Marcus & Millichap formed the basis of the career advice I have given ever since: don't think about the next job; focus on doing the very best you can with the job you have. Learn everything you can from everyone you can. Focus on the possibilities of each job, not the limitations. Look for the people who will take a chance on you.

George Marcus and Bill Millichap paid me the tremendous compliment of asking me to train to become a broker for their firm. Their confidence in my abilities gave me the courage, ultimately, to pursue an MBA. And they taught me an invaluable management lesson: a boss's confidence is a powerful motivator. Because they saw potential in me, I began to look for it in myself.

4 | New Fears

I THOUGHT TODD WAS A GOOD MAN, and he was someone I had known throughout college. He knew exactly what he wanted to do and where he was going. He seemed sure of himself, and for me he was comfortable and familiar. And perhaps that is why I fell in love with him—I was so unsure of what I wanted and where I was going, and he seemed safe, providing continuity and security. My mother was tremendously disappointed for reasons she couldn't completely articulate and which only later I would understand. At the time I resented her criticism. Todd and I were married in June 1977 and immediately left for Italy, where he was studying at the Bologna campus of the Johns Hopkins School for Advanced International Studies.

We lived in a shoe-box-sized apartment. I loved Italy, loved Italians and loved the whole crazy adventure that was our first year of marriage. I learned to drink coffee, learned to drink wine and learned to make Italian food. Todd was, in very real ways, my teacher. He had lived in Italy before, and I was following him as he pursued his studies and his career. I admired him and relied on him to make the decisions about our life. While we were husband and wife, we were not peers.

Todd was studying full-time and we needed money. I didn't have a work permit, but I could work as a private language tutor. So I taught English to Italian businessmen and their families and built up quite a clientele by word of mouth. At ten dollars an hour, the teaching work supported us.

I was often asked by my businessmen clients to "explain American business." Of course, I knew very little about it, but, determined to try to respond, I began reading as many American business journals and newspapers as I could get my hands on. Then I would use the most interesting articles to both teach English and talk business. While I hope I earned my money and satisfied my students, those lessons were also a great experience for me. I perfected my Italian but also furthered my knowledge and interest in business. So after thinking about it for quite a while, I concluded I would seek an MBA. Applying to graduate school from Italy in 1978 wasn't an easy process. I traveled to American military bases to take the GMATs, the entrance exams for graduate business studies. My first attempt was stymied by the Italian postal service—the exams were literally lost in the mail, so after arriving at the base, we were told to go home and wait four months for the next opportunity.

If I had been looking for a sign to reassure me that I was making the right decision, the signals so far weren't all that encouraging. Having finally completed the exams, I filled out a single application: to the Robert H. Smith School of Business at the University of Maryland. At that time, it was the only accredited business school in the immediate area of Washington, D.C., where we would be living while Todd finished his second year of studies. I received a rejection notice.

It turned out my application had been late. The Italian postal service went on strike regularly, as did the railway workers. Besides missing the deadline, the application itself wasn't very impressive. Sure, I'd scored well enough on the GMATs and I'd graduated from Stanford with honors and distinction, but I was a history and philosophy major, a receptionist and an English teacher. It wasn't exactly a recipe for success—I sounded lost and directionless. And if I couldn't get into business school, I had no alternative plan.

I decided I had to talk to someone. I knew I was an unlikely student from the school's perspective, but I was convinced I had chosen the right path. After several weeks of trying to get through the various admissions committees and officers, I finally got to talk to the head of the Admissions

Council, Dr. Ed Locke. I called him on a regular basis while he deliberated. My stomach was in knots for every call, and I practiced each in advance, writing down the key points I wanted to make. As hard as those calls were for me to make, though, the thought of getting thrown off my game plan before I'd even started was much worse.

I knew how to be a good student, and I was a good business school student, graduating with straight As. The fact that I could learn all these new disciplines—marketing, finance, accounting, organizational behavior and so on—gave me some confidence that I could actually succeed in business. Yet I also worried because I knew that being a successful student wasn't the same as being in the real world, and so what happened outside the classroom had a great impact on me. Once again someone believed in me, and that encouraged me to believe in myself. And when I became a teaching assistant, I realized I could make a difference for others.

For whatever reason, the dean of the business school, Dr. Rudy Lamone, saw something in me, and one afternnon he asked me to come to his office. I was very nervous; perhaps I'd done something wrong. Instead, he asked for my help in devising a more effective alumni program. I was amazed. Whatever did I know about such a thing? He gave me an opportunity to work with him; and learn from him; and most important, be taken seriously by him. He treated me as an adult and as a peer. He thought I had potential and wanted to help me explore it. I have embarrassed him by telling this story many, many times to students at the university over the years. It was a simple thing he did, and yet it made all the difference for me. Believing in someone else, so they can believe in themselves, is a small but hugely significant act of leadership.

In one of Dr. Locke's courses I wrote a paper on the famous Hawthorne experiments. Much had been previously written, but I thought I saw some aspects of the subject that others had missed. He reassured me that I had brought a new perspective to an old subject. He believed in my contribution enough to put his name alongside my own and publish the results. I felt as though I could conquer the world the day the journal was published.

Dr. Bill Nichols was a marketing professor. I needed to work, and he hired me as a teaching assistant. Watching him teach, I learned the power of humor and the impact of storytelling. And working as a teacher myself (I taught eight undergraduate classes a week), I had also discovered that people sometimes learn best when they have to figure out things for themselves. And so rather than lecture on the importance of brand, for example, I devised an experiment for my students. I sent them to stores, identified types of articles they should buy, and then asked them to explain their purchases. It was fun and rewarding to literally see the lightbulbs go on when a student realized how often their decisions were based almost exclusively on that amorphous but potent emotion that surrounds a great brand.

I found out that some of my students were afraid too—afraid they couldn't make the grade, afraid they wouldn't measure up. They explained their fears when they asked for my help, and I found that I could make a difference for them by building both their confidence and their capability. I think it was the first inkling of what ultimately became my favorite description of leadership: "The good leader is he whom men revere. The evil leader is he whom men despise. The great leader is he of whom the people say, we did it ourselves." (From Sun Tzu, *The Art of War*.)

Dr. Locke encouraged me to consider getting my PhD, but the real world beckoned. I wanted a job in business that wasn't secretarial, so I made the interview rounds with all the big firms that came on campus to recruit. I splurged on my one blue interview suit. I talked to consulting companies, accounting firms, automobile manufacturers, banks—you name it. If they arrived on campus and were willing to talk to me, I was willing to talk to them. I really had no idea what kind of industry or business I was looking for. The company that finally intrigued me was the one most of my professors advised against: Ma Bell, the phone company. In 1980 the Bell System was huge—with over one million employees. It was a mammoth bureaucracy by any measure and included local telephone service, long distance, telephone equipment and Bell Laboratories. It was a complex, regulated corporation whose stock every widow and orphan should own and whose familiar bell-shaped logo implied safe, secure, reliable and ubiquitous service.

People told me it was too slow, too bureaucratic, too dull. Nevertheless, I was interested. Communications itself seemed fascinating; it was a basic tool and yet a complex technology. There were rumblings of industry change in Washington. An upstart firm named MCI was shaking things up and demanding new rules. We'd talked about the telecommunications industry a lot in my economics courses at Stanford and about the difficulties of maintaining a monopoly position when technology changed rapidly. Beyond that, the Bell System had something called the Management Development Program, where young managers were rotated throughout different departments. It was known as an up-or-out opportunity. You either performed well enough at each assignment to be moved on to other new responsibilities, or you were asked to leave the company.

I thought it sounded like a great challenge. I figured I'd get a lot of training in the industry, which was clearly growing. I liked the exposure to many different departments, since I didn't know which would be most interesting to me. Even if I left after a few years, which seemed probable, it would be a valuable experience. I signed up.

The first decision I had to make as a brand-new recruit to AT&T was choosing the department I would start in. I could go to finance, engineering or sales. After much agonizing, since I really didn't know much about any of them, I picked sales. I'm not sure how I made this decision, other than that the only businesspeople I'd known previously were the brokers at Marcus & Millichap, and they sold things. I do remember someone telling me that sales was a good place to start because you had to learn all about the company's products. That made sense. Over time I also discovered that you learn not only a lot about a company when you sell its products, but you also learn a lot about yourself and how to communicate effectively with other people. I believe every aspiring business executive should have at least one sales experience.

The beginning of my Bell System career seemed a lot like school. I was sent off to nine weeks of sales and product training. I sat in a classroom with other brand-new recruits, and for a while it was a lot of fun to be with new colleagues. But it wasn't very challenging. After a few weeks it was time to put the books aside and actually start performing—literally. We were learning something called the Seven-Step Selling Process. It was easy to study, but soon we were involved in competitive role-playing exercises where instructors played the part of customers, and we had to develop complicated proposals and sell them. It began to get pretty tough. I'd never experienced role-playing before, and I'd never sold anything. Actual selling, as opposed to reading or talking about it, was a lot harder than I'd realized.

I almost didn't make it past the very first role-play. It involved having to convince a gatekeeper—a prospective client's secretary, as played by an instructor—that what you had to say to this client was important enough for the secretary to allow you to speak with her boss. I was put into a window-less conference room with a telephone. This was a simple exercise, but I was literally paralyzed with fear. I remember sitting in that room, staring at the phone, trying to gather my courage to dial the number. I was sure I would make a fool of myself and fail the first test. I told the instructor several times that I wasn't ready, that I had to postpone the role-playing. I was afraid to fail, and so I was afraid to try.

Eventually, I had no option. The rules were clear: if you couldn't make it past this first exercise, you couldn't continue in the course. My first sales call was pretty pathetic, but the instructor, probably out of pity, let me past the dreaded gatekeeper. I felt tremendous relief and triumph—not because the exercise itself was all that important, but because I had mastered fear and moved forward. I approached the rest of the role-playing with newfound energy and confidence.

Over the years I came to recognize this same pattern in others; I wasn't the only person who was afraid. And like me during that role-playing, when confronted by something new and unfamiliar—even something relatively simple and meaningless—people often become immovable because of their fears. In the course of those long hours in the conference room, I'd learned, once again, that each time I overcame my own fear, I was stronger. There are some who would argue that a manager's job is to use fear to motivate people, but I believe a leader's job is to help people overcome their fear.

5 | Not Till the Lady Leaves

SALES SCHOOL, like every school, presented an idealized version of its subject. It still took a lot of hard work, but in sales school the customers were always willing to spend time with you if you had a good idea, it was possible to talk directly to the decision maker, and your teammates were always willing to help you. When I finally arrived at my real desk and started my real job, I was in for a rude awakening.

I joined Government Communications—that part of AT&T that served the federal government. I didn't know it on my first day of work, but I was the first MDipper to join the sales team to which I'd been assigned. MDipper was the not-so-flattering term used to describe people like me who came in with graduate degrees through the Management Development Program. Everyone knew who we were, and some of us quickly developed reputations for being arrogant and impatient to move on to the next assignment. The sales district I joined was very successful, and they didn't think they needed any help from someone like me.

I approached my first day on the job with great anticipation. I was on my way! I was going to do real work! I don't know what kind of welcome I expected, but what I got was a big letdown. My boss said good morning and directed me to my desk. It was stacked two feet high with books and papers.

He said, "I've written down the accounts we're assigning you to. You can read up on them. Welcome aboard." On a single sheet of paper were the letters USGS, BIA, WPRS. I asked what they meant. He said, "You'll find them in there" as he motioned to the stack of reading material.

I don't know whether I was being tested or whether my boss just didn't know what else to do with me. I did as I was told. I started reading. Five days later I was still reading. I knew that BIA was the Bureau of Indian Affairs, USGS was the United States Geological Survey and WPRS was the Water Protection and Resource Service. I also knew what the AT&T billing was on each account, what the account team was hoping to sell them, and what each agency's mission was. Then I started talking to my new colleagues. I did what I always had done when encountering a new situation. I asked a lot of questions, and I'd read enough so that I could appreciate something about the answers. I asked questions about our customers and what we were trying to accomplish. And I asked questions about each of my teammates: how long they'd worked there, what they liked about it, what they didn't like about it.

My boss was well intentioned, but he was having a romantic relationship with a woman upstairs, and he didn't have much time for me. We sat in low-walled cubicles, and my desk was directly across from his. I came to recognize the particular way he sounded when he was talking to his ladylove, and I learned to make my interactions with him short and to the point. His boss, who ran the entire sales district, seemed very impressed with his own importance and was always busy bustling somewhere else.

Marie Burns had been in customer service for many years and was heartened to have another woman on the team. She would freely offer counsel and perspective. Steve Frantz was in customer service and was willing to work with anyone who was willing to work with him. Bill Allan had been on the team the longest and was reserved and thoughtful. He would wait and see how I measured up before committing himself.

And then there was David Godfrey. David had been brought into the Washington, D.C., office from Oklahoma. He was legendary for the relationships he'd built with the Bureau of Indian Affairs. BIA was the government agency responsible for managing relations with the country's Indian reservations, and it was a very large Bell System client. They had a massive, nationwide network connecting regional BIA offices, and each Indian reservation had its own communications systems. David was very protective of his turf and close to retirement. He came in early and always disappeared at lunchtime, usually not to return until the following morning. It was said he could sell anything. I was assigned to "comanage" the BIA with him. No one knew what this actually meant, or who was supposed to do what. David thought the whole thing was a very bad idea—dreamed up by our bosses, "who," David informed me, "don't know what they're doing anyway."

One day David let me know that the two most important regional managers at BIA were coming to town. They held the purse strings for the national network and approved all the network upgrades. David was going to meet with them to discuss our latest proposal. I thought it was important that I meet them as well, so I asked if I could join him. David seemed genial enough about it and invited me along. I was delighted. It would be great to have my first introduction to these customers come from David: it would almost be an endorsement from him. Maybe he thought I could help after all!

The day before the meeting David came to my cubicle. "You know, Carly, I'm really sorry. I know we'd planned to have you meet the two directors. The thing is, they have a favorite restaurant here in D.C., and they've requested that we meet there. You know, I always do what the customer wants, and so I don't think you'll be able to join us."

"Why not?" I asked.

"Well, we're going to The Board Room. Sorry." And he walked off.

I needed to consult with Bill. He gave me a slight grin and said: "Carly, it's a strip club."

The Board Room was more than a strip club. As its name implied, it was an upscale "gentlemen's club" on Vermont Avenue. It was famous not just for what happened on stage. Between acts, the young women who worked there would dress in see-through baby-doll negligees and dance on top of the tables while the patrons ate lunch.

The BIA customers wanted to go there, so David and Steve were going to The Board Room. As all of this dawned on me, I was both very embarrassed and very anxious. I went and sat in the ladies' room to think about it in private. I thought for a couple of hours and worked myself into a state of near panic. I had no idea what I was supposed to do in this situation. I couldn't tell myself it didn't matter—it clearly was important to meet these clients and to convince David that I should be taken seriously. It never occurred to me to be outraged and demand that they not go—it wouldn't have worked anyway. I had been presented with circumstances that others had created. Fair or not, it was my problem to solve and decide how to respond.

Finally, I went to David's desk and said, "You know, I hope it won't make you too uncomfortable, but I think I'm going to go to lunch anyway. I'll meet you all there." You could have heard a pin drop in the office as everyone watched the scenario unfold.

The next day arrived and I was scared to death. That morning I chose my outfit particularly carefully. I dressed in my most conservative suit and carried my briefcase like a shield of honor. "I am a professional woman," I whispered to myself. I got into a taxicab and, feeling like an idiot, gave the driver the address. He turned around to stare at me. "You're kidding, right? Are you the new act?" This wasn't starting out well.

I arrived at the destination, took a deep breath, straightened my bow tie (Dress for Success for Women, a must-read in those days, recommended floppy bows tied at the throat of all blouses), and stepped into The Board Room. It was very dark and very loud. There was a long bar down the right-hand side of the place and a large stage to my left. There was a live act going on with probably ten or more women. My colleagues were sitting as far from the door as possible, and the only way to reach them was to cross in front of that stage. I clutched my briefcase tighter and walked to their table, looking seriously out of place and quite ridiculous.

I was cordial and tried to appear relaxed, tried to sound knowledgeable about BIA business, and desperately tried to ignore what was going on all around me. David was in high spirits and really didn't have much interest in working. He was slugging back gin and tonic and kept calling the women over to dance on top of the table. The other men were either amused or slightly embarrassed, but no one tried to stop him. In a show of empathy that brings tears to my eyes still, each woman who approached the table would look the situation over and say, "Sorry, gentlemen. Not till the lady leaves."

After a few hours, having made my point, I left them all there. They heaved a sigh of relief, I'm sure, but the next day in the office, the balance of power had shifted perceptibly. I had shown David and Steve that I would not be intimidated, even if I was terrified. I had proved that I wasn't just another MDipper; I truly cared about doing my job even when it meant working in difficult circumstances. Having tried to diminish me, David was himself diminished. He was embarrassed. And Bill decided that he would take me under his wing and help me succeed. We cannot always choose the hurdles we must overcome, but we can choose how we overcome them.

We never spoke about what happened at The Board Room, and David and I became a great team. It was Bill who told me that David drank too much to be effective. He knew everyone, though, and the customers liked and respected him for his work over the years. So he would get our meetings set up, and then I'd do business. There was a lot of business to be done; we provided communications systems to every Indian reservation in the country, as well as data and voice networks to the Bureau. David would sit looking like a proud father and let me work with the clients. I trusted his judgment about whom to see, and when and where to see them. I traveled to a great many Indian reservations all over the country. I addressed tribal councils. The Bureau of Indian Affairs turned out to be a great account and a great experience.

We met in bars a lot. In part it was because David liked to drink and in part it was because many of our customers wanted to get better acquainted in a relaxed setting. Really getting to know who they were dealing with was just as important to them as what we were talking about. Trust was important to business. Years later I learned that drinking rituals are an important part of doing business in many cultures, particularly in Asia. I wasn't much of a drinker, but I drank gin and tonic, as David did. And as the night wore on, and my colleagues grew more comfortable, I would slip away to the bar and tell the bartender, "From now on, anytime I order a gin and tonic, make it just tonic. And this is just between us." I don't think anyone ever figured it out. I was paying respect to our clients by letting them choose the settings in which we'd do business. And I was doing what was necessary to protect myself.

I traveled all over the country visiting BIA, USGS and WPRS customers. When I called on customers at Washington headquarters, I learned things. When I traveled to meet with people in the field, I learned more. In every job since, including as a CEO, I've found that if you really want to know what's going on, you have to travel. The farther from headquarters you get, wherever headquarters happens to be, the more you find out about what's actually going on.

It was on one of my trips to Denver that I first met a regional manager with the Bureau of Mines, part of USGS. He was frustrated by his current telephone system, a PBX, and said no one on the local Mountain Bell sales team would listen to him. He said they kept trying to solve his problem with existing technology, and it wouldn't work. USGS needed a way to handle a huge number of incoming calls and track the data that resulted from those calls. More important, in emergency situations they needed a way to convene huge teleconferences quickly and pull together a large number of participants in diverse, remote locations. While this is easy to do today, in 1982 the technology didn't exist. When I talked to the local sales team, they complained that it would take too much time and energy to work on this opportunity. There were easier sales they could make.

The regional manager was a potential customer who needed someone to actually make the investment of time to understand his problem and then be willing to design a solution to fit his needs. I didn't argue with him. I listened hard and asked a lot of questions. After several long meetings I told him that although I didn't know what the solution might be, I really did understand his problems and his objectives. I promised I would work on it.

Around this time I was given the opportunity to rotate to a different department. By now, though, I was committed to my customers. I had unfinished business with them, so I decided to stay in my current job, even though as an MDipper I was overdue for another assignment. Many coworkers told me I was making a mistake. The colleagues I really cared about appreciated that finishing the job I had was more important than moving on to another one.

Over many months I talked with several Mountain Bell people about the USGS opportunity. I knew there was something big there, even if I couldn't define the answer. Most of them dismissed me pretty quickly, saying I didn't really understand the technology challenges involved or perhaps I'd misunderstood the customer's situation. I was new, I was young, I was a woman—I clearly didn't know what I was talking about.

I thought I'd finally found someone who took me seriously. I was a first-level manager and he was a second-level manager with Mountain Bell. He was very encouraging. He listened carefully and then suggested we spend the day visiting various customers and talking more about the opportunity. That day it seemed to me we were in the car more than we were with customers, but I didn't question his judgment. I was eager to be treated as a professional peer and thought he was sincere. When we finally returned to the hotel at the end of the day, he suggested we have a drink. Sitting in that bar, I suddenly realized I had been foolish and naive. My colleague wasn't interested in a customer; he was interested in a conquest. I excused myself and spent the rest of the evening in my room. He called throughout the night and was angrier every time.

When I went to the local Mountain Bell office the next day, I noticed people staring a bit too intently at me. Eventually I was told that the man I'd rejected the previous evening had come into work that morning bragging about the great sex we'd had the night before. I was horrified and humiliated. I wondered what I had done wrong. I felt as though everyone in that office was laughing at me behind my back. It made me more determined than ever to prove that there was an important sale to be made to the Bureau of Mines, and to be the one to make it.

I gave up on Mountain Bell and began talking with people at AT&T in New Jersey and Washington. Eventually, after lots of dead ends, I found someone who took me at my word, understood the problem and was willing to design the solution. He looked at me, smiled and said, "Do you realize how big this is?" His name was Frank.

When all was said and done, the system that finally was sold, designed and installed was the largest of its kind that had ever been implemented by the Bell System to date. It was the Dimension 2000 with the Emergency Communications System (ECS). I brought food to the installers every day to keep their spirits up and to show them my appreciation for their round-the-clock work. The system was based on a prototype that was just coming out of Bell Laboratories and the installation was extremely challenging. Later, based on its successful performance, the ECS would become a standard part of the Dimension, the company's flagship PBX system. I won a national award and was promoted to sales manager.

I learned many things during that year and a half. I learned that sometimes you have to have faith in what you know even when most everyone else tells you you're wrong. I learned that if I focused all my energies on the job I had, and performed to the very best of my abilities, opportunity would knock. I learned, once again, that we can only be diminished if we choose to allow it. I learned that the more difficult challenge is sometimes worth going after. I learned that those kinds of challenges take a whole team.

And I met Frank.

6 | Choices of the Heart

FTER I LEFT GRADUATE SCHOOL and had entered the workforce, something had changed in my marriage. As my career at AT&T progressed, I became surer of myself. As I came into my own and grew up, Todd and I grew apart. Todd's choices had always driven our lives. Now that we were peers, the marriage no longer worked. He began to travel for weeks at a time, and one weekend I discovered that he wasn't at the office working as he'd said he was.

I decided I had to consult an attorney. She advised me to go through all our papers when he was away. I will never forget her words: "This guy has it made. You're making the money, and he's managing it. You need to find out what he's doing with it." I had paid no attention to our finances. I never saw any of his paychecks and had no idea what he actually made, although I knew I was the primary wage earner. Todd seemed to enjoy looking after our finances, and I trusted him. I remember sitting at home at my desk going through bank statements and other records.

When the truth of it all finally settled in, I saw the whole world differently. I could not believe that someone I thought I knew so well, someone I had trusted and loved, could behave in this way. It was the first time I fully understood how threatened some men are by capable, successful women. I would experience it again and again in the workplace, but to discover it in my marriage was a searing revelation. I had been raised to believe that what you are is God's gift to you. What you make of yourself is your gift to God. How could someone who loved you resent that? In retrospect, this all sounds hopelessly naive, but to this day I underestimate people's capacity to abuse my trust and the insecurity that sometimes drives them.

M OST OF THE TIME when God closes a door, He also opens a window. During that terrible time when I was agonizing over what to do about my marriage, I met someone who became a lifelong friend and role model. One day I was waiting for the bus on my way to work and, as usual during that period, crying while I waited. Suddenly a car veered across four lanes of traffic and came to a stop. The door opened and a woman said, "Get in. You look as if you could use a friend." I surely did, and Carole Spurrier has been a wonderful and beloved friend ever since. She also happened to be the highest-ranking woman in AT&T's Washington office, and she became a constant source of guidance and motivation. Carole and her carpool mate Judy Hudson spent the next many months engaged in marriage counseling as we drove to work. We laughed and cried together, and they eased my fear and loneliness. I'm not sure what I would have done without them. I said good-bye to Todd and vowed I would never again trust anyone the way I'd trusted him.

I would break that vow. Although I didn't know it at the time, I think I fell in love with Frank at first sight. He was the office heartthrob—a dark, handsome, charming guy. His father had died when he was thirteen, and he'd been surrounded by women his whole life: his gentle but indomitable mother; his tender and devoted older sisters, Ursula and Claudia; his aunts. He understood and appreciated women, and they all loved him in return. I loved him because he loved that I was capable. He told me he thought I would run the company some day. I laughed and told him it was ridiculous, and although I truly thought it was, I loved him for thinking it was possible. More than that, he found it thrilling, not threatening.

Over time, I learned that he also had been betrayed. Neither one of us thought we could trust again. And so we called it off several times.

He had two young daughters, Tracy and Lori. I was afraid to meet them because I knew I'd be pulled deeper into his life. Tracy was grown up beyond her years and protective of her father. Lori was starved for affection. I fell in love with both of them too, over our first meal together—Chinese takeout. From then on there was no escape. Frank asked me to marry him as we sat in the car in his mother's driveway on Easter Sunday. Tracy was discreet enough to be with her grandmother, but Lori was bouncing up and down with great excitement in the backseat. She'd picked the ring. Saying yes was the best decision I ever made.

I had one last panic attack the day of our wedding. It was the only time in my life I actually had to breathe into a paper bag, but when I finally walked out and met Frank's eyes, my anxieties disappeared. We were married in a small ceremony in Carole's home. I gave each of the girls a delicate gold bracelet. I told them I would not try to replace their mother, but I loved them with all my heart and would be their special guardian. Frank and I tried to have more children, but as disappointed as we were, that wasn't God's plan. We felt complete with the family we had, and it seemed a miracle to both of us that we had found each other.

All through the twenty-five years we've been together, my trust in Frank has been absolute. His faith in me has been unwavering, his candor uncompromising. And he brought so much with him: two wonderful daughters; a large, welcoming and affectionate Italian family; a whole new life. Today our daughters have husbands of their own, Lowell and Chris, so Frank finally has some guys in the family. And there are two more girls—our granddaughters, Kara and Morgan.

Every year on Easter Sunday, I say a special prayer of thanks for my own rebirth.

7 | Our Token Bimbo

I N 1982 I BECAME a manager for the first time. I didn't know anything about being a boss and there weren't any training courses for
bosses. So I thought about my own bosses and how they'd managed
me. I remembered feeling mostly ignored and on my own. They
seemed to have a sink-or-swim philosophy about management. I decided I
could do better. I would be interested in my subordinates.

It was a small team, and we served the Department of Health and Human Services. Pattie Espey, like me, was one of the young women who'd
been hired after AT&T settled a lawsuit by signing a consent decree with the
federal government and committing to hiring and promoting more women.
She was bright, energetic, frustrated and always about to quit. Don Haynes,
the customer service manager, had been around a long time. He'd forgotten
more than the rest of us knew, but he'd disengaged and was essentially retired in place. He didn't think much of women in management. Bill Cash
was overtly gay, which was unusual at the time, and he'd been marginalized
and ridiculed as a result. He was funny and self-deprecating, and pretended
not to care, but I recognized the desire to be taken seriously. He was desper-
ate to prove himself.

I met with each of them. I asked them what they thought about our customer. I asked what they thought we did well and what we didn't do well. I asked how they thought they could best contribute. I asked what they thought I should be doing. It was pretty clear nobody expected much from this team. In fact, they'd been thrown together because the higher-ups thought the customer didn't have any potential; there certainly wasn't much action on the account. I'd been given the team for the same reason: my new boss didn't expect much from me either.

The district manager, my new boss, knew he was born to lead and seemed unusually proud of his monogram—RWP—which he put on everything. He knew he was about to be promoted at any moment to something much bigger and better. He knew all about the consent decree and why AT&T had to hire women. The numbers had to look good. That was just the way it was.

He decided we should visit customers together so he could introduce his newest sales manager. At our first meeting he opened up by saying: "I'd like you to meet Carly. She's our token bimbo." Then he laughed and said, "Actually, she's your new sales manager." I laughed too, and did my best to dazzle the client with my knowledge of their mission. After the meeting I took my boss aside and said, "You will never do that to me again." My anger outweighed my fear of speaking to him like that. He looked me up and down and replied, "Okay. Sorry. Tell me, were you ever a cheerleader?"

I decided that my new team and I would exceed others' expectations of us. We would set more challenging goals for ourselves, and then we would beat them. We would not be content to be underestimated. So I gathered my team together and fed back to them all the opportunities they'd told me about that we weren't pursuing. I reminded them of all the things they'd told me we should be doing differently and better. I replayed for them what they each thought they were good at. I told them we were going to put this team on the map at AT&T. I didn't know how exactly, but together we were going to figure it out. I remembered how I'd felt when people had taken a chance on me at Marcus & Millichap, and now I told the team that they could do more.

Pattie and Bill were game and enthusiastic. They had nothing to lose. Don was skeptical and didn't know how he'd ended up with such a strange group of people. He was tired of being bored, though, and his curiosity got the better of him. He'd give it a try. We met together until we'd roughed out a basic game plan—how we would work together and which opportunities we'd go after. And for the next year we worked to put ourselves on the map.

Each one of us brought different experiences and points of view to the table. We each had different hang-ups and different ambitions. And yet when we all contributed, the outcome was better. It wasn't always easy finding common ground, but to get what we were after, we needed one another. We all wanted to be treated with respect and asked to deliver.

I needed a team who would cut me some slack while I figured out what being a sales manager was all about. This was long before the days of 360-degree feedback. Nevertheless, every three months I would give Pattie, Bill and Don a little questionnaire I'd devised and ask them to tell me what I was doing right and what I was doing wrong. They took the request seriously, were thoughtful in their responses and helped me tremendously. We also had fun with it. Occasionally Bill would stray from the assignment and give me wardrobe advice. He was usually right.

Working together, we didn't accomplish everything we'd set out to do, but we accomplished much more than we'd been asked or expected to do. We were different people bound together by a shared purpose. I had experienced both the power of diversity and the impact of common goals. Pattie and Bill got promoted. Don became the highest-rated customer service manager in the district—and decided women bosses weren't so bad after all. He worked very well with another one before he retired. I enjoyed proving RWP wrong.

ONCE A YEAR managers rated and ranked their employees. Each employee would receive a rating for his or her performance: Superior, Excellent, Satisfactory, Unsatisfactory. Each would also receive a numeric ranking that represented how they stacked up against the other employees in the organization. In my first job I remembered watching my boss and all the other second-level managers go into a room early in the morning and finally come out at the end of a grueling day. Several weeks later my boss would tell me how I'd been rated and ranked. I never understood much about what went on in those sessions. The whole process seemed very important and pretty mysterious.

Now I was a second-level manager, and I had to represent my own employees. I was proud that I had achieved this level of responsibility but also nervous because I didn't know what I was supposed to do. Besides, I would be interacting as a peer with people who had not so long ago been my superiors. I prepared carefully. I wrote up each of my subordinates' accomplishments, their strengths and the areas where improvement was needed. I talked with some other second-levels about how the meeting worked.

I went to Marie Burns, who'd always been so helpful to me in my previous job. She described a very rational, thorough process in which the supervisors presented their employees and proposed ratings and rankings. When they had completed their presentations, there was a general discussion and then everyone came to an eventual agreement on the distribution of the ratings and how each employee was ranked in the total universe. Sometimes they also talked about an employee's potential to move up in the organization. This all seemed very reasonable—we were professional managers coming together to talk about all the subordinates for whom we were collectively responsible. We would discuss and deliberate together, eventually reaching consensus. It made sense to me why these were long, grueling meetings. There was much important work to do.

Then I talked to Ron Ketner, the manager whose team sat next to my own. I didn't know him all that well, but he seemed experienced, caustic and sexist. He was always making off-color jokes and once told me that he saw nothing wrong with a female salesperson sleeping with a customer as long as she made the sale. I didn't think much of his jokes or his point of view, but he was well respected in the office, so I wanted to get his take on rating and ranking.

"Listen, Carly, I don't know what Marie told you, but here's the bottom line. Rating and ranking is just a big horse-trading session. Every boss wants to be sure to have as many of their people at the top as possible; otherwise they don't look good to their own boss when it's their turn to get rated and ranked. So we're all competing against each other in that room, and you have to do your friends some favors if you want them to do you some."

"But, Ron, isn't it about the people we're evaluating, not us?"

"Nah, this is politics pure and simple. Good luck."

I was a brand-new manager with not much of a track record. Office politics, like real politics, are based on power—who has lost it, who wants it, who's got it. I didn't have any of it, so I played the game the only way I could.

I decided ahead of time what rating I thought each of my subordinates really deserved. I decided whether they were at the top of that category, the middle, or the bottom. This gave me a rough feel for the ranking they should receive. When it was my turn to present, I laid out my conclusions and refused to budge for the rest of the meeting. Others coaxed, or cajoled or threatened. Some actually reasoned and compromised. The meeting turned out to be a little like Marie had described and a lot like Ron had predicted. And I was a stubborn, immovable object in the middle of the swirl. When everyone became convinced I really wouldn't change my mind, they gave me what I wanted. If I couldn't persuade them, I would outlast them.

I wasn't particularly proud of my performance. I hadn't contributed much to the discussion. Maybe I could have done better some other way, but I had walked out with what I'd come in for. And I could honestly tell Pattie, Bill and Don why I supported the rating and ranking they received.

Because I hadn't said much, I'd listened all day. And I'd learned a lot about how things actually worked. First, just because someone was a second-level didn't mean they were any smarter than a first-level. That sounds pretty basic, and it is, but as someone who had never been in a big corporation before, I'd just assumed that level and title must have some correlation to character and capability. If someone had been promoted, it must mean they were better. I found out that day that I was wrong. Some of these managers were smart, some weren't. Some were honest, some weren't. I knew first-levels who I'd thought would be better managers, and I knew second-levels who should never have become managers.

People are people no matter where they are or what position they hold. Some are worthy of their titles, some aren't. On the one hand, I found this revelation somewhat alarming. I couldn't assume anymore that the boss always knew best. On the other hand, it was empowering somehow. It reinforced what I'd learned growing up: value isn't measured by title or position but by what someone is made of and how they choose to use it.

I'd also observed that managers seemed more enthusiastic about subordinates with whom they were comfortable. As a practical matter, this meant those subordinates whom managers had known a long time, or someone they knew had known a long time, or those subordinates who were a lot like the bosses in their habits and interests, or subordinates who fit the bosses' image of what success looked like; these employees did much better in the rating and ranking than those who were different, or challenging, or less well known. If a boss was uncomfortable with a subordinate, it showed up in how he talked about her or him.

Seniority and familiarity could, and did, sometimes trump results. When you're thinking about whether you're comfortable with someone, you focus on their personality and characteristics. So looking and acting the part could also win out. There was one very handsome salesman who'd worked on the same sales team I once had, who was the most obvious case in point. He looked good, he presented well, he talked football with all the managers, and he was fast with a good joke. He was truly likable. He also frequently dropped the ball with his customers and always had a good reason why he couldn't make the numbers. He was consistently ranked at the top of the pile. He was a classic 42-long, his suit size. "Forty-two-long" was also the expression for a manager who looked and acted the part but was more show than substance. Comfort and familiarity have nothing to do with merit other than by coincidence. I was getting my first glimpse of how prejudice can linger in an organization, and why a meritocracy is so difficult to achieve.

Finally, the horse-trading that went on didn't just affect the decisions of that day. People did favors for one another in that room in return for other favors that might pay off on a different day and a different subject, or maybe even in the next round of rating and ranking the following year. These managers had to work together on many issues over time. The particular people they were discussing at that particular time were important subjects in and of themselves, but they were also pawns in a bigger game. It's unfortunate that there are many people who find it exceptionally difficult to put their own agendas aside and focus solely on the best outcome for the challenge at hand.

I myself became the subject of such a horse trade. It was my turn to be rated and ranked as a second-level. Ron Ketner had become an acting district manager because of his boss's prolonged absence, and so he was in the room with the other districts. When the meeting was over, he came to see me.

"Carly, I shouldn't tell you this, but I think you really got screwed. You were very highly rated, and I argued that you should be ranked number one. Lots of people agreed with me. You did a great job with HHS, but one of the districts said it was their guy's turn to be number one; he'd been promised that slot last year, and he'd told his guy already. None of us wanted to go along with him, so he decided to deal some dirt on you."

"What? What did he say?"

"He said when you worked for him, you took credit for [the 42-long's] work all the time."

"But that's ridiculous. We didn't even work on the same accounts! I couldn't take credit for his work."

"Well, we didn't know any of that, so no one could contradict him. Anyway, you ended up as number two. That's pretty good, you know; I just think you deserved number one."

The result was, in fact, much more than I had expected. I wasn't focused on that, though—I was outraged by what had happened. This would not be the last time someone falsely maligned my reputation to serve other ends. Indeed, it happens to all kinds of people all the time. It is the everyday stuff of organizational resistance and petty politics. Still, it was the first time for me. Someone had fabricated a story about me, impugned my character and done so purely for his own purposes. I felt an injustice had occurred.

I was so furious that I got up and stormed into that district manager's office. I had recently worked in his district; he had been my first boss's boss. I certainly had no position power, and I wasn't even supposed to know what I knew. I hadn't planned what I was going to do, but somehow I had to make my point.

I startled him. He was a short man, and he was sitting behind his desk. He started to get up. I said, "Sit down" and strode quickly to his desk and stood beside it as close to him as possible. I literally towered over him.

"Did you have a problem with me while I worked for you?"

"No, Carly. Why?"

"Did you think I took credit for others' work?"

"No, Carly."

"Are you sure? Because if you did, you should have told me."

"No, Carly, honestly. You were our best account executive. You know that."

"Then don't ever say it again; and from now on, if you want to say something behind my back, you'd better be willing to say it to my face."

And I walked out.

I was literally trembling, both with fear from what I'd done and anger at what had been done to me. I lay awake and worried all night about it.

It was the first time I had experienced the triumph of personal power over position power. Granted, it wasn't a very elegant display. Cinnamon (of *Mission: Impossible*) would have done it more subtly—standing over him in my high heels, I'd been physically intimidating. But it had worked. The next day, to his great credit, the district manager came to my desk and apologized. By then, he'd already gotten the number one slot; but still, it took humility, and I think his remorse was genuine. Either that or he was afraid of running into me in a dark alley.

And what about caustic, sexist Ron? I'd learned that sometimes you never know who your friends are going to be. My own bias had led me to underestimate him.

8 | I Can and I Will

RWP DID GET PROMOTED to division manager, and he moved upstairs to Public Affairs. This was the organization that interacted with the government on a policy level. It was a very important position, particularly since by then, divestiture was a reality. On January 1, 1984, the vaunted Bell System would be split apart. The regional telephone companies would become the Baby Bells and be responsible for local telephone service. AT&T would become AT&T Long Lines, or the Bell regulated entity (BRE), which would maintain the long-distance network, and the AT&T independent subsidiary (IS), which would sell equipment. AT&T IS and the BRE had already been created. Now the final, most wrenching step, pulling apart the network itself into local and long-distance service, would occur.

It was a very complicated solution to a complex problem: how to accelerate innovation and create sufficient competition in a vital industry while at the same time maintaining the existing quality of universal services that the entire country relied upon. I'd spent a great deal of time during 1983 explaining to our customers how this would actually work, from a technological, billing and regulatory perspective. I'd traveled all over the country visiting field offices, carrying large poster boards that I'd created to show people what the networks would look like and how we'd manage and charge for them post–January 1, 1984. I spent enough time learning it myself and then explaining it to others that I really understood where the problems were going to be. In the process I'd learned what really good teachers know: if you want to truly understand something, try explaining it to someone else. The problems were going to be at the demarcations between local and long-distance companies and their networks. In telco jargon these points of demarcation were known as Points of Presence, or POPs.

IN EARLY 1984 my new boss approached me and said, "Carly, it's time to move out of sales. Where do you think you want to go?" I deeply appreciated that he was asking me what I wanted, and I appreciated that he was willing to help me get it. So I thought about it for a while and finally said, "I want to go to Engineering and work in Access Capacity Management."

"Carly, why would you want to go there? It's a zoo! I hear it's chaos over there. No one really knows how to do what they're supposed to do. I hear they're working 24/7, with three engineering shifts a day. You've never been in Engineering."

The Access Capacity Management Center (ACMC) was where AT&T Long Lines and the Baby Bells came together. It was a brand-new organization because it had never been necessary before. This was where, from a technical and engineering perspective, different companies' networks would be brought together at the POPs. Any service that needed to be provisioned after January 1, 1984, would have to come through the ACMC. And because every long-distance call and circuit terminated somewhere in a Baby Bell's territory, the Baby Bells would charge AT&T (and MCI) for that termination. These access charges would become the single largest expense for AT&T, running into the billions and billions of dollars every quarter. (Almost twenty years later, methods used by some long-distance providers to account for these same access charges brought down WorldCom in one of the biggest corporate frauds in history.) The ACMC was where the problems were going to be.

My boss was absolutely right, and it was why I wanted to go. It was brand-new. Everyone was trying to figure it out. Maybe I could help. It was chaotic—maybe that would be exciting. It was difficult work—I wanted a challenge. It didn't bother me that it wasn't a typical move. I was looking for interesting work where I could make a real difference.

My boss thought it was a risky move. I might fail, and so far I'd been pretty successful in my career. He suggested several possibilities that he'd been contemplating: jobs that he thought might offer me a better opportunity to build on my previous work. But I wasn't focused on the risks, although I acknowledged they were there. I wanted to learn something new and I wanted to help solve real problems. He knew the district manager in charge of ACMC, Bob Cann, so my boss called him. Bob was delighted. He had so many challenges, he'd take on anyone who wanted to help. And so I left Government Communications and went to work in Oakton, Virginia, headquarters of AT&T's Eastern Region.

When I arrived, I saw a beehive of activity. ACMC occupied almost the entire first floor of the building. Desks were separated by low partitions, so everyone could see everyone else. People were standing at their desks shouting at each other; engineers were running back and forth with reams of paper. It really was chaos. Bob Cann's office was in the far corner of all this activity. He was friendly but stressed. Everyone was working long hours, and Oakton engineers were accustomed to being able to provision service smoothly, with quality and on time. Now nothing was on time, and there were too many errors. Worse, the previously cordial relations that had existed between local Bell and Long Lines engineers were badly frayed. Lots of finger-pointing and arguing went on. No one wanted to take the fall for someone else's screw-up. Most of the engineers thought divestiture was a really bad idea, dreamed up by a bunch of politicians and executives who didn't have a clue about how a telephone network actually worked.

Bob had decided to put me in charge of the group that designed the circuit layouts. These were the engineers who determined how service should be provisioned and then created the engineering diagrams to support it. These blueprints were then passed to the teams actually provisioning the service, and they'd work with the local company engineers and talk to the customers. All this documentation was necessary because provisioning was now a contractual process between two independent companies, and access charges were determined based on these blueprints.

I think Bob gave me this group because it was the smoothest-running organization. I couldn't get into a lot of trouble, and maybe I'd learn something. Although Bob didn't see me solely as a fifth wheel, I was brand-new to engineering. He couldn't afford to have my ignorance hurt the business. I began my new job in the same way I'd started every other one. I met with my new employees and asked a lot of questions. What did they do? Why did they do it?

The engineers seemed friendly and open. They were pros, and were very patient in describing what they did and how they did it, but it was pretty clear they didn't need any help. They would be better coaches to me than I would be a boss to them. One of them, Jim Psioda, was in his midfifties, shy and reserved. He felt underutilized but didn't know how else to help. I didn't get much out of him during our first meeting. Carol Swann was one of the few female engineers. She seemed unhappy and tense. She told me at our first meeting that she really should have been promoted a while ago. I knew she thought she should have my job. She was conscientious and hardworking but stuck to herself and seemed isolated from the rest of the group.

After this first round of meetings, it was pretty clear that I could add no value by telling these people how to do their jobs or getting in their way. They knew more about what they were doing than I did. They had enough frustration to deal with; they didn't need me hanging around trying to "help." I wanted to show them the respect they deserved, so I needed to know something about how they did their jobs, but to make a difference I'd have to focus my time on something no one else was doing that needed to be done.

I started studying circuit layouts—those blueprints my team was creating. I noticed that they identified each relevant POP by its unique numeric indicator and described the specific kind of circuitry and the exact mileage required. The tariff or pricing arrangement was also noted. All in all, there was a lot of detailed information involved in every record. I asked someone whether I understood correctly how it all worked. I did. Then I asked if anyone ever looked at the access bills we received that were based on these records.

"Not really. We look them over every month when they come in, and they look right. They're just billing us based on the records we send them."

Those bills represented a lot of money: $2 billion in our region alone. I thought it was worth double-checking, so I started to look at access bills. They seemed okay and they had all of the same information that we provided to the provisioning teams. Still, I looked at the chaos all around me on the first floor and figured it must be equally chaotic over at Bell Atlantic, the local telephone company we interfaced with. People can make mistakes in such an environment, so maybe they were making some. I didn't know what I was looking for; but I was learning something in the process, and I was trying to find something worthwhile to do. I sat at my desk with a bill, books of circuit layouts and a pricing reference. And I started checking and cross-checking.

I found mistakes. I found a lot of them. Some weren't worth much, but some could be worth a lot of money over time. I was surprised, so I wanted to double-check my work. I went to Jim, who felt underutilized. "Hey, Jim. I wonder if you could help me out on something." Jim perked up right away. I asked him to check over the work I'd just done. I told him why it could be important. I didn't want him to think it was just busywork. "These bills are for a lot of money. If they're wrong, it's costing us plenty."

Jim was dubious we'd find anything but accepted the assignment graciously. He appreciated being asked for help. It made him feel useful. He was slow and thorough in his work. When he was finally done, he came back with a big grin on his face. He'd found more mistakes than I had. "Carly, this is great! We can save the company lots of money."

We needed to be sure, so we started looking over lots of bills. I asked Carol to help verify records with us. After several weeks it was clear that we had been overbilled by tens of millions of dollars in a single month. Now it was time to call in Bell Atlantic. I figured we were paying them, so they should come to us.

Levels and titles mattered a lot to people in the Bell System, as they matter a lot in most big companies. People become attached to the symbols of their power and authority. At AT&T the protocol was that a superior can call a meeting with a subordinate but not the other way around. I was a second-level manager, and the person in charge of Access Billing at Bell Atlantic was my superior, a district manager. He was also the only person who had the authority to fix the problem we'd identified, and so I asked him to come see me.

He was polite and agreed to come. Jim, Carol and I sat across the table from him and his team. I started slowly walking through every bill and pointing out every error. Each time they asked a question, Jim or Carol would have the backup documentation. We gave them all the cases where they'd undercharged us too, but most of the mistakes went the other way. We overwhelmed them with data.

Finally, they said, "Okay. We believe you. What do you want us to do?"

"Pay us the money."

Jim was triumphant. He'd been in the Bell System almost thirty years, and he liked making a big district manager squirm. Even Carol was starting to have fun. This was serious work worth serious money, but we were also doing something no one had ever done before. On our own we'd discovered something that mattered, and it was exciting.

By now we knew there was a lot of money at stake, and that we could force Bell Atlantic to rectify their mistakes. And so we started checking every bill. There was soon too much work for our little team, so I got Bob's permission to hire temporary workers to help us. We had boxes and boxes of paper and more than fifty people poring over every detail of every bill. It wasn't sexy work. It was tedious, detailed, boring work, but it was important. So every time we brought new temporaries in, I'd have a meeting and explain to them how their work made a difference. I'd tell them how much money they were helping us save. I explained why all the boring details they were looking at mattered. They needed to understand the value and context of their work if they were to do it with quality. And at the end of every week we'd tell everyone how much money we'd saved. Everybody works better if they're motivated, and they were motivated because they knew they were making a positive difference.

Bob had seen enough to know that if we were having this problem in the Eastern Region, every region must be having the same problem. And so he asked for a meeting at corporate headquarters in New Jersey. He wanted to bring together all the other ACMC organizations around the country and our company attorneys to tell them what we were finding. He told me to get ready to make a presentation, and we went to headquarters.

We were in a big conference room with lots of people crowded around a huge, long table. Bob introduced me and asked me to describe what we were doing. I'd only been to headquarters one other time, and that was to accompany a customer on a tour. This was a pretty intimidating setting, and the people in the room had been at AT&T and Engineering a lot longer than I had.

People challenged me immediately. They argued and interrupted. Their questions revealed deep skepticism, but there was something else as well. They were almost offended that I could have discovered something they didn't know about, but for every question they asked I had an answer. I wasn't attacking what they were doing; I'd just been looking for something that wasn't getting done. As the session wore on, I realized I knew more about the subject than anyone else in the room. They had power and position, but I had the facts. And I had Bob Cann, a man with a great reputation who, having called the meeting and brought me to it, was staking at least part of that reputation on me. I will never forget him for that. It was generous, and it made a big difference in that room and for my career.

Resistance to a new idea or a new way of doing things is interesting to observe. It is an emotional reaction to fear of the unknown or fear of losing power or influence. It does not always yield to facts and reason, and such was the case at that meeting. Bob and I returned from New Jersey disappointed and discouraged.

On our way back, Bob said, "I loved watching what happened in that room. When you stood up, the look on everyone's face said, this gal doesn't have anything to tell us. And then as you talked, their looks changed; and you could see them deciding that maybe you weren't so dumb after all. Look, Carly, people see me and even if they don't know me, they assume I'm pretty good or I wouldn't be in the job I'm in. People see you and they don't assume that. You have to convince them."

I was thirty years old, but believe it or not, this was the first time it had ever occurred to me that my gender alone could deny me the presumption of competence. Because I was a reasonably attractive woman, some people assumed I wasn't capable. Sure, I'd been harassed and propositioned; some men were just like that, but Bob Cann was telling me that many other people wouldn't give me the benefit of the doubt. They wouldn't assume I could do the job I had. I would have to actively dissuade them from their presumptions about who and what I was before I would earn their respect. I'd have to work harder and be better prepared.

He was also telling me that I could see this bias in their faces and body language. He was giving me great insight. Over time I learned to study people carefully and look for the nonverbal cues. Some people's mental blinders are so strong that they can't take them off. More often than not, though, I learned that if I could convince people that I knew what I was doing in the first twenty minutes or so, they'd listen to the rest. If you can get people to put their prejudices aside, whatever they are, and actually listen to you in those first twenty minutes, then you can stand on your capabilities.

That summer Bob was sent away for an eight-week executive training course and he put me in charge of the district. When an ambitious attorney involved in a major set of legal disputes with Bell Atlantic showed up, he had to deal with me. This attorney had been at that New Jersey meeting and thought that what we were doing could be useful to his case. He was impatient, belligerent and rude. He was the first truly abusive executive I'd run into. He routinely belittled everyone he worked with, and shouted at people to get his way. He knew a lot about the law, but he didn't know anything about access engineering and billing. He had a real problem and we could really help him, but he'd have to slow down and listen long enough to let us.

We battled back and forth all summer long. He'd ask for things that made no sense, and instead of just giving them to him, I'd try to convince him that he'd be better served with something else. Most of the time he would eventually listen to reason because he was a smart man, but it took a lot of energy. He had no appreciation for the work anyone else was doing. His requirements were always the top priority in his mind, and he couldn't understand why we weren't just dropping everything else to answer his requests immediately. So we argued a lot about time frames.

I didn't particularly like how he talked to me, but I could appreciate the pressure he was under. So I let it ride. Sometimes, when he didn't get the answer he wanted, the attorney would work around me to get a different one. He would call Jim. Jim was a slow talker and cautious. This attorney talked a mile a minute, so he got frustrated and called Jim an idiot. He called Carol and got her so upset she threatened to quit on the spot. And then one day I came in to find both Bob's secretary and my own in tears. He'd shown up at their desks and screamed at them, demanding they find me immediately wherever I was. The attorney was a division manager—he was a level higher than Bob. When he threw his weight around, it had a big impact. They were afraid they were going to lose their jobs. And at a basic human level he'd been disrespectful in the extreme. I remembered being a receptionist and a secretary. I remembered how it felt.

A boss isn't paid more than a subordinate because he or she is better. A boss is paid more than a subordinate because the boss has greater responsibilities. One of those responsibilities is to stand up for people when it's necessary and to shield them from things they shouldn't have to deal with. I had to call this man on his behavior. The way he was berating people wasn't right. I was very nervous because he was a high-level, fair-haired lawyer with a lot of clout. Despite my trepidation, though, it was necessary. I wouldn't be living up to my responsibilities if I didn't confront him. So I went into Bob's office, shut the door and made a phone call to the attorney.

"I have some very upset people over here."

"Oh, tell them to get over it. I'm in a hurry; I need the data, and I can't get anyone to help me."

"We're all doing everything we can to help you. My people are under a lot of pressure and working long hours too. But you cannot speak to them the way you do. It's disrespectful, it's abusive and it's wrong."

We went back and forth like this for quite a while. I honestly thought that if I could just make him see the impact he was having on people, he'd realize he was shooting himself in the foot. For him it was a matter of pride and power. He was too proud to admit he was wrong, and he thought he would lose power if he backed down.

All my life I had worked hard to be liked. Most of us want to be liked, but I think women feel a special pressure to be pleasant and accommodating. That day I decided that sometimes it's more important to be respected than to be liked. When I get really angry, my voice gets very low and very steady. I don't get louder, I get quieter. I could not reason with him, so now I would talk to him in a language he understood: the language of power. I had something he needed.

I said very quietly: "You will apologize to the two women you abused. You will never speak to them in that way again. You will not talk to Jim or Carol. And until you apologize, you will not get one more piece of data, one more shred of help from me."

"You can't do that," he howled into the phone.

"I can and I will."

I was shaking like a leaf and burst into tears when I hung up the phone. I was exhausted and scared. I was also furious. He could not treat people like this and get away with it. I told our secretaries that if he called again and was abusive, they should hang up the phone. I said I would take responsibility. I told Jim and Carol the same thing. And then we waited. We stopped working on his outstanding requests. We didn't send the data that was due. After two days he called and apologized.

Never threaten if you're not prepared to follow through. Never threaten if reason can prevail, but if you must, threaten something that really matters and stick to it. There are, unfortunately, too many abusive people. In the business world they are frequently tolerated because they deliver results. Abusive behavior is unacceptable. Everyone deserves to be treated with courtesy and respect. Sometimes the only solution is to fire the abusers, but I would learn that later. As it was, I felt lucky that I hadn't been fired, and relieved that this lawyer's desire to get on with his case had overcome his pride.

Eventually the people in New Jersey caught on. We were getting refunds while no one else was. Now "corporate" decided that the whole country needed to be systematically verifying access billing and demanding remuneration. A corporate officer was put in charge of a new, nationwide program. They brought all of us into headquarters again and told us how we were going to proceed, and they gave us a lot of forms we needed to fill out and send in every week to report on our progress.

I'm not proud of how I reacted. I was upset. We'd discovered this problem and had a fine solution, and they were changing it! Worse, we had to fill out all these stupid reports every week. In fact, after that I would spend every Thursday night at my kitchen table filling out reports of the previous week's activity. With my calculator in hand, I would usually be up until 3:00 A.M. making sure we'd got it all right.

I was totally demoralized by the fact that I no longer owned what we'd started. Jim and Carol and Ed reacted the same way. It had become bigger than we were. Bob Cann wisely reminded us that we'd really gotten what we wanted. We'd succeeded in changing how the company did business, and we'd helped save literally hundreds of millions of dollars. Still, it was hard to share and hard to let go—we'd become possessive of our success.

You have to remember, this wasn't glamorous work. Our teams of temporaries sat in the basement of the building. We had so many boxes stacked up that we'd been moved out of our own space and were using rented, metal desks. Finding a way to keep motivated was important. For a long time it had been the excitement of doing something new and being the only ones doing it. We knew something others didn't. Now that motivation wasn't there anymore. Eventually we decided that we would compete with the other regions and be the absolute best ACMC team in the country. Our reports would be the most accurate, our work the most thorough. When we challenged Bell Atlantic, we would be right and we would prevail. We took great pride in the fact that no one ever found an error in one of our reports, and that we had the highest hit rate of any team.

One day in March of 1985, Bob asked me to come into his office. He closed the door, and when I'd sat down, he said, "Congratulations, Carly. You're going to be promoted to district manager. You're going back to Government Communications to run their largest civilian government account, the General Services Administration. You're going to have a big team reporting to you."

Of course I was pleased. It was a big move, going from second-level to district. It had happened sooner than I'd imagined. But I wasn't as excited as I thought I'd be. I didn't say anything to my team. I sat on the couch with Frank that night, and when I told him about my big promotion, I cried. He was both bemused and frustrated with me. "Why are you crying? This is huge. You got promoted, and it's a great job. You know a lot already about the federal government. This is perfect!"

I was crying because I didn't want to leave Jim and Carol and Bob. I loved seeing them every morning, loved seeing their delight when we achieved a small victory, loved that special camaraderie that comes from working really hard together on something that's really difficult. I was crying because I didn't want to leave Engineering. I'd gotten comfortable there. The engineers liked me, and I liked them. Now I would have to start all over. I was crying because I was scared. There was a big difference between a second- and a third-level management job. Was I really up to it?

I met with each of my team separately to tell them I was leaving. Jim Psioda was one of the most loyal and dedicated employees I've ever seen. He was dogged and persistent in his work and loved the challenge. He wasn't flashy or fancy (he got tongue-tied a lot), but he was the Rock of Gibraltar.

When you needed him, he was there. Jim was one of those people you know you want in the trenches with you. I told him how much I appreciated his work, his counsel, his companionship and his contributions. I told him I would miss him tremendously. He told me that in his thirty years in the Bell System, I was the best boss he'd ever had. We both had tears in our eyes. Jim gave me a great gift: he told me that I'd not only earned his respect, I'd earned his trust.

Carol started crying almost immediately. It wasn't just that we'd miss each other, although she didn't have many friends. She had been carrying something around with her for a year, and whatever it was weighed heavily on her heart. I could see it in her, but I didn't know what it was. So now she told me. She wanted to have a baby. She wanted to devote more time to her marriage. She didn't want to work full-time anymore, but she felt guilty saying it. She'd worked hard to earn her engineering degree. She hoped she would get promoted soon (I'd put her name in for a couple of second-level openings, and she had a good shot). It was the 1980s and somehow she felt she wasn't sufficiently ambitious.

I said, "Carol, you cannot sell your soul. Don't become someone you don't like because of the pressure. Live your life in a way that makes you happy and proud. If you sell your soul, no one can pay you back." And we had a good, long hug.

It was the first time I had used the word *soul* at work. As the years went by and I saw how the pressure to succeed can affect people, I would say these same words to myself and others many times. That day I was trying to tell her that how she measured her own life was so much more important than any position or any company. I was also trying to reach out in a conversation between two human beings, not between a boss and a subordinate.

Sometimes bosses forget to see employees as people, but sometimes it's just as hard to see the person in the boss. A boss represents authority and power. Maybe you respect the boss, maybe you resent them. The higher up the boss, the more people see the position rather than the person. As I rose through the ranks, the work would become more challenging and in many ways more rewarding, but the higher I climbed, the lonelier it became.

When I went to ACMC, I'd chosen challenge over safety. When I got there, I'd looked for the possibilities. Bob, Jim, Carol and I hadn't been afraid to try something new. Challenge comes from the reality that your best is required and falling short is possible. Learning comes from rising to meet that challenge. Sometimes the riskier choice gives you a better opportunity to prove yourself to others, and you'll always prove something important to yourself. You'll know yourself and those you work with better.

9 | Saving My Tears

THE GENERAL SERVICES ADMINISTRATION was the procurement arm for the federal government's civilian agencies. Among many other responsibilities, GSA also provided data and voice communications services for these agencies. The team I now led maintained huge national networks and switching systems for GSA. We responded to all the procurement requests for upgrades or additional service. We competed for every opportunity to meet their new communications needs. GSA was worth hundreds of millions of dollars a year to AT&T. GSA's Requests for Proposal (RFPs, the documents government agencies use to describe their procurement requirements) were already worth almost $20 billion.

GSA had huge purchasing power and immense clout in the marketplace. Their job was to demand the best prices, the most advantageous terms and the latest technology. They got it by using their market power and through the tortuous, complex, carefully orchestrated and highly regulated RFP process. Their procurement officers were tough, demanding, well aware of their institution's power, and extremely difficult to deal with. Despite all the challenges of working with GSA, their business was ferociously competed for by every telephone company, systems integrator, and computer manufacturer. If GSA bought what you sold, you wanted their business.

GSA's purchasing decisions could literally change the competitive land-scape. They could make markets for new technology and destroy or salvage companies. And so GSA officials believed it was also their job to advance the public policy and regulatory goals of the federal government. GSA wanted to make divestiture work. That meant AT&T needed to face as much competi-tion as possible, and if we lost a lot of our existing business it was all to the good. Rumors were swirling that GSA was about to put a new RFP out on the street. Its purpose was to rebuild the entire Federal Telecommunications Systems (FTS). AT&T would have to compete for, and stood to lose, all of its existing business. The rumored RFP would be called FTS2000. The name meant that whoever won the right to provide the new Federal Telephone System would do so until the year 2000. FTS2000 would be worth about $25 billion. It would be the largest nondefensive systems procurement ever awarded.

I didn't know any of this when I arrived for my first day on the new job. Sure, I knew what GSA and our team did, but I didn't know what GSA was contemplating or how high the stakes were. My superiors didn't seem to know either, which is probably why they weren't worried about putting me into the job. GSA was a big account, but it had been pretty sleepy for a long time. A little over a year after January 1, 1984, the fact that GSA had a vested interest in accelerating the impact of divestiture wasn't appreciated by Government Communications executives or headquarters. All the action seemed to be on the military side of the AT&T business.

That first day I did discover some important things that distinguished this job from my others. I had an office for the first time. I had a large team—almost sixty people. And when I started making the rounds to ask people about their work, it was soon clear that some of the second-level managers didn't like my talking directly to their subordinates. It wasn't true for everyone, but a lot of these managers thought that access to me and the knowledge we would share with one another was a privilege of their rank. It was the first time I'd been high enough in the organization to see that some managers think they add value merely by being between their boss and their employees. These people thought that a layer of management was valuable in and of itself. They ferried information back and forth. I'd heard the old saying "Information is power"; now I saw people who practiced it.

The worst offender was a guy named Ethan Downs. He seemed like a 42-long type. He'd been on the account a long time and had a vague set of responsibilities for "new business." He had been positioning himself for the district-level job for years. He'd been bitterly disappointed when he was passed over, and was even more disappointed when I arrived. I was younger and less knowledgeable about the account. This alone could have accounted for his resentment and condescension. The fact that I was a woman can't have helped.

I first heard about FTS2000 from Ethan. He hadn't exactly volunteered any information, but I'd asked enough questions that he couldn't avoid telling me. It sounded pretty important to me, so I asked him what we were doing to prepare for it. In an offhand way he said, "Don't worry, Carly. I have it under control—I'm meeting with some network planners up in New Jersey."

I had plenty of other things to worry about as I settled into my new role, so I let it go that day. Every couple of days, though, I'd wander back to Ethan's cubicle and ask him what was happening on FTS2000. His uncooperative attitude began to irritate me. It also alarmed me. The amount— $25 billion—was a lot of money, and all my instincts said we were underestimating the situation. No one other than Ethan seemed to be focused on it, and that just didn't make sense to me.

I asked Ethan to arrange a trip to New Jersey. I told him I thought it was important for the two of us to meet with these network planners to determine their level of preparedness for the RFP. I knew how many people we had working on the other $20 billion worth of GSA RFPs. I thought I could make some rough comparisons to decide if the yellow caution lights flashing in my brain were real or just an outcome of the obvious tension that was building between Ethan and me. Ethan told me it wasn't necessary, threw out lots of logistical complications, and did everything to talk me out of it. I insisted, and eventually he had no choice.

Our trip was revealing. The folks in New Jersey, in particular the district manager who ran the network planning team, were obviously as frustrated as I was. They didn't have enough information about the customer's requirements; they really needed to talk to the customer directly at some point.

What was our strategy for the response? We had lots of technical options; how would we decide which to choose? What was our sales strategy? How did we want to position our response against the existing network? They asked all these questions and more.

Instead of allowing a free flow of information between everyone at the meeting, Ethan attempted to answer every question. His tone was one of fatigued tolerance. He had explained all of this so many times, but for the good of the business he would do it again. Ethan had set himself up as the single conduit of communication and information between New Jersey and Washington. If New Jersey needed to know something about the customer or our strategy, they had to ask Ethan. If Washington needed to know something about what the network planners were doing, they had to ask Ethan. Perhaps Ethan didn't realize that people frequently want to hear things firsthand, particularly if they're important. Maybe he didn't appreciate that real problem solving requires the give-and-take of conversation, not the orchestrated flow of bits of information over time. Maybe he really thought he was helping by filtering and interpreting a complicated set of facts. More likely, he was defensive because he'd lost the job he wanted and was determined to build up his power base by holding on to important information and forcing people to come through him to get it. Information is power. Today the Internet has changed everything. Ethan's game is harder to play, but people still play it.

On the way back from the meeting, I tried to explain to Ethan why he couldn't control every information exchange. FTS2000 was going to be huge. The stakes were high. We could lose everything—our existing business with the customer and the new business. We needed a lot of help. He couldn't carry all of this on his shoulders alone. Now was not the time to be a hero; now was the time to be realistic. Realistically, we weren't adequately prepared for what was coming. Ethan could play a huge role in the solution because he knew more about this than anyone else. Or he could be part of the problem.

I really did want Ethan to succeed. I needed him to step up to a new role. And I felt for him. I knew why he was disappointed. If I'd been in his shoes, I might have reacted the same way. I remembered how I'd felt when everyone had descended on us at the ACMC and we'd had to let go, but there was no getting around the fact that Ethan had to change. My responsibilities demanded that I maximize AT&T's preparedness to compete effectively for GSA's business.

Ethan and I would have this same conversation many times over many weeks. Each time he would assure me he understood and promise me he'd do better. Nothing changed. Finally, despite my disappointment and apprehension, I stepped up to what I had to do. If Ethan would not or could not change, he had to leave. I was disappointed because I actually thought I could change him. I was apprehensive because I'd never had to fire anyone.

No one likes to hear bad news. We particularly don't like to hear it from people we resent—so we resist hearing it. Think about how often two people in the same conversation have totally different recollections or interpretations of it. When the news is bad, and the messenger is unwelcome, the signal sent is often glaringly at odds with the signal received. When resistance is inevitable, words alone are never enough. Many nonverbal details can either support the intended message or undermine it.

I thought a lot about how to communicate effectively with Ethan. How should I explain it? Where should the meeting be? When? There are circumstances where it's important to let people come to the right conclusion in their own way on their own time. Only then can they truly embrace and support the decision. That approach takes time, however, and I'd let the situation linger long enough. Ethan was hurting the business, and we needed to move on. So whether Ethan agreed or not, we needed to understand each other right away.

I picked a Tuesday afternoon at five o'clock. Ethan could leave the office right after the meeting and think about it that night. He wouldn't have to face the team until he'd prepared himself. Wednesday morning we could discuss the next steps, and we'd have the rest of the week to lay out a game plan. Three days seemed like the right amount of time to agree on how to transition his responsibilities, prepare him to find another position and then communicate it all to the broader team. I didn't want anyone agonizing over the weekend about what might happen. I wanted Ethan, and the rest of the team, to go into the weekend thinking about the future—so everything had to be resolved by Friday.

When I meet with people, I usually sit with them at a conference table or come around from behind my desk. It's easier to talk when there are fewer barriers, and people are more open when they're not intimidated. For this meeting, though, I sat behind my desk. Ethan didn't think I should be his boss. He resented my authority. Now I needed the symbol of that authority to stand squarely between us; he might not like it, but he couldn't ignore it.

Since we'd talked past each other so many times, I would use language I knew he'd understand.

"Ethan, you're a football fan, right?"

"Sure, why?"

"On a football team every man plays his position. Every position is important, but there's only one quarterback. Why is that?"

Ethan didn't know where this was going, but he'd play along. "Because the quarterback calls the plays."

"And when the play is called, the team runs the play, right?"

"Right."

"Ethan, on the GSA team, everybody has an important role to play, but there's only one quarterback. That quarterback is me, not you. You may think it should be the other way around, but it's not. I'm the quarterback; and since you're not willing to run the plays I call, you need to leave the team."

We understood each other. Ethan was professional and polite. I thanked him for his many contributions—and meant it—and offered to help him find his next assignment. At the end of the week, when we had an agreed-upon transition plan, I called my peer in network planning at headquarters and informed him.

"I was wondering how long it would take you to do that. It was the right thing to do."

I was surprised. My peer had never said a word about Ethan needing to go. Perhaps he didn't want to take on the responsibility of that recommendation, but he was glad I'd confronted the situation. Confrontation isn't easy—at least not for me. I have to steel myself, and I agonize over it every time. I much prefer the camaraderie of a team working together over the conflict of a team at odds. When confrontation becomes necessary, it needs to be honest, clear and respectful. Every time I've asked someone to leave a job, it's been painful, certainly for them but also for me. And every time I've done it, people have come forward and told me I'd done the right thing, even if they'd lacked the courage or candor to tell me beforehand.

Headquarters' network planning and my team started meeting together on a regular basis. Meanwhile, the people at GSA were beginning to hold meetings with vendors to share their preliminary thinking about the huge procurement. Interesting groups of companies were lining up to compete. The aerospace companies were going to play because they had systems-integration expertise that would be vital for such a complex program. In addition to AT&T, MCI and Sprint were competing. And, of course, all seven Regional Bell Operating Companies and GTE were planning to participate (this was long before the wave of consolidation that swept the telecom industry). Every time I attended one of these GSA sessions, I had a feeling in the pit of my stomach that we were being outgunned. Our competitors' teams were much larger than ours, and they had higher-level executives.

By this time, I'd done my homework, and I knew as much about GSA as anyone else in the company. I'd read every relevant document and met with every relevant GSA official. And I began to wonder whether I was trying to be a hero like Ethan. When the draft FTS2000 RFP was released, I knew I needed help. Although I could continue to rely on New Jersey for support, I was in way over my head.

It's important to have confidence in what you know and what you can do. You can't make decisions effectively without confidence. It's equally important to be realistic about what you don't know and what you can't do: without realism, confidence becomes hubris. Realistically, I didn't know enough to make all the right decisions about how to compete for GSA's business. Besides, I couldn't commandeer sufficient resources within AT&T—I didn't have the clout, or the connections or the experience.

Mike Brunner was the executive vice president in charge of Government Communications. He was a wonderful leader with strong values. He was tough as nails, demanding and sometimes impatient. He also laughed often and encouraged others to do the same. If I was going to get help, Mike would have to authorize it. He was many, many levels above me, but he was always approachable. He was the one who'd promoted me.

Monica Archambault was Mike's secretary. She was a beautiful, lively, intelligent woman who was a joy to be around. Like most really good secretaries, she knew everyone and everything that mattered. It didn't hurt that men loved to talk with her—she found out a lot during their visits to her office. It was my great fortune that she befriended me. Like most executives' calendars, Mike's was impossible, and I wasn't an especially high priority in his mind. We tried and tried, but days dragged into weeks, and I still couldn't get in to see him. I was probably a pest, but finally, Monica said: "Carly, why don't you slip in there and ask to have a drink with him tonight. I'll explain it's important that he talk to you; and really, if it's not after work today, I'm not sure when he'll ever do it." Mike trusted Monica absolutely, so when Monica told him he should have a drink with me, he believed her.

I don't know why she suggested we have a drink instead of sitting in his office. Maybe she just thought he'd be more relaxed after a long day and wouldn't be so irritated about having to squeeze in one more meeting, or maybe she was smart enough to see that I was pretty uptight myself about this meeting. Telling him "I can't do this on my own—I need more help" didn't feel like the best way to impress the big boss.

We went to a bar in the courtyard of our building. We went because it was close, but it wasn't a particularly conducive setting for a business conversation. It was a loud, smoky singles bar. Mike and I sat huddled around a small table, shouting over the music while the rest of the patrons circled each other, assessing the possibilities. I felt foolish for having made the suggestion, and mortified that I was wasting Mike's time. Mike was gracious and encouraging, and made a joke to put me at ease. I took a deep breath and said: "Mike, FTS2000 is bigger than me. If we don't approach it differently, we're going to lose."

At least I had his attention. I was as blunt and straightforward as I could be because he deserved the truth, but I also knew I couldn't just describe the problem and lay it at Mike's feet. If I was going to ask for help, I also had to propose a solution. I knew that drawing upon the resources of the entire company was critical; our competitors were going to throw everything they had at this. Besides, GSA didn't particularly want us to win; AT&T had been the sole provider of service to them for decades, and they thought it was someone else's turn. If others won this contract, GSA would be advancing the public policy goals of telecommunications competition and getting a better network all at the same time.

I made my pitch to Mike: "We need a full-time vice president assigned to this. Headquarters needs to be completely behind our approach here, so it can't be solely a Government Communications program. The vice president has to be someone New Jersey will trust because it has to be someone who can marshal all the corporate resources that are required. My team and I will work for him, but he's going to have to go get a lot more executive talent."

Business is about producing results. If you're going to work for a company, large or small, then you must be prepared to embrace the objectives of that business. If you can't, you should work someplace else. Those business objectives are more important than any individual ambition or the desire to "get credit." I believed that then. It is why I told Mike someone else needed to be in charge. I believe it to this day.

When our hour-long meeting was over, Mike agreed. From that evening on, Mike became a wise mentor to me. I was fortunate to have his counsel during my career, and I am equally fortunate to still be able to call him my friend. We've laughed often about that night over the years: how tense—and intense—I was. How out of place we both looked and felt.

Mike went to headquarters to meet with the AT&T chairman and his staff. He asked for a full-time vice president and several directors. This was a huge commitment of resources, but Mike insisted that we really did need the cavalry. As is often the case, the arrival of the cavalry didn't bring all good news. As the new team assembled, I had to engage in a massive education effort so everyone had the same base of knowledge to work from. This took a lot of time and effort, and as is frequently the case when new teams come together, decisions that I used to make quickly became major deliberations among many new players. Everyone had a different point of view about what we should be doing, and we didn't know each other well enough to have sorted out roles and responsibilities. Until we were aligned around our strategy, and learned how to work with one another, everything would slow down. It was frustrating, but it was necessary. Sometimes you have to go slow first to go faster later. We had to take the time to build a broader, coordinated team now so that we could act quickly and effectively later.

Lou Golm, the new vice president, was the perfect choice. He had been rising in the ranks of AT&T for a number of years. This was his first officer position, and he was enthusiastic about the opportunity. He seemed to know everyone in the company, so he could get the people he needed. He had an easygoing style that encouraged give-and-take. The other senior executives who'd been chosen were more problematic. Part of my frustration came from their eagerness to dismiss me; just because I'd asked for help didn't mean I couldn't add value. Some of them, clearly, had not worked with many women before, and I was a very junior midlevel manager.

One of the executives was put in charge of the actual RFP response—ultimately it would exceed forty-five volumes. He bragged too often about his support of women, but he could not talk to one without a constant, lecherous leer on his face. Before his assignment was completed, he would be forced out because he had propositioned one too many women. I had encouraged each of these women (one was my friend Carole Spurrier) to bring their complaints to Lou Golm, who ultimately acted on them.

Another executive was in charge of technology and network design. One evening at a team Christmas party he told me that he didn't know whether "to hate me or fall in love with me." Frank was observing our conversation from across the room and said I kept clenching my fist while I talked. I don't recall that, but I do remember how I ended the conversation:

"Do you want to step outside?"

"Sure," he said, wondering what I had in mind.

"Good. Because I'm going to punch you full in the face."

The guys from Boeing were the worst. FTS2000 was going to be a massive, complex program with many moving parts. AT&T lacked program management expertise in-house, so we partnered with the Boeing Company's Systems Integration Division. Watching the discipline and expertise involved in professional program management made me a believer for the rest of my career. Ultimately we would build this capability at Hewlett-Packard, but before we did, we would buy it or partner for it.

We needed the support of Boeing's top management as well as AT&T's, so we decided to bring the executives of both companies together for a meeting. We held a full day of reviews and then adjourned for a dinner. The day had gone well, and everyone was in good spirits. At dinner, the senior-most executive present from the Boeing Company turned to me and said: "That was a great presentation you made today, Carly. You really understand this market and the customer and what we're up against. Tell me, how tough do you think the orals are going to be?"

In large federal procurements, vendors are required to submit written responses as well as engage in oral presentations and technical demonstrations. During oral presentations, vendors highlight the key aspects of their proposals. The customer asks questions and assesses both the responses and the management team. In an intensely competitive procurement, bids are frequently won, or lost, during these "orals." The government can request as many cycles of written response, oral presentation and technical demonstration as it desires. It may eliminate competitors at each phase or keep all competitors in until the end. We expected to have to perform through multiple cycles, and we were reasonably certain no one would be eliminated until the final decisions were made. Orals were going to be absolutely critical to our success.

I was pleased by the question. I also appreciated the compliment, particularly from this executive, and I was eager to give my views on what our strategy should be. Not everyone is effective in an oral presentation. Some of our best technologists wouldn't hold up under the pressure, so we'd have to pick our team carefully. I knew the personalities of the customers who would be asking the questions, and I had some opinions on how we could communicate most effectively with them.

I took his question seriously and I was answering it seriously, but after a minute he laughed and interrupted me: "Carly, we'll have plenty of time to decide on our strategy. I was just wondering: maybe you shouldn't be one of our presenters. I know some of you women can't take the pressure. We don't want you losing your cool in there. Why are you doing this anyway? Don't you want to spend more time with your husband and have children?"

I could feel the blood rush to my face. Then everyone was laughing because I was so obviously blushing. I said almost inaudibly, "Don't worry. I won't lose my cool."

Lou rushed to my defense and said, "Carly keeps her cool better than almost anyone else here." It was true. The two executives Lou had brought to the team were legendary for their temper tantrums. If either of them was in a bad mood, meetings were rescheduled. Their behavior would not have been tolerated in a woman. Lou was the coolest under fire; nothing, absolutely nothing, rattled him.

That night I lost my cool. The Boeing executive wouldn't get off it. He kept asking me about my husband, what he did for a living, how long we'd been married. He did not ask my male colleagues about their wives or their marriages. Finally, I excused myself from the table and walked outside. I found myself crying alone in the parking lot. I was embarrassed I was crying. I was angry I was crying. Most of all I was demoralized that I was once again being underestimated, and I hadn't seen this coming. Eventually I returned to the table and received a halfhearted apology, but I was distant and disengaged for the rest of the evening.

When I got home that night, I called Carole Spurrier and told her what had happened. Carole was fuming too, but she can find a way to laugh at anything. "You should have told him you'd be all right as long as you weren't having your period." She was right. It would have been the perfect response—ridiculing and embarrassing him at the same time. Too bad I wasn't clever enough to have thought of it.

That night, after I'd cried long enough, I made a decision. I would not cry again over others' prejudice. Sure, what people thought or said about me might hurt. What people did to me might hurt as well, but I would not carry their narrow-mindedness or bias as my burden. Life isn't always fair, and it is different for women than for men. I decided to accept that reality and refuse to be diminished by it. I would accomplish all I was capable of. I would concentrate on doing what I believed were the right things for the right reasons to the best of my ability. Some, perhaps even many, might believe I couldn't, or shouldn't, do what I chose. That would be their problem, not mine. They would not wound me again. I had decided once that my life was my own. Now I decided my heart would be my own as well.

I came close to crying during the proxy battle at Hewlett-Packard, and closer still when I left HP, but since 1986 I have saved my tears for more important things: my family, the beauty of nature, Beethoven, a dear friend, the goodness of people, their wisdom, their tragedies or their triumphs.

10 | The Stuff of Triumph

MONEY AND POWER can corrupt, so it was probably inevitable that a $25 billion award and the careers that would be made or broken would corrupt both GSA employees and vendors. Still, it was shocking when it happened, and for quite a while none of us believed it. Most GSA officials were honest, hardworking professionals, and most of the competitors were the same. But it only takes one person at the right place with the right opportunity for an entire process to be compromised.

It would take several years for GSA to award the FTS2000 procurement and several more for the network to actually be implemented. Meanwhile, the current FTS network needed upgrading, so GSA decided to issue an interim procurement for all the switching centers on the network. A vendor could win some, or all, or none of these centers, and the winners would have some important advantages going into FTS2000. When we lost 100 percent of these switching centers to the local telephone companies with prices we knew were competitive, we realized something was wrong. Ultimately we came to believe that money had changed hands, although we couldn't prove it in court. We did prove that lies had been told and favors repaid. Before it was all over, there would also be media reports of drugs and sexual favors, and several people would lose their jobs.

In federal procurement law, a vendor can protest an award. The case is heard by a special judge and the award can be overturned or upheld. Although the laws governing federal procurement are specialized, the way the case is tried is familiar: plaintiff's and defendant's attorneys argue their case before the judge. The facts at issue are presented through witnesses for each party. AT&T now had to decide whether we would sue our customer and bring our protest to the court.

I knew what decision I would make. As a citizen and a taxpayer, I was appalled by the dishonesty of the process. As a manager, I knew that if we allowed a corrupt award to stand, we were throwing away our chances of winning FTS2000. If we couldn't change the game now, then we couldn't play to win. And if you can't play to win, you might as well not play. If we were going to lose, it had to be fair and square. This was not a decision I could make, though; this was one of those times when it was necessary for all the players to come to their own conclusions in their own way in their own time. This was too big and too important. Ultimately the chairman of the company, Jim Olson, had to weigh in on this one.

Corporate headquarters sent down teams of lawyers, led by the legendary John Zeglis, the general counsel. They brought in outside counsel, headed by the famous Washington lawyer Stanley Dees. Because my team was responsible for the current FTS network, I had managed our response to the procurement in question. I spent all day describing to these lawyers what I believed had happened and what our case could be. My good friend Harry Carr, the counsel for Government Communications, was adamant that we should sue and that we could win. At the end of the day, John, a trial lawyer by trade, could smell a good fight and recommended we file the lawsuit.

Thus would begin one of the most extraordinary periods of my career. It was my first experience in a courtroom, although it would not be my last. It was my first experience with the media. It was my first experience watching people lie under oath.

Stanley and his lawyers wanted my full participation in the preparation for the case, so he asked me to sit in on some of the GSA officials' depositions. I sat across the table from people I'd worked with and thought I knew, and I watched some of them lie about events, about themselves, about me. I knew they were lying because I knew the facts. Stanley knew they were lying because he'd seen so many others do the same. That was interesting to me: that if you'd seen enough people lie and enough tell the truth, the difference was perceptible in how they held their heads, where they focused their eyes, the tone and tenor of their voices. Watching them made me both angry and sad. The experience reminded me yet again to watch people carefully because the words people say aren't always the best indicator of what they're really thinking, feeling or intending. There will be times in every career when it will be vital to know whether what someone says is what he or she means. When I've missed this in my own career, the consequences have always been dire.

Stanley pulled no punches with me. Because my team had been at the center of this procurement, I would be the lead witness and the key to our case. I could win the case, or I could lose it. The facts were with us, but they were complex. We would have to convince the judge that we were telling the truth and that others were lying. GSA was joined in its defense by all seven of the Regional Bell Operating Companies who had won the procurement. So our one team would be arrayed against eight teams. The pressure was enormous. I definitely could not lose my cool. So I did the only thing I could: I worked harder, prepared longer, asked every question I could think of until I knew every fact that mattered. Ultimately I would rely on the same things that have sustained me many times: team members who knew what they were doing and believed in the same goals I did, realism about what we were up against and confidence that we had prepared diligently for every eventuality, and enough stamina to outlast just about anyone.

THE FIGURE $25 BILLION is pretty big news everywhere, so the procurement, and our court case, was routinely reported in the media. One morning I arrived at work to find we were front-page news in the *Washington Post*, the *New York Times* and the *Wall Street Journal*. And the news wasn't good: GSA, feeling the heat, was accusing one of my employees of misconduct. She had done nothing wrong, and for that reason alone I thought we needed to defend her reputation. I also didn't want our team put on the defensive before we'd even gotten into the courtroom. I argued strongly to Lou that we needed to respond aggressively.

AT&T normally maintained a pretty low profile in the press, so both Lou and Mike felt they needed to consult with headquarters. My first introduction to the AT&T vice chairman, Randall Tobias, and the executive vice president of Public Relations, Marilyn Laurie, was on a hastily arranged conference call in Lou's office. We debated issuing a press release. I argued that facing reporters directly, and answering their questions, would be more effective. They had to be convinced, both by what we said and how we looked, that we were telling the truth.

I had never talked to a reporter before, but I knew more about the charges and the case than anyone else. If we were going to face reporters' questions, I was the only one who could do it. So Randy and Marilyn put me through my paces. Finally Randy said, "Can you do this, Carly?" "Yes, sir." I remember feeling a huge rush of appreciation for his confidence in me when he said, "Okay. Let's do it."

Typical AT&T press conferences were held in a large room on the fifth floor. An executive would stand behind a podium to speak, and reporters would sit in chairs in rows. But credibility would be everything here, so Herb Linnen, the Washington press director, and I decided that the podium had to go. These reporters needed to get a good close look at me. So we all sat around a large table.

It's an understatement to say I was scared. I remembered going into a brand-new school on the first day and how terrible it was until I met the first person I could actually talk to. And how once I'd been engaged in conversation, I was all right. So when I walked into that room, instead of thinking about the reporters and the stories they would write, I just thought about new people I was about to meet. I shook every reporter's hand and introduced myself. And then I just talked—about why I was there, about why we had filed a protest against GSA, about why the charges against the employee were false. And then I let them ask every question they had. Today, every time I give a speech I get nervous ahead of time. And each time I walk out on a stage, I think about one person and having a conversation.

I learned a lot that day that helped me later. We always talk about "the media," which sounds like an institution or a machine. In truth, reporters are just people, and like people in every walk of life, some are good at their jobs, some aren't. Some reporters are honest, some aren't. People, and reporters, are swayed by emotion, and sometimes the herd can stampede. All reporters, like the rest of us, come to a story with a set of opinions, or biases, or preconceived notions—whether they're prepared to admit them or not. Sometimes that point of view changes over the course of a story; sometimes it doesn't. And all reporters advance their point of view by deciding what to put in the story and what to leave out. The one thing every reporter, and every one of us, has in common is this: we all love a good story. For some reporters a good story is more important than the facts. In this case we had both the story and the facts: junior, unknown female manager defends another woman's honor against the powerful federal government. We didn't score every point, but we advanced our cause that day.

THE COURT CASE OPENED, and almost immediately, at about 8:15 A.M., it was time for me to take the stand. I had never been in a witness box before, never been sworn in. The discovery phase of this trial had been extensive, and I knew the opposition had everything from my personal calendar to my expense vouchers. Eight sets of attorneys watched and waited as Stanley Dees took me through more than four hours of direct testimony.

Direct had gone well, but it took intense concentration to listen to the question and to explain my answers in clear terms that would mean something to the judge, all the while wondering why the GSA attorneys scribbled furiously during some answers and not at all during others. I was also well aware that because this day was so important, there were many AT&T executives from headquarters in the courtroom. Tommy Thomsen, who was Mike Brunner's boss, told me he was there for moral support. He meant it, but he'd also shown up to evaluate for himself how the case would go. Eventually I had to forget about everyone else and think about just one person, the judge, and whether I was communicating truthfully and effectively.

Stanley was pleased when direct was over, and he wanted to finish the cross-examination that same day. I was tired, and it would mean I'd need to be on the stand another six hours or so. GSA went first. After a few hours of cross, they decided to go through my calendar page by page. They took particular interest in a page that read "Jim Olson." I smiled at the memory of that meeting. It was good they asked about it because I needed a burst of energy in the middle of what was by now an extremely tough day.

Lou Golm and I had gone to meet with people at the Office of the Chairman. Jim Olson held regular meetings with the twelve senior executives of AT&T. We were asked to present our strategy for FTS2000. The last time I'd been near this group was when Mike Brunner and I had gone to New Jersey to ask for a vice president. Mike had asked me to come along in case there were any questions he needed me for, but I'd waited outside. I remember the afternoon slipping into evening and the windows I sat near growing dark. Mike came out only once and stepped back inside after a brief question.

This time, with Lou, I assumed I was there once again as a resource, not a participant. I was about to sit down outside when Lou said, "Come on in, Carly."

"Are you sure?" I said tentatively.

"Absolutely."

I was thrilled; this was the real inner sanctum. Inside there was a long, rectangular table. The meeting was in progress when we entered the room. Lou sat at the table, and I sat in a chair along the wall. Lou made introductions, and then Jim Olson said, "Pull up your chair, Carly, and sit at the table." And he motioned to a spot at his left hand. I was touched—he had acknowledged me in a very personal way. I was also grateful—he had signaled to the other executives that he was prepared to listen to me.

This memory made me feel ten feet tall all over again. GSA seemed very excited about the entry in my calendar.

"Why does your calendar read 'Jim Olsen'?"

"Because Lou Golm and I were meeting with him."

"Why were you meeting?"

"We were talking about FTS2000."

"What were you discussing about FTS2000?"

"Our strategy."

"What aspects of your strategy?"

"Well, mostly our political strategy actually."

"Did you talk about pricing at all?"

"Yes, we did, but our principal topic was upcoming meetings Mr. Olson had on the Hill with members of Congress."

"Why would Mr. Olsen be interested in meeting with you on these subjects?"

By now I'd noticed that the GSA attorney seemed both anxious and excited; all the lawyers at his table were scribbling furiously. I was getting nervous. What was it they thought they had?

"Well, it's an important procurement for us and . . ."

The lawyer cut me off. "Mrs. Fiorina, are you aware that meeting with a GSA official on pricing and strategy for FTS2000 outside the procurement process is strictly forbidden?"

Suddenly I understood. GSA Procurement reported to a GSA member of senior executive staff named Jim Olsen. I had him. "Certainly, I'm aware of that, but I was meeting with the chairman of AT&T, Jim Olson."

The courtroom erupted in laughter. Even the judge was amused. And the GSA attorney knew he was finished. He tried a few more halfhearted attempts to find incriminating evidence in my calendar.

"I see here you show a notation for a meeting at two o'clock."

Finally, the judge had had enough. "It also shows she went to the hairdresser at six o'clock. So what? Move along, counselor." Years later the subject of hair and hairdressers would become the stuff of infuriating and inaccurate media reports, but that day I was delighted the subject had come up.

Each of the seven RBOC attorneys also cross-examined me, but by then the wind had gone out of their sails. At 7:40 p.m. the last attorney stood and said, "Your Honor, please bear with me. I know it's very late, but it's hard to do this when the witness is smarter than the attorneys. I only have a few questions." Ten minutes later the judge said, "Well, I guess we can finally adjourn." And Stanley Dees stood up with a big grin on his face and crowed: "Your Honor, at least give me the pleasure of saying 'No redirect.' "

That night we drank a toast to the judge and to the hapless GSA attorney who hadn't prepared as well as he should have.

OUR OVERWHELMING VICTORY in the court case could have made us cocky. Instead, it made us wary. We had to be realistic, and the truth was that GSA wanted us to lose more than ever now. We had won the battle, but we still needed to win the war. During the meeting with Jim

Olson, we were discussing a split in the award for FTS2000. At this point, FTS2000 was a winner-take-all procurement: one company, or a consortium of companies, would win 100 percent of the business. I had become convinced that under these circumstances we were going to lose. It would not be politically feasible to have the new ten-year award for the FTS network go to the same company that had been providing service for the last quarter century. Everyone would claim that AT&T had had an unfair advantage. Everyone would protest. Everyone would conclude that GSA had done something wrong. Congress would weigh in. Our win would become a pyrrhic victory. The whole award would become so controversial that neither we nor GSA would be able to move forward. The current game was stacked against us. So we'd have to change the game.

Why didn't GSA split the award between two consortiums? It was a radical idea, but once the environment we were competing in was clearly understood, the logic would be compelling. Eventually GSA embraced the idea because they understood that this was a lower-risk strategy for them as well. They also added some twists of their own to ensure perpetual competition throughout the ten years: one vendor would win 60 percent of the business, one 40 percent. At specified intervals over the life of the contract, the two winners would compete for the swing 20 percent.

That day in Jim Olson's conference room we were getting the final blessing on this strategy. We were also asking Jim Olson to call several members of Congress to relay our strong support for the idea and articulate why it was in the best interests of the government to move forward with two awards. Finally, after everyone had agreed to this approach, Jim turned to me and said, "Well, Carly, what do you think I ought to say to this congressman? Why don't you write something up for me?" I sat for the next ten minutes scribbling furiously in longhand, writing down how I thought the conversation should play out—how he should open, how he should close, what questions he should ask, what facts he needed, how he should make the case. When I was finished, he read it out loud to his executive team. Then he made the phone call.

I've often thought about those ten minutes. If I'd known what he was planning to do with my work—make the phone call as is, no questions asked, no modifications made—I probably would have been too intimidated to focus on the job at hand. For me, the chairman of the board of AT&T

making a phone call to the chairman of the House Appropriations Committee was a very big deal. Sometimes it's important to see what's coming down the road. And sometimes it's important just to put one foot in front of the other and not look too far ahead. This was one of those times when I had to concentrate on the job at hand—"What do you think I should say? Write something down for me"—and not focus too much on what would come next. ("Oh, my gosh, my words are going to come out of his mouth. What does a chairman sound like? What if I use words he wouldn't say? . . .") I had learned to think of only one person and what I wanted to say to that person, and to overcome my fear of talking to many, unknown people. I also had learned that sometimes I could think of only one step at a time.

In the end, we would win 60 percent of FTS2000. The GSA official who was responsible for both the procurement and the network (Ben Bennington) would remark: "Everything was stacked against AT&T. They won it because they were just so much better than anyone expected and better than anyone else." (I named a parrot we once had after Ben because he always bit me.)

It had been a tremendous effort. There had been plenty of naysayers within GSA, on the Hill, in the media and within AT&T. Like everything in life, some things broke our way, some things broke against us. We won because we had the unfailing support of Lou Golm and especially Mike Brunner, as well as Tommy Thomsen and Jim Olson. We won because the right team of people had been assembled, and those people both complemented and relied on one another. We won because we worked as hard as we had to and prepared for everything that might come our way. We won because we kept the end goal in mind—winning as much of FTS2000 as we could—and were willing to change our strategy and tactics to meet the goal. We did not change the goal just because it turned out to be tougher than we anticipated. We did not think about how we might lose. We thought about how we could win. We won because we chose to.

All triumphs are made of the same stuff: the right support, the right team, the determination to achieve the goal, lots of really hard work. And all triumphs are much more about choice than they are about chance.

11 | The Journey, Not the Destination

WHEN LOU GOLM HAD TAKEN OVER FTS2000, he'd decided to let me do my job and not try to do it for me. He had lots of work to do that he didn't need me for, but where he did, he'd relied on me. He treated his other subordinates in the same way. Because of his decision not to micromanage, to do his job while we did ours, we were all more effective. More than that, Lou's confidence in me earned him my gratitude, my loyalty and my best work.

In January of 1988, Lou began to talk to me about the Sloan School of Management at the Massachusetts Institute of Technology. The school offered a one-year intensive program of study that culminated in a master of science in business administration. Companies sent midcareer managers to the program for development purposes. AT&T sent two or three people a year, and many candidates vied for those slots. Many of Jim Olson's Office of the Chairman executives had attended Sloan. Lou himself had gone, and now he and Mike Brunner wanted to sponsor me to attend. This was a program for people who were being groomed for senior management roles.

It was the first time I thought I might make it to vice president at AT&T. When I joined the company in 1980, I'd figured I'd stick around for a year or two. Maybe I wouldn't like it, maybe they wouldn't like me, and maybe I wasn't really cut out for a big company or a career in business. AT&T had an employee savings plan in which the company matched the employee's contributions; however, if you left, you couldn't receive the company's portion of your savings until you'd been at AT&T for at least five years. I declined to join the plan because I knew I wouldn't last that long. On my five-year service anniversary, Frank and I had just been married and I'd been promoted. It seemed there was quite enough to celebrate, and I wasn't thinking about what came next. In fact, for the entirety of my now eight-year career, I'd poured all my energies into the job I had and didn't think about the career ladder that might be in front of me. Now Lou was telling me it was time to think about it. More than that, he was telling me I had the potential to climb several rungs.

Of course I said I was interested, but the whole conversation had a surreal quality to it. Frank and I were visiting Carole Spurrier and her husband, Greg, in Key West, Florida, the day I got the phone call from Lou telling me I'd been selected to attend Sloan. When I hung up the phone, I just kept saying, "I can't believe it. I can't believe it." It seemed as though my life were happening to someone else.

Sloan turned out to be both a great sacrifice and a great gift. It was a sacrifice because Frank had a very important job of his own, and he couldn't just suddenly move to Boston. So he stayed at home with the kids and the dogs and visited as often as he could. I commuted back and forth. It was a real strain on everyone, but we learned how strong our marriage really was. It was a gift because of all I learned and the people I met. And in the course of that year I came to accept that the life of a senior business executive didn't just happen to someone else—it could happen to me.

MIT is full of rocket scientists—literally. Everywhere you go you run into geniuses—Nobel Prize winners, those who will be Nobel Prize winners, students and teachers of incredible mental strength. It isn't just how smart everyone is that charges the atmosphere, however. It is also a school where discipline and hard work are mandatory. At Stanford people are plenty smart, but when I was there, the atmosphere was quite relaxed. I, and many others, worked extremely hard, but you didn't have to. At MIT everyone did—and you had to. The curriculum in every department, including the Sloan School, is rigorous and quantitative, and in this pressure-filled world it is expected that everyone will focus on performing with excellence. It was an intimidating academic environment to enter, particularly when I hadn't been in school for more than a decade.

The required courses for the MS degree included economics, finance, accounting, operations research and organizational behavior. I had studied many of these subjects before, but they had a different impact now that I'd been in the workforce for a while. Certain insights stand out for me still. I remember studying game theory in Jake Jacoby's Applied Economics course. Economic theory posits that people will always behave rationally based upon their own self-interest. Markets, in economic terms, are collections of people behaving rationally. Game theory is a quantitative discipline that attempts to predict and explain nonrational decision making. In essence, so the theory goes, people can behave irrationally simply because they believe someone else is going to.

Fear and uncertainty can drive behavior. Emotion can determine a decision as often as reason. Large groups, or responsible executives, or individuals can be motivated to shoot themselves in the proverbial foot through their actions. These are commonsense statements to anyone who has actually observed people in the real business world. Apparently, the frequency and consequence of nonrational decision making in the marketplace spawned an entire field of study devoted to explaining it.

I remember Gabe Bitran's course, Management Decision Support Models, which gave me great insight into the requirement for holistic systems thinking. If only one part or parameter of a complex systems problem is understood or acted upon, the problem cannot be solved. Only by comprehending the whole system—its interactions, dependencies, constraints and pressures—can a real, sustainable improvement be made. Many systems and problems are simply too complex to be approached adequately through a change in organizational structure or the application of subject-matter expertise. You've heard the old saying To any complex problem, the simple, obvious answer is wrong. This course proved the point.

In Organizational Psychology, taught by Ed Schein and John Van Maanen, we conducted elaborate negotiating sessions through role-playing. This time the role-playing didn't scare me, but observing the behavior in those sessions was sobering. Everyone would go into them knowing that solutions could only be found by creating win-win scenarios; both parties had to feel their most pressing issues had been addressed. It was startling to see how quickly people could dissolve into I-win-you-lose behavior, even when they knew rationally that it wouldn't work. Once this pattern was established, and emotion and ego took over, it was very hard to recover and find a solution.

I remember reading a book by Alfred D. Chandler in our strategy course. He wrote, "Strategy should be ennobling." This made sense to me; an organization's effort must be sustained through worthy purpose. Fear, the so-called "burning platform," is a temporary motivator. We all read a case study on a CEO's undertaking major change at a company. Everyone in the class criticized the CEO for moving too slowly; he'd failed to generate enough momentum to sustain his change efforts. After a while I raised my hand and said, "We all could have made the same mistake. If he'd moved any quicker, he would have been criticized for being too radical." I would later be called a radical myself.

I can't say I loved writing a thesis, but when it was over, I felt a real sense of accomplishment. Now I'm grateful that I recognize the twin poles of panic—"I'll never start . . . I'll never finish"—that a writer swings between.

I took electives in manufacturing management. I'd never been exposed to manufacturing before; the disciplines and challenges were fascinating and complex. When I left Sloan, I returned to the manufacturing arm of AT&T. I studied international dimensions of business management. One can tell a lot about the times in 1989: we still talked about "international" instead of "global." Without this course I don't think I would have had the confidence to make the choices I did when I left Sloan.

I took a fascinating course by Michael Lee: Business Implications of Advanced Technology. I wrote a research paper on neural networks, and beyond the intricacies of the science itself, I began to see the connections between not only biology and technology, but also between biology and organizational structure and behavior. These insights would help shape the Leadership Framework I would later introduce at Hewlett-Packard.

All of these courses shaped my business thinking. The course that caused me to do the most personal soul-searching, however, was Readings in Power and Responsibility with Abe Siegel. The most profound experience for me was reading *Antigone* by Sophocles. It is the story of a woman who stays true to her principles despite enormous pressure to sacrifice them, and the isolation and ostracism she faces as a result. My study group had major debates over this book. Was Antigone merely stubborn rather than princi-pled? Had she truly understood the criticism she would face when she made her decision? Antigone was courageous, lonely and resolute. She knew her soul and she kept it. Moral choice was a personal private decision, not a public display.

Ever since reading *Antigone*, I have taken the time, once a year, to deeply examine my own behavior and motivation. It's sort of a year-in-review exercise that happens around New Year's. Each year, alone and in private, I ask myself whether I am at peace with the choices I've made. Is my soul still my own?

I met one of my dearest friends at MIT. Deborah Bowker was one of the few other women in our class (there were nine of us out of a class of fifty). Like me, she lived in downtown Boston, while most of the rest of the class lived out in the suburbs. At first we were thrown together out of necessity because we were two women, whose husbands were elsewhere, living alone in Boston. Over time we became virtually inseparable. We decided the class was much too serious, so we threw parties for our classmates and their spouses every Wednesday evening in our apartments. It became a Sloan School tradition. We roomed together on every class trip. We became as comfortable as an old married couple. When a big exam was looming, I'd go off to the library and prepare our study plan for the evening. Deborah would prepare our dinner. I'd ring her doorbell and say "Honey, I'm home!" and then we'd eat and study. Her nickname for me was Antigone.

I observed a lot of CEOs that year. They would come to campus every few weeks and spend an evening with our class. Each would lecture for an hour or so, and then we'd have dinner together. Perhaps by then it shouldn't have been a surprise, but it was: CEOs were people too. Just like people everywhere, in every walk of life, some were good at their jobs; some weren't. Some were straightforward; others dissembled. Some got to the top after a lifetime of preparation; others still seemed surprised they were there. Some practiced intimidation; some were engaging. Some you could see yourself having a drink with; some you hoped you'd never see again. Some impressed me; others depressed me. Mostly the interactions took the mys-tery out of the CEO. And so for the very first time, I told my father when he came to visit that perhaps one day I, too, might become a CEO, just as Frank had predicted so many years ago.

Interacting with the other Sloan Fellows was a year's worth of learning all by itself. I developed new skills in collaboration because most assignments could not be completed alone. I gained new insight into other cultures because my classmates came from all over the world. We formed friendships that have endured. We studied hard and laughed a lot. Some of us discovered a great Irish pub near Harvard called the Plough and Stars. It became the setting for one of our favorite games: "If you could spend an evening with anyone in the world, living or dead, who would it be and why?"

The Plough and Stars was also the scene of an important revelation that came on our very last day, after graduation exercises. The people who made it to the Sloan program were very driven, type A overachievers who were focused on goals and accomplishments. We had just completed a year that was a great luxury—a sudden intermission in our lives when we could change the pace, tempo and nature of how we spent our days. That night we all wondered aloud whether we had savored the year sufficiently. Had we been too focused on getting that A and not fully absorbing the learning that went on in the process? Had we been so worried about the job we might go back to that we'd failed to appreciate our time without one? Goals are important, but that night I realized that life is about the journey, not the destination. The steps along the way are what make us who we are.

12 | Confrontation and Understanding

UPON MY RETURN to AT&T, I had to decide which job to take. One had all the backing of the AT&T executives who had sponsored my studies at MIT. The other was in what they called "the wrong part of the business."

I had entered Sloan from AT&T Long Lines, the network services side of AT&T. One of the most lucrative and important lines of business there was 800 Service. I was offered the director position, responsible for managing this business. I would report to one of the most influential officers at AT&T, Joe Nacchio, a real rising star. Everyone assumed I would accept the offer, and I was strongly advised that this was the fastest ticket to officer.

Meanwhile, Bill Marx, the president of Network Systems, had come to Sloan to visit me. He wanted me to work in the manufacturing side of AT&T. Network Systems, which had grown out of Western Electric, was definitely the black sheep of AT&T. They pretty much stuck to themselves and everyone left them alone. The job was ill defined, but they were just starting to build up their international business, so I would have some sort of role in this effort.

I decided I needed to meet Joe before I made my decision. I made an appointment and traveled to New Jersey to his office. Almost an hour past our scheduled time, a secretary told me I could go in. Joe was perfunctory. He did not come from behind his desk. I thanked him for his time and asked him to tell me a little about the job and what he thought needed to be accomplished.

"Listen, Carly, I'm not sure this meeting was necessary. It's a great job, and 800 Service is probably the most important profit generator for AT&T. We've laid out a five-year strategic plan, and now we need to follow it. I think this is an important step in your career."

I tried to ask some follow-up questions, but it was clear Joe found this a waste of time. It was equally clear that he thought the opportunity to work with him should have been a compelling enough reason for me to accept the job immediately. I didn't like him; he seemed arrogant and slick. When I visited with Network Systems, they seemed enthusiastic about the business they were building. They didn't have a real plan, but they knew there was a lot of opportunity outside the United States and that they needed to grow.

I agonized over the decision. I knew I would be disappointing a lot of people, most especially Lou Golm, if I didn't stay in Long Lines. Yet Network Systems seemed more exciting—ill defined but ripe with possibilities. It was a challenging environment, and I thought I could make a contribution. The best advice I got came from Mike Brunner: "Evaluate all the pros and cons and then go with your gut." I decided to go to Network Systems.

The reaction was instantaneous. Joe Nacchio was furious, and he could be formidable when angry. He involved his boss, the executive vice president, who sent me a very clear message through the Human Resources director. "Carly was Long Lines property. She'll never have an opportunity here again."

My first response was to be cowed. I'd made a terrible mistake, and now I would pay for it. I had no idea these executives would feel so strongly about this. After a couple of hours, I became more angry than intimidated. How dare they think of me as "property"! Joe Nacchio hadn't been particularly interested in what I'd actually do in the job. Indeed, he seemed to want me to do as little as possible beyond following his instructions. He just wanted to say I worked for him. I'd made my decision, and now I was going to make the best of it. It wouldn't be the first time in my career that I'd ignored the conventional wisdom.

My first few months were not encouraging. My job title was director,

International Strategy and Business Development (ISBD). It sounded good, but the reality was more complex. First, my predecessor in the job was still in his office, and working on the most important international relationship Network Systems then had: a joint venture with Italtel, the Italian version of Western Electric. He was deeply resentful of my presence and wasn't going to help out in any way. Second, unbeknownst to me, my position was a pawn in a political power struggle among three officers in Network Systems: the vice president of Strategy; the vice president of Marketing; and the vice president of Network Systems International. Each of the three executives thought he should be in charge of international strategy and business development. I reported to the vice president of Strategy, a smart but somewhat eccentric boss who valued orderly written plans above everything else and demanded that every document that came to his desk be fastened with a very particular kind of paper clip. If you didn't have enough of these regulation paper clips, his secretary was happy to supply them.

My first month on the job felt a lot like my first month as a brand-new employee. No one was much interested in helping me understand the lay of the land, so I listened hard in every meeting, asked a lot of questions and spent every evening reading all the documents I could get my hands on until ten or eleven o'clock. I was trying to understand how decisions were made in this new organization, and eventually I realized that the organization chart wasn't always a useful guide to who could influence or make a particular decision. I would read memos and simply couldn't figure out why certain people were included in the distribution list and why others were left off. I couldn't accurately predict who would attend certain meetings and be absent from others. Unexpected people answered my questions. It was an important introduction to the reality that organizations don't always function the way they're designed on paper. Many decisions are made or strongly influenced by individuals outside the formal organizational structure that theoretically has decision-making authority. These individuals have access to and relationships with others from whom they derive their power. And sometimes formal decisions can be very effectively undermined by simply refusing to acknowledge them.

These are the realities of how large, complex organizations work, and it's particularly true in businesses where people have been together a long time

and where relationships are deep and long-standing. The relationships become more important than the organization charts. It's very hard for outsiders to come into these insulated worlds. Everyone should understand how
things work on paper and how things actually work when they get a new job
or enter a new organization. Stop, look and listen is good career advice, not
just wise counsel for crossing the street.

I have never been screamed at more than during those first six months
in Network Systems. Every time I did something, someone would be in my
office or on my phone yelling at me—and I do mean yelling. Every organization has its own way of hazing newcomers; the Network Systems way was to
verbally beat you up hard and often to see what you were made of. There
was only one other woman in Network Systems at the director level, and she
was the head of Human Resources, an accepted position for a woman. The
Network Systems guys had grown up in a rough, loud manufacturing culture. My boss was also an outsider from Long Lines, and no one much liked
him. They didn't know me either, and I, too, came from Long Lines, so what
did I know about their world? Besides, I probably wasn't tough enough for a
"real business" like Network Systems. In part they screamed at me to see if I
could "take it like a man."

It was so different from the politesse of the Long Lines crowd. There
everyone was polite. There confrontations were avoided. There I'd been
counseled frequently that I was "too direct" and needed to be "more diplomatic." Now, in Network Systems, everything I said and did was challenged
openly, with a raised voice and usually a few choice four-letter words to go
along with it.

By Christmas, I was exhausted. Frank and I were trying to move into a
new home in New Jersey. I'd commuted to D.C. every weekend for four
months, and now he was commuting to New Jersey because he didn't want
to leave his own job. All the battles in Network Systems were also taking
their toll. I told Frank I might not make it there. With the time and rest the
holidays afforded me, I finally came to a different view. I decided that in
many ways I preferred the confrontation of Network Systems over the courtesy of Long Lines. Many people before had presumed I would fail or
thought I shouldn't be where I was. At least these guys were up front about
it. I was quite sure many had said behind my back what was now being said

to my face; but if I had to choose, I'd much rather someone said it to my face. And people weren't just hazing me; in some cases we had honest disagreements. I believed we should be taking a more systematic, strategic approach to our international opportunities, selecting which we would pursue, playing to win by applying the appropriate resources, and then ensuring we could deliver. Others felt this approach was too confining and believed we should be more opportunistic, pursuing business across as wide a field as possible to maximize our chances of winning. It was a legitimate debate, and I would rather debate it with people than be ignored. I returned to work in the new year of 1990 with a determination to give as good as I got, both in the logic of my arguments and the strength of my own defense.

As with many New Year's resolutions, this one was tested almost immediately. I had to make a trip to the Netherlands. This was the headquarters of Network Systems International (NSI), where Jack Heck presided. Jack was an officer from the old school. He liked to imagine himself as "a regular guy," since he'd come up through the ranks from the manufacturing floor; but, in fact, he lorded his rank, his title, his palatial office over everyone. He could be funny and charming, and his people were intensely loyal; but he was also loud, rude and uncouth. He was a very intimidating man, and I was going to deliver a deeply unpopular message to Jack and his team. They were responding to competitive bids all over the world, and the larger organization that had to support the sales and implementation process was neither aware of their efforts nor prepared to deliver against them. As a result, NSI was losing far more than they were winning, and we had botched a couple of very important installations. If we did not come to some kind of agreement on which opportunities we were going after and align our resources behind them, we were going to continue to lose, or worse, disappoint our customers.

My boss was enthusiastic about this trip because if I succeeded, his organization would have gained power in his ongoing struggle with Jack. If I failed, he'd lost nothing, and he wouldn't have damaged his own reputation by going to Jack and coming home empty-handed. Everyone on both sides of the Atlantic knew that Jack and my boss detested each other; they were like two mean old dogs circling each other and growling. Jack Heck was not about to let me prevail; he wanted absolute autonomy for himself and his organization. He had no use for headquarters. They were just a bunch of pencil pushers who didn't know anything about what it was "really like out here." I was keenly aware of the politics involved in my visit, but I also knew we had to change how we were doing things. We were running people ragged, chasing after business and then desperately trying to respond with too few resources.

I went and talked through the merits of a changed approach with everyone in Jack's organization who was involved. Virtually all of them agreed with me. They could see the toll all this frenetic activity was taking, and they bore the brunt of customers' complaints. Some even concluded that I might add value, but no one was going to do anything unless Jack said so. This wasn't about logic, it was about power: Jack's power over them and Jack's power vis-à-vis his peers. Many, many decisions in business, in politics, and even sometimes in life, are all about power, not about the actual substance of the issue. Sometimes this is obvious, and sometimes it's very hard to discern.

Finally, after getting nowhere for a few days, I asked to see Jack. One of his habits was to refuse to talk to anyone from headquarters unless one of his own people was there. He did it out of respect for his team but also out of disdain for his visitors. Whatever they had to say was actually beneath him; he was just being polite. I was fortunate that Bill Rohrbach was asked to sit in on the meeting with us. Bill understood what was going on. He was trying to help me in his own way. And later he would be a useful witness to what happened.

After a few pleasantries, I began to explain yet again why I was there and why we needed to find a compromise on how we did business for the good of the company and our customers. Jack didn't let me get very far before he exploded. He was literally ranting and raving—about me, my boss, about headquarters, about how difficult it was to do business, about how I was wasting his and his people's time, about how no one really knew what they were talking about unless they'd been there. His face was crimson, his language was blue and he was doing his best to frighten and intimidate me. He was doing a pretty good job of it, and I could tell that Bill was taken aback as well. Jack's temper was well known, but as tantrums go, this one was apparently extraordinary even for him. Of course much of it was for effect, but I also represented an opportunity for him to vent all his frustrations.

It was a very long, very difficult forty-five minutes, and I'll admit I was afraid of him. Finally, though, I'd had enough, and I didn't much care what the consequences were. I would not be diminished any further. I'd read somewhere that anger can be effective as long as it's controlled: use it, don't lose it. So I decided to use it. He was midsentence when I slammed my open hand down on the conference table. "Enough, Jack! That's enough!"

He looked shocked, but he stopped.

"Jack, I am not stupid. I am not evil. I do not get up every day trying to f—— up your business. I am trying to do my job. And I am sick and f——ing tired of being yelled at by you and grinf——ed by your people."

It was the first time I'd ever sworn like that, much less at work. But I was speaking to Jack in language he understood: the rough language of the factory floor. And I was standing up to him, which, as a player of power politics, he also understood.

"What's grinf—— mean?" he asked. His curiosity had gotten the better of him. It was a profanity he'd never heard, a rarity in itself. It came from Long Lines, where the politics of saying exactly what you didn't mean had been raised to a fine art. With this question Jack had given me an opportunity to finally connect with him.

"That's an expression they use at Long Lines. You know, all those smooth 42-longs over there are so polished and political, they smile to your face and f—— you behind your back."

"What's a 42-long?"

I explained. Now I'd connected on two levels: I spoke his language, literally, and I also had disdain for those guys over in the long-distance business. They were pretty boys, and they didn't actually make anything—they just sold "minutes of use" of the network. What's more, in my own way I was telling Jack I appreciated the Network Systems' trademark: straight talk.

Jack and I didn't come to agreement that day, but he listened and he gained respect for me. When I arrived at the airport for my flight home, I called my boss and told him I thought Jack would be calling Bill Marx to have me fired. I believed it, but I was still glad I'd done what I had. If I didn't respect myself, no one else would. And my self-respect demanded that I not endure what was, by any standard, completely inappropriate and uncalled-for verbal abuse.

I didn't get fired. To the contrary, in an unexpected way my exchange with Jack bolstered my reputation. Bill Rohrbach told everyone at NSI about it. Most of them had never stood up to Jack; they were all afraid of him too. The fact that I could do so meant something; it was a little bit like taking on the school bully and surviving. My new reputation for both toughness and persistence began to influence the people in my organization. They started to walk a little taller and press a little harder when they got into confrontations of their own. They now knew they had a boss who wouldn't wilt under criticism. And so, little by little, we started making progress. My team and I started to matter in both the day-to-day operations and the strategic choices of Network Systems.

NOTHING IN A BIG ORGANIZATION happens quickly. In a complex organization there are too many people operating too many moving parts for change to occur overnight. But it's equally true that large organizations have a lot of momentum. Once a real shift in an organization's thinking and behavior occurs, even if it's imperceptible at first, the momentum behind the new direction will continue to build and gather strength. My confrontation with Jack signaled an important shift in how Network Systems thought about its international business. The idea that we had to be more strategic and systematic began to take hold.

Of course, it wasn't simply because I hadn't backed down. It was also because we just kept at the idea that there was a better way of doing things. An organizational psychologist once told me that a person needs to hear a new idea at least six times before he or she can acknowledge it. A lay person would say "Change just takes time." And it's true. It takes time to hear a new idea, time to understand it, time to accept it, time to support it. And of course it takes time to see it work.

Leaders who are driving change need credibility. My credibility in talking about our international opportunities required me to really know something about them—through experience, not study. And so I traveled a lot. And as I traveled, I once again marveled at how different things are when you're actually out there doing them. In New Jersey I'd read all day long about our Italian joint venture. I'd listened to my predecessor talk about it, but when I was actually engaged in negotiations with Italians in Italy, I understood the complexities in a deeper and different way.

Our relationship with Italtel and their parent, STET, had reached an impasse. We were trying to negotiate a change in our respective ownership positions, and we were deadlocked. Our day-to-day operating relationships were becoming frayed as a result, hurting our collective efforts in the marketplace. I was asked to take over the negotiations. I had lived in Italy and spoke Italian; what had been a lark then became an important asset.

I knew that Italians, like many people, place high value on protocol. I was more junior than the executives I would be negotiating with, both in title and in age. Although I certainly could have demanded that they travel to the United States, given our ownership position, it would have been disrespectful. I would go to them, and they would set the agenda for how we would proceed through negotiations. I asked them to send me their proposed agenda in advance of my trip so that I could be adequately prepared.

The agenda I received was meticulous in its allocation of time. When we would start, when we would take a break and when we would conclude our discussions were all laid out for each of two days. The food at each break and meal was detailed in a complete menu. I knew in advance what we would be having at each coffee break, the wine we would be drinking at lunch and the sauce that would accompany the pasta. Left out completely was the substance of what we would discuss. This same pattern would be repeated for six months. I would ask for an agenda in advance, and I would receive a timetable and a complete menu—and nothing more. At first I thought I'd failed to communicate. Later I thought it was a negotiating tactic. Finally, I came to understand that for these Italians, productive discussions required personal relationships. Personal relationships took time to develop and were built while eating and drinking around a table together. After quite a lot of time together, and a great deal of fabulous Italian food and wine, we had made substantial progress and had agreed upon a change in our ownership positions.

STET was the government entity that owned the Italian telephone companies as well as Italtel. As such, our negotiations encompassed network services and systems issues. From my perspective, this meant that both AT&T Long Lines and Network Systems had interests in these discussions, so I was representing both of them. When I wasn't negotiating in Italy, I was negotiating in New Jersey, trying to find a solution that would satisfy all parties.

We had achieved this accord, but now an executive vice president from Long Lines decided to come to Rome to solidify his part of the deal we'd reached.

His first mistake was to pick a date that was convenient for him because it occurred in the middle of an already planned visit to Europe. Unfortunately, it coincided with one of the many national holidays in Italy. When our STET counterparts objected to the date, the EVP's staff sent word back that this was a crucial meeting and the only time possible. The Italians canceled their holiday out of respect for this executive vice president—whom they had never met. When he arrived, he brought with him some staff members he hadn't warned them about. This was his second mistake.

We sat at a square table in a conference room. The AT&T executive sat opposite the Italians. He said STET was an important partner, and he appreciated the meeting. I believe he sincerely meant it, but from the Italians' point of view, everything he did contradicted those words. He read from a set of notes. He rarely made eye contact. He didn't engage in social chitchat. He talked a great deal about the purpose of his broader trip and the relationships he was crafting with other partners. When an hour had passed, he indicated that the meeting was over. He said he had no time to join his STET counterpart out on the terrace to enjoy the view of Rome and the Vatican along with a glass of wine. And this last mistake only added to the disastrous nature of the meeting he had just conducted. It wasn't the substance of what he'd said that was the problem. It was how he'd said it, how he'd behaved, and how he'd treated them.

When the executive and his entourage had departed, the Italians exploded. I had never seen them angry like this before. I tried in vain to calm them down and focus them on the substance of his words, but they were insulted in the extreme. All the progress we had worked so hard to achieve vanished. They declared that they could not do business with a company that behaved in this way, and they would have to "reconsider" our agreements. We spent many more months trying to regain lost ground; but it was never the same again, and the agreement we'd had eluded us. The agreement we eventually achieved was less advantageous to AT&T, and we'd lost a lot of time.

Companies are big, abstract entities. People don't do important business with a company; they do business with people who represent that company and can commit its resources and support. And people the world over do business with people they trust and respect. To some of us, the Italians' reaction might seem petty, but trust and respect mean different things in different cultures. Trust in the United States might be built through a detailed legal contract. Respect might come through a difficult, protracted set of negotiations, where each party learns how vigorously the other will defend its ground. In Italy, trust and respect are built through time while enjoying the good things in life together, with proper attention paid to the details of gentility.

If you want to conduct effective negotiations, know whom you're dealing with. Pay them respect by respecting what's important to them, and take the time to build trust. Trust and respect are the foundation for successful agreements and the emotional glue that binds people together during disagreements.

In many Asian cultures trust and respect are built around drinking. Everyone gets to know one another better when the restraints of sobriety and the trappings of office are removed, and a person's stamina, fortitude and judgment can be assessed. In the early 1990s the drinking customs of Asian nations were quite distinct. My first visit to Korea occurred for many of the same reasons I had traveled to Italy. We had an important joint venture with the Korean chaebol Lucky Goldstar. Our relationship was longstanding; but now some changes were required, and the local team was having difficulty achieving them. We had arranged a meeting between me and the president of the LG subsidiary that was our partner.

My gender was an issue from the moment I arrived. There were really no women in positions of authority in Korea, and these Koreans had never done business with a woman before. There were many, many women at Lucky Goldstar, but they all wore uniforms and white gloves; they were either elevator operators or secretaries. When I entered the building, everyone stared and pointed and whispered. I wore no gloves, and I was clearly the superior of our local manager; it's easy to tell because Korean protocol demands very specific seating arrangements in every venue, including the seating in an arriving automobile. I was to go upstairs in the president's private elevator. Everyone I met was polite, curious and deeply skeptical.

I had prepared carefully for the meeting, although I couldn't hope to understand as much about the details of this complicated, multifaceted relationship as the people who'd been engaged in it for years. Yet here was a case where that Stanford philosophy course helped me. I'd reviewed the history of our negotiations, and it appeared that the two sides were getting confused and bogged down by the complexity involved in trying to achieve one overarching agreement. The heart of the matter seemed to be that we had three relationships, not one, and we could make progress by understanding the differences between them.

After the president entered the room, I had only about twenty minutes to convince him that he should spend his time dealing with me. All his cultural mores told him that dealing with a young woman was beneath his stature and position. My title was sufficiently impressive that he would grant me a meeting, but he'd decide how long to stay. I said that the AT&T/Lucky Goldstar relationship was of great importance to both of us, that our successful history together prepared us well for the future, but the new competitive realities required us to think differently about our relationship in the future. I drew a picture of three interlocking circles and said we actually had three partnerships: one in manufacturing, one in R&D, and one in sales to our mutual customers. Our success in each was measured differently. Our success as a whole was measured by our return on equity.

These were simple words, simple pictures and simple concepts. And yet they represented a way out of an impasse. They represented a way of simplifying a complex reality so that people could understand and deal with it. Sometimes simple concepts are deceptive because they distort reality by hiding important details. This kind of simplification might be called spin. Sometimes simple concepts are vital because they magnify reality, stripping away the less-important details so that people can focus on those that truly matter. A focus on the essential is necessary to prioritize effort and make progress.

In this case, my focus on the essential persuaded the president to stay. And so we spent all day together with our teams. About four o'clock in the afternoon the president's aide came up behind me and whispered in my ear: "Excuse me, Mrs. Fiorina, I need to inform you that our president entertains in the traditional Korean fashion. He'd like me to ask you whether you want a man."

I was, of course, taken aback and perplexed by the question. I didn't know what "traditional Korean fashion" meant, and I certainly didn't like the sounds of "whether you want a man." So I improvised: "I don't want the president to make any special arrangements on my account. Whatever he would normally do for a Korean business colleague will be fine." The aide smiled and disappeared. When I asked my American teammates what he had been talking about, they looked very nervous. One of them explained, "Well, the traditional Korean evening is a barbecue called a *kisaeng* party. You sit on the floor and drink a lot of scotch. Women are never invited, so we assumed he'd choose a European-style dinner." My Korean host had made compromises by meeting with me at all. He would not compromise his traditional, and preferred, method of entertainment. Besides, it would be a good way for him to test me. So we all went off to the *kisaeng* party.

We entered a traditional, wooden Korean hut. The small space was dominated by a large, rectangular, low table that was mostly a very hot metal cooking surface. We sat on the floor with our legs hanging into a recessed pit below the table. Bottles of Four Roses scotch had been placed within easy reach of every seat. The president sat at the head of the table, and I sat to his right. As soon as we got comfortable, a large number of young, beautiful, traditionally dressed Korean women entered, each carrying a small wooden bucket. One sat down to the immediate right of each guest. Now I understood the aide's question earlier that day. I would have a Korean woman as my dinner companion, just as all my male counterparts did. I did not yet understand the purpose of the bucket, but I would come to appreciate it—and my companion—soon enough.

In Korea an individual offers a toast to another individual. Each fills his glass and drinks to the other. It is a sign of respect and a drinking game all at the same time. I was the highest-ranking guest. Everyone was feeling pretty proud of themselves for dealing with me all day, and we'd made a lot of progress. We'd even found we liked each other. I was the recipient of endless toasts, both to honor and to test me, although I suspect it was mostly the latter. It is impolite to refuse a toast; and because a proper one takes time, each person reserves his turn by placing a full glass of whiskey to your right. When you drink and toast your way to that person's glass, it's his turn. Very quickly I found I had eight glasses of whiskey lined up beside me, and eight beaming colleagues waiting to toast me.

I had never drunk whiskey before. I had never drunk this much of anything before. All the while we drank, meat and vegetables were being cooked on the hot table. The steam and the heat in that small hut, combined with the whiskey, made staying sober out of the question for even the most experienced drinker, which was, of course, precisely the point. Pretty soon the beautiful woman to my right was whispering in my ear: "You must not lose face. You must not become too drunk or get sick. I will help you." And while no one was looking, she would quickly and surreptitiously take a glass of whiskey off the table and pour it into the bucket. She did save me, and soon I noticed that all the other women were doing the same thing for their "patrons." So we toasted and drank and saved face by having toasts disappear off the table without ever really offending anyone.

The truth is I had a wonderful time that evening. I liked our Korean hosts tremendously—they were warm and funny and full of life. I thoroughly enjoyed the time with my companion the *Kisaeng* girl. She was not only beautiful but also highly educated with a near-perfect command of English. Her job was to flatter and entertain me, and she did an excellent job of both. She was witty, interesting and totally captivated by the most unusual opportunity to do her job for another woman. I could see why men absolutely loved this style of entertaining. (Today in Korea there are establishments where women can enjoy a traditional *kisaeng* party with male companions, but this is a recent phenomenon.) And to complete the evening, we all sang songs—at the top of our lungs and off-key.

The truth is I was very drunk and got very sick later that night. And in classic Korean fashion, our meetings recommenced the next morning promptly at nine o'clock. The conference room was hot and stuffy, and every movement was an immense effort; but I stood at the front of the room and led us through the day. I would not fail the test of my stamina. The Koreans and I came to trust and respect one another. At the end of the second day, the president walked with me through the halls of Lucky Goldstar. He was showing me off, and showing off how open-minded and flexible he could be.

To this day I have great respect for the nation of Korea and what it has achieved. I have great affection for the Korean people and their warmth and good humor. And they taught me never again to play a drinking game unless I'm prepared. Over the years I would participate in many drinking rituals in

Korea, Japan and China. I would learn to prepare myself mentally, to prepare myself physically by eating the right kinds of foods ahead of time, and to toss liquor straight back in my throat, not sip it, so that the alcohol is absorbed more slowly into the system.

I came to appreciate these rituals. I made good friends in China because of them. It is true that trust, respect and shared experience make it easier to do business. It is true that participating in others' customs lays foundations for common understanding.

13 | The Consequences of Strength

A BIG PART of my job while I was director of International Strategy and Business Development was to build a team that was capable of actually performing the role. When I arrived, I found in the organization many very bright people with no agreed-upon purpose or self-respect, people who were willing to do whatever work was asked of them, grateful for the opportunity to contribute in some way. They became helpers; when other groups asked them for help, they provided it, with little concern about whether there was something else more important or worthwhile for them to do. They were not respected as peers or real players—they were viewed as a free resource.

As human beings, we need both purpose to motivate us and confidence to move us forward. Both are necessary to gain self-respect and the respect of others. Organizations are made up of human beings, so it's not surprising that organizations need exactly the same things. A leader's job is to build an organization's skills and capabilities and to develop its capacity for producing quality results. A leader's job is also to define a worthy purpose and to build the confidence to perform.

Briefly put, we decided that ISBD's purpose was to analyze, propose, advocate and ensure implementation of a strategic framework for evaluating and pursuing our international opportunities. In other words, our value-add would be to get everyone on the same page. Any organization is stronger when people are aligned to act together, instead of working at cross-purposes. I say "we" decided because our mission was designed as a team. This kind of collaboration was required if our mission was to be more than a nice slogan on the wall. A purpose which directs people's behavior must be fully understood and embraced. Specific tactics—"execute this specific action in this specific way"—can be imposed on an organization from above. Indeed, sometimes they need to be if speed and precision are important, and if the action is controversial. A mission or purpose or strategy is designed to guide decision making for the longer term. It channels people's energies so the boss doesn't have to direct every action. An organization that requires the boss's involvement in every decision can't function effectively over the long term; it's simply too complex and time-consuming. Besides, smart people want to contribute their talents—they don't always want to be told what to do.

And so my team and I labored together to create a mission and purpose we could all rally around, one that truly served the larger organization of which we were a part. We held a series of off-site meetings and argued and debated and finally coalesced around a mission statement and a strategic framework. And then we began to roll it out across the broader organization in a series of Strategy Forums. People are motivated by both reason and emotion. So are organizations. And it was in the course of this work that I learned that a leader must capture hearts as well as challenge minds.

Part of the strategic framework we agreed upon was a set of "focus countries": markets that would receive our highest-priority attention. There were also "exception countries": markets where we would not pursue opportunities without a level of executive approval that would permit us to divert resources from our priorities. And then there was a set of markets that we would not enter because either the conditions or our capabilities did not provide sufficient probability of success to warrant the expenditure of scarce resources. Intellectually, everyone understood that a framework for deciding how to allocate our resources to international opportunities made sense. Intellectually, people even understood that our win rates would improve if we operated within these constraints. Yet although reason supported such a prioritization, it felt limiting emotionally. As we talked to the various organizations in Network Systems, people would invariably spend all their energies on which countries weren't on the focus list. At first we would try to counter these objections with all the facts and figures around why our focus countries represented higher value, higher probability markets. It wasn't enough. Emotionally, people felt they were giving something up: the freedom to act autonomously and the possibility of some wonderful, unknown opportunity.

To be motivated to give something up, as opposed to being depressed or resentful, people need to feel they're getting something in return. We are motivated, for example, to give up sweets in return for a leaner physique. To motivate members of the organization to give up how they'd always done things—which represented freedom and possibility—they had to get something in return. That something was a more exciting future and the confidence to achieve it. Excitement and confidence are emotional states, and although they can be bolstered by logic, ultimately the mind does not think them, the heart must feel them. And so I became involved in the strategy and goals of the broader Network Systems organization.

Western Electric had been a captive supplier to the Bell System. Network Systems, the successor organization and a subsidiary of AT&T, hadn't actually moved much beyond the familiarity of its domestic telco customers. Now we needed a goal that represented people's aspirations for what we could and should do. We could challenge the market leaders in terms of growth and profit—and beating competitors is always fun and exciting. We could really move beyond the constraints of historic relationships—and the AT&T parent—by striving to become a world leader. It would take the discipline of rigorous prioritization and our strategic framework, but it could be done. This was something people could get excited about. Yes, their logic told them the revenues and profits could be better also, but their emotion told them this meant respect in the marketplace and just as important, respect inside AT&T. Emotionally, we would get a chance to show people how good we really were. People rallied around this new future. Now we had to build confidence that we could achieve it and that we had the discipline, the capability and the moxie to pull it off.

The confidence to chart a different course is built by experiencing success. Individuals or teams can experience success in individual efforts. An entire organization can experience success by celebrating the success of its members. Communicating and celebrating success stories is thus a critical part of building confidence, and so we began sharing success stories from all over the world—examples of where teams of employees had won against our competitors by sticking to priorities and acting with discipline. Then the organization began to move forward toward the possibility of a bigger future, operating within the parameters of a framework that represented where and how we would go get it.

N OT ALL MEANS ARE JUSTIFIED by the ends; so as important as it was to communicate success stories to build confidence, it was also important that people understood how they could not, or should not, operate. In international business our most important constraint had to be the honesty and integrity with which we did business. Many of the markets we were operating in were corrupt. Many of our competitors engaged in business practices that violated U.S. law and the Foreign Corrupt Practices Act. You can talk about values like integrity all day long, but actions always speak louder than words.

Around this time, I traveled to Brazil to meet with our joint venture partner and some important customers. Our managing director there was smart and savvy with a lot of experience in Brazil. He was well regarded, well liked and he delivered results. The Network Systems offices were in São Paulo, but one evening we had a dinner meeting in Brasília, the capital, with some very important ministers. Our managing director had set up the meeting; and although I wasn't quite clear on its purpose, the ministers were obviously worth meeting.

We entered the private home of someone described as a "friend and business associate" of one of the ministers. It was a beautiful, sprawling, one-story mansion surrounded by lush foliage. Multiple sets of French doors were open throughout the living and dining rooms, and it was pouring outside. The effect was like being in the middle of a rain forest while surrounded by candlelight and priceless art and furnishings. I felt as if I were in a Fellini film.

The conversation meandered around without direction. Brazilians can be quite efficient in their communications, and I kept trying to steer the conversation toward our areas of mutual business interest. My hosts resisted my efforts. It was a lovely evening with interesting, accomplished people;

but as the night wore on, I became more and more uncomfortable. Something wasn't right, but I couldn't put my finger on it. Then I felt the prickle of goose bumps on my skin. I don't remember exactly what was said, but suddenly I knew that the purpose of the evening was to test whether I was prepared to participate in bribery. I was being educated about how business was done there and how our competitors played the game. Our managing director was watching me silently.

I played dumb and made excuses about my fatigue, and the evening came to a merciful end. After I'd slept on it, I asked the managing director what his reaction was.

"Look, Carly, you don't need to get involved in this if you don't want to, but I'm going to have to if we want to achieve our goals down here."

I asked, "Do you think you can do that without getting caught?"

"Oh, sure. I used to do it for my other employer [a non-U.S. company] all the time, and we can control it all down here. Our budget is big enough. Look, I know you're worried about FCPA, but this is Brazil and I'm not American and we can just pretend this conversation never happened."

Two days later he was fired. Although he didn't work for me, I'd persuaded his boss to take the action. The organization was shocked, but the message was clear: the ends do not justify any means and we will not tolerate dishonesty and corruption. Values trump results. Values are what guide our behavior when no one is looking and no one can find out. I could not assume that this managing director would act with integrity when we couldn't watch him or catch him, which would be most of the time. A lack of integrity puts a whole organization at risk in ways that can't always be predicted. We declined to participate in a number of opportunities in Brazil and lowered our goals as a result. Now when we celebrated success stories to build confidence within the organization, we also served up a cautionary tale to build character.

BY NOW I was regularly involved in meetings with Bill Marx's officer team. Bill used me effectively to accomplish his purposes and supported me appropriately. He let me fight my own battles when it was important to demonstrate my strength in the organization, and he intervened only when necessary. Bill was smart enough to know that there would be times when he'd have to give me some extra support. It was true for many reasons: I was an outsider and would make mistakes; I was one of very few women and would ruffle some feathers; I was driving a change that was necessary but difficult and would encroach on some established turf in the process. Bill's interventions were important because enemies always come along with success.

People both appreciate and resent strength and success in others; for the same reasons, strong, successful people are both admired and attacked. Some people see inspiration for themselves in others' success. Some people who think they cannot accomplish their objectives alone ally themselves with strong people when their goals and agendas are aligned. Some people, who are equally strong and successful, may choose open confrontation if they disagree, but they do so with real respect. And some people simply resent others' strength because it highlights their own perceived inadequacies. Some are jealous of success they see as greater than their own. Jealousy and resentment are feelings of inferiority or inadequacy, and they breed resistance and the instinct to engage in an unfair fight. And at a very fundamental level, on the school playground, boys don't like losing to girls, and girls sometimes compete against each other for a boy's attention.

Jack Heck fought fair. We frequently had our differences, but we disagreed out in the open and with mutual respect. The vice president of Marketing didn't fight fair. He was ambitious and flamboyant, but his impact didn't match his bluster. As he watched me accomplish things he had not, or could not, he began a whisper campaign against me. He began by telling one of the female managers who worked for me that I wasn't supportive of her. It wasn't true, but she had no reason to doubt him and he was an officer. He said he would need her help from time to time, that she would have to keep it confidential, and he promised her a job in his own organization. (He never delivered.) He went to my boss and told him I was disloyal and critical behind his back. That wasn't true either, but my boss was insecure enough about his own position, and jealous enough of my relationship with Bill Marx, that he aligned himself with the vice president who had become my enemy.

I didn't know any of this at first, but I began to notice that my boss and this VP would frequently challenge me in meetings with data they said came from my own organization. I found myself in a very awkward position. If I said I'd never seen the data, which I hadn't, people wondered if I knew what was going on. If I ignored the data, I looked stubborn and illogical, since it did indeed contradict my conclusions. Of course the facts were selective and chosen to make a particular point, but the other meeting attendees didn't know that. Later, when I would seek an explanation so I could understand the data or our differences, or I would ask these two VPs to give me a heads up before the meeting so I could respond more effectively, they'd always claim I'd misunderstood. I was just "overreacting."

Sometimes you never discover an unseen enemy, and you never know what really happened. In this case I eventually got lucky. Jack Heck knew what was going on because he'd been around a really long time, and he'd seen it all before. He knew his colleagues well. He told Bill Rohrbach, who was his closest confidant. Bill, who had become my friend and supporter, told me.

One day Bill Marx asked me to come see him. He asked how it was going. We talked for a while and finally he said, "Anything giving you trouble, Carly?" I've always believed an honest question deserves an honest answer. I told him I was having trouble with the vice president of Marketing. "I just don't seem to be able to get on the same page with him." Bill had hired this VP and he liked him, so he suggested a meeting between the three of us.

I didn't quite know what to do in such a meeting. I didn't want it to degenerate into my becoming a tattletale, forcing Bill either to take sides between us or reprimand both of us. Fortunately, my enemy took care of this. Bill could be blunt; it is one of his best qualities, so he started off by asking, "So how are you two getting along?"

I waited and said nothing. The VP's insecurities and resentments got the better of him. Instead of saying "Carly and I get along great. I just think she's wrong about a few things," or something else calm and rational, he started to talk fast. And then he talked faster. And the faster he talked, the more emotional and defensive he became. I sat and watched him self-destruct. Part of me was relieved; Bill could see for himself what the problem was. Part of me was depressed—what was it about me, or the things I was doing, that could cause such an extreme reaction? One thing was certain: the vice president of Marketing had created the very situation he feared most—he had weakened his position and strengthened mine.

I had a long talk with the female subordinate who'd been manipulated. I told her she was being used for someone else's purposes and that no matter how she felt about me, she was doing herself no good. She learned a lot, I think, and eventually got promoted. I continued to treat my boss with courtesy, but I never trusted him again. And like everyone else, I now ignored the vice president of Marketing.

Several months later I received a call at home from Bill Marx. Could I urgently see him in his office? When I arrived, he informed me that my boss was being transferred back to Long Lines; the Marketing VP was retiring and their jobs were being combined. I would become the new vice president of Strategy and Marketing. To my complete astonishment, I had just been promoted to officer.

I had raced out of the house without looking at my gas gauge. As is frequently the case, I was running on fumes. Now, as I drove home in a state of shocked euphoria, I realized I had to get gas. I sat at the pump and called my mother. I told her I had just become an officer of the AT&T Company—long before I'd expected. We both started laughing and crying at the same time. And when I moved into my new office, she sent a beautiful Baccarat bud vase and enough money for my secretary to buy a fresh rose every week for three months.

14 | The Inspiration to Change

S OME THINGS WERE IMMEDIATELY DIFFERENT about being an officer. The office was bigger and so was the authority. I felt like the same person, but many others no longer saw me in the same way. I learned to be more careful about what I said and how I said it; there was no such thing as an offhand comment anymore. In any organization where hierarchy is important, words that come from the higher-ups always carry more weight—even if they shouldn't. I also began to experience the "Carly says" phenomenon. People would attribute words to me to advance their own agendas; sometimes they reflected my comments accurately and sometimes merely what they wished I'd said but hadn't.

Some things didn't change at all. I remember going into my first rating-and-ranking session as a vice president. One of my peers was presenting his subordinate; everyone else in the room had issues with this particular director and voiced them strenuously. After they'd all spoken, I was asked to give my opinion as well. I'd worked closely with this director and confirmed both his strengths and the serious weaknesses that had just been highlighted by all my colleagues. Although I'd said virtually the same things as the others, the reaction to me was different. Now the director's boss said, "Well, Carly, you just don't like him. You're being emotional, not objective." He was trying to dismiss me with the old women-are-too-emotional line. Later, after I'd been promoted to senior vice president, a peer angrily accused me of sleeping with the boss to get my way; he'd vigorously argued against one of my recommendations, and I'd prevailed.

I certainly had a wider field of vision in my new job. Throughout the previous year the aspirations of the organization had changed. The people of Network Systems had once been content to focus their energies on Western Electric's traditional domestic customers. Now we raised our sights and looked out over the whole market. International opportunities and new kinds of customers were no longer a sideline—they were core to our new ambitions. And we wanted to invest in these growth opportunities. As our investments increased, so did the tension with the rest of AT&T.

Network Systems had always been a predictable producer of profit for AT&T and had required virtually no management time and attention from its parent. AT&T was one of a very few network service providers in the world that also owned manufacturing and basic research capability. Now Network Systems was trying to sell communications equipment to AT&T's partners as well as its competitors, while at the same time supplying AT&T's own network. The partners sought to leverage this unique situation; the competitors were fearful of it. And so as our ambitions grew, so did our challenges. Our customers and potential customers were less and less likely to simply negotiate a deal with Network Systems alone. Increasingly they either wanted assurances that Network Systems did not have a conflict of interest in serving AT&T and a competitor, or they wanted a better deal with AT&T because they were doing business with one of its subsidiaries. Meanwhile, AT&T kept demanding greater profits from its subsidiary.

I also had greater insight into what Bill Marx was actually thinking and worried about. He was now frustrated by the position his organization was in. From his perspective, AT&T kept getting in the way in the marketplace and yet wouldn't lessen its demands for financial performance. At the same time, Network Systems' traditional customers, including AT&T itself, were increasingly looking to diversify their supply base and move away from their longtime, and in some cases, sole, supplier. Bill wanted me, in my new role, to try to negotiate a set of operating agreements between AT&T and Network Systems that would govern how we each operated in the marketplace.

He hoped this would create more predictability for both our sales forces and our customers.

My goal was to build these agreements on a country-by-country basis, taking into account the specific relationships each of us had in those markets. We went through endless analysis and discussion to try to create "rules of engagement" that were both specific enough to be useful and general enough to be comprehensible. It was difficult work, and I'm sure my counterparts at AT&T were as frustrated with me as I was with them. Either we couldn't agree in a market, or conditions changed as soon as we did, or we couldn't get people out in the field to follow the rules that we'd agreed to. We were a bunch of staff people focused on theory and paper when the real action in the marketplace was both faster and more complicated than we could handle. The conflicts between us were so numerous that even when we did reach agreement, we were both unwilling to sacrifice what was required.

Synergy is a fancy word for the whole being greater than the sum of the parts. In business terms it means that when different products or services are combined into a solution, or different parts of an organization work together out in the marketplace, there is a greater opportunity for growth, market share and/or profitability. When we sat in meetings at headquarters, we were arguing that synergy still existed between Long Lines and Network Systems; and the theoretical case we made for it looked very compelling. But if you want to know if synergy in a business is real, don't ask headquarters and don't ask people doing analysis. Ask the sales force. If customers actually are willing to spend more for a combination, or award more of their business, synergy exists. If they're not, it doesn't; and only members of the sales force, who talk to customers day in and day out, really know the answer. The synergies that once had held AT&T together were disappearing.

At the end of a long process, my counterparts and I produced a report. It outlined the arrangements that theoretically could work in each of our focus markets. We presented it with as much enthusiasm as we could muster. It was as good a compromise as we were going to achieve, and on the margin it would probably help some. We didn't oversell, but we didn't say it was a waste of time either. After the meeting Bill asked me what I really thought. I told him this wasn't going to work for long.

A few weeks later Bill asked me to lead an effort to prepare a strategic presentation for an upcoming AT&T board meeting. Three different scenarios were being developed by three separate teams: one maximized AT&T's emphasis on computer systems, one maximized AT&T's emphasis on Network Systems, and one maximized AT&T's emphasis on the Long Lines services business. AT&T's chairman, Bob Allen, asked that the work be kept confidential.

A small team of us labored for many weeks. We argued that Network Systems could not achieve its potential unless it was separated from AT&T, free to pursue its own interests, unfettered by AT&T's issues. We quantified in exhaustive detail the likely outcome of remaining in AT&T versus the alternative. Bill Marx went to the Board convinced that our recommendation was sound and hopeful that the Board would agree. He was instead deeply disappointed. So was I, but we both knew that sooner or later the inevitable would occur, for while the Board's deliberations and our work were confidential, the Network Systems sales force was restless and worried. They could see and feel the impact of the constant conflicts between us and our parent in the field.

Sometimes you have secret enemies. Sometimes you have secret friends. A few months after I'd arrived at Network Systems, while everyone else was yelling at me and telling me I didn't have any value to add because I didn't understand the business, I got a phone call. On the other end was a man named Jim Brewington, and he was responsible for Network Systems' sales to the U.S. West telephone company. He said he was calling from Denver and needed my help. His customer was doing business with the Russian telephone operator, wanted Network Systems to do business with them in Russia, and he didn't know what to do.

"I read here that you're in charge of International Strategy, so I figure you know more about this than I do." This alone made him a friend in my eyes. Here was someone who was willing to give me the benefit of the doubt just because I was in the job.

"Jim, thank you for calling me. I can't tell you how appreciative I am that you thought I could help out."

I guess he didn't know what I meant exactly, because he said, "Well, you are in International Strategy and Business Development, right?"

"Right, right. I just meant that not everyone assumes I know anything."

"Oh, don't pay much attention to these Western Electric guys. We've all got pinheads and size nineteen necks."

He made me laugh. He took me seriously enough to explain the whole opportunity. We arranged that I would travel to Denver to meet with him and his customer and see what we could do together.

J IM HAD GROWN UP on a cattle ranch in Idaho. He was rough around the edges and did not suffer fools gladly. He was book smart and street smart and liked to play dumb. He was a workhorse who never tired, and if you were his friend, he was as loyal as a dog. He was blunt but charming. He could not lie if he tried. He and Bill Marx were very much alike, which is probably why Bill considered Jim both friend and protégé. I didn't know about his relationship with Bill, but by the end of our first meeting in Denver, I knew I'd found a friend and a mentor. Bill asked Jim's advice a lot. Jim wouldn't play politics with anyone, and Bill knew he'd get a straight answer. Jim and Bill could violently disagree sometimes, but they trusted each other. Bill asked Jim whether I was ready to be promoted to officer. I think he also asked him whether I could take over the sales force.

Bill asked me to lead Sales East, field operations for the eastern half of the United States and Canada. Later I would become head of all North American field operations. Bill and Jim believed in me. They both took a chance on me. I trusted them to support me when I earned it, and to tell me the truth when I needed it. In return for all they gave me, they got my best work, my absolute candor and my unwavering loyalty.

A leader's job is to add value, not get in the way, or preside or take credit. If things are working, people actually don't need your help. Go find where they do need you. Sometimes, if things aren't working, people can see that there are problems, but they can't identify the cause or, consequently, the solution. A leader's job is to find and address the cause, just as a doctor's job is to try to cure the disease rather than simply treat the symptoms.

The North American business was the cash cow of Network Systems. These teams always brought in most of the revenue and profit. Now, with the company's increased emphasis on international opportunities and new growth, they felt undervalued and underappreciated. At the same time, their customers were aggressively looking for competitive alternatives; closing deals was becoming more difficult. The intensifying conflict between their customers and AT&T didn't help the situation. The sales force felt caught in the middle and demoralized.

The symptoms of all this were the numbers. Revenues were shrinking. Expenses were growing, profit was declining. The directors of each team knew their results were unacceptable. They were too professional to say otherwise, but when it was time to agree on plans and budgets, they would expend enormous energy saying they couldn't do any better, and then miss their commitments just to prove the point. Their revenues were down because their customers didn't trust AT&T and didn't want to give any money to its subsidiary. Their expenses were up because they spent so much of their selling time explaining what AT&T was doing. Their profits were down because they were competing against companies who didn't have to carry the same baggage as we did, so they had to cut the prices to win the deals. Of course, all the things they pointed out about the marketplace really were happening. It was also true that the emerging strategic conflict between AT&T and Network Systems had become an excuse for their failure to address the issues that lay well within their managerial control. And the fact that the new business outside the United States was getting so much attention became the excuse for the failure to motivate their own teams; it was the "no one cares so why should we?" syndrome.

Sometimes people stop striving for improved performance because they don't think it's necessary; their lack of aspiration comes from overconfidence. Sometimes people stop striving because they don't think it's possible; their lack of aspiration comes from defeatism. Whenever people stop striving for improved performance, inevitably execution gets sloppier and results deteriorate.

Steve Carson was the chief financial officer of Network Systems and another wise counselor. He used to say "Operational cause drives financial effect." What he meant was that numbers don't just happen. Numbers are a direct result of operational cause. And operational cause is a fancy way of saying people's actions, decisions and behavior. If you want to make a positive impact on the financials of a company or a business or a product line, you have to understand what people are actually doing. Then you need to understand how their actions must change to produce better results. And then you have to understand how to motivate people to behave differently.

Every environment is different. What motivates changed behavior on a factory floor is different from what works in an R&D lab. What works in one company won't work exactly the same way in another. However, no matter what the environment, a vital starting point for motivating changed behavior is real agreement and real belief that improved performance is both necessary and possible.

I spent two days in meetings with my new regional vice presidents. I insisted we examine every opportunity for increased efficiency. We looked at every sales funnel. I pushed and probed and prodded. There was a lot of resistance. "We're spending too much time in meetings; we should be out with our customers." "We've done all this before; why do you think it will be any different this time?" "This is our job, not yours; why don't you just let us do it." Their litany of ways I was wasting their time was long and oft repeated.

On the afternoon of the second day, I finally stopped the discussion. "Look, guys. Forget about me. You used to be the heroes around Network Systems. You always delivered. Now everyone thinks you're a bunch of crybabies. You whine all the time, and the people who used to count on you are getting tired of it." There was a long silence. It got increasingly uncomfortable, but I would not break it. I would not let them off the hook. Finally, one of them spoke—Tom Carter. "Really? Do people think we're crybabies? Who said so?"

"Jim Brewington and Bill Marx." It was true or I would not have said it.

Another long silence. Now they were contemplating the fact that two very important people they'd known longer than I had were talking to me about them. Then Tom said to his colleagues, "Look, guys, I don't like that. I'm not willing to live with that. So let's just give it a try, okay?"

It was a breakthrough. It took a no-nonsense appeal to their egos and their self-respect. And it took Tom Carter's decision to become a change agent. Change doesn't require 100 percent of the people to go along. It doesn't even take a majority. It does take critical mass. In this particular case, among this group of peers, Tom represented critical mass. His results were always among the best, and his peers admired him for many reasons. Besides, this was a group that had worked together for a very long time; every single one of his colleagues owed him one.

With renewed energy we talked nuts and bolts, and by the end it was clear to all of us that despite all the issues that made our jobs difficult, we could make very real improvements in every aspect of our business. The exercise had been long and difficult, but everyone felt better when we'd finished. No one actually wants to be mediocre, and these guys had once been much better than that. They could see a real path to better performance now.

Nevertheless, things actually were tougher now than before. People really were working harder and harder just to stand still. Improved performance would take even harder work and greater discipline. We couldn't pay people any more; we didn't have the budget. So how could we reward them? The answer was simple, and it was the only one we had: we'd make it fun.

We began to recognize achievements large and small. I'd call people to thank them, and especially for someone who'd never heard from a vice president before, that small gesture was meaningful. A balloon might show up at someone's desk. I'd send silly cards. We had weekly teleconferences to track our progress, and each regional vice president would get to highlight his team's important accomplishments of the week before. Pretty soon people got to know if their work was going to be mentioned on the teleconference, and they started to compete for the honor. I constantly traveled all over the territory to meet with our teams and our customers. At every stop we'd talk about our issues and how to resolve them, but we'd also celebrate our victories. We held contests. We gave silly prizes.

A cynic would say these simple things couldn't possibly matter. Anyone who's ever led people would know that they do. The difference between missing the performance mark and making it is often only a matter of persistence—you can't give up too soon. It's easier to keep going when you're having some fun along the way and you know someone cares.

Our teams competed every day out in the marketplace to win their customer's business, but they also competed fiercely with one another. If internal competition gets in the way of serving customers, it's counterproductive. Then, teams need to be focused externally. When internal competition spurs higher performance, it should be encouraged; and that was the situation here. Tom Carter and Joe Mauriello were the two senior-most regional vice presidents. They had the biggest customers, Bell Atlantic and Bell South, and the biggest teams. They complained the loudest and delivered the most. They were consummate professionals, deeply passionate about their business, fun and funny. And they competed with each other for everything, from the best results to my attention. Joe and Tom set the pace for all the others.

As the final quarter of the year approached, I needed to rally the teams. Although we had performed well so far, we wouldn't make our goals unless we ratcheted up our performance. I decided to use Tom and Joe's competitive spirit in a more systematic way. We would have a horse race. We made a video tape to introduce the race. I went to a local stable, stood next to a horse and announced that the race was on. Then we filmed the large plasterboard race course we'd designed and hung up on the wall outside my office. Each team was represented by a small plastic horse attached with Velcro to the race course, in a position relative to one another based upon their percentage completion of our performance metrics. We showed them the large winner's cup I would present to the team whose horse crossed the finish line first. Every team had to name its horse. And from then on, every weekly conference call would begin with the sound of the bugling call that starts the horses down the track.

Was it corny? You bet. A number of regional vice presidents said so, but Joe and Tom couldn't help themselves. It was a contest—a silly one at that—but both of them wanted to win it. And so they got into the spirit of it, and the harder they competed with each other, the more difficult it became for the rest of their colleagues to sit on the fence. They could see their own plastic horses falling farther behind while Joe's and Tom's were running neck and neck. Every week, after the bugle, the skeptics would hear ". . . and trailing as they round the bend . . ." So eventually everyone's pride got the better of them. Besides, it really was fun.

Lots of other organizations in Network Systems thought we were crazy. There was a lot of talk similar to "What does Carly think she's doing over there?" Frankly, I didn't care. If it got us the results we needed, it was worth taking some flak over. When the year finished, we'd delivered better results than even we had predicted. And as soon as the winner's cup was presented, everyone wanted to know what next year's contest was going to be. We decided on the slogan "Run the Rapids, Feel the Rush." I sat in a raft wearing a life jacket and carrying a paddle to announce it.

Of course we couldn't have achieved anything without detailed plans for improved performance and all the heavy lifting that operational excellence requires. We also wouldn't have achieved as much without the extra motivation. And hard work becomes drudgery unless you have some fun along the way.

. . .

AS 1993 BECAME 1994, whatever synergies existed between Long Lines and Network Systems had been replaced by clear, strategic conflict. Every time I would visit with a customer, I'd have to spend 75 percent of the meeting listening to their issues with the rest of AT&T. One day I received a handwritten note from the AT&T chairman, Bob Allen. This was extremely unusual. I'd never received anything directly from him before and now he was asking, in a casual way, for a meeting the next time I was in Basking Ridge. While of course I knew Bob, and had been in large meetings he'd attended, I'd never met with him alone. I was very curious and a little unnerved.

We met in a conference room down the way from his office. Bob was friendly and polite. He asked me how I liked Network Systems. I told him I loved it. I had grown to feel at home there, and running North America was the best job I'd had yet. I told him how great Bill Marx had been to work for. We talked about all this for what seemed too long, and finally Bob asked, "How's it going with the RBOC customers?" I told him the unvarnished truth. "Bob, it's getting harder and harder. We've become whipping boys for all their complaints about AT&T." I told him about a recent meeting with Pacific Bell. The president had spent the first thirty minutes playing a videotape of AT&T's most recent commercials over and over. He found their tone and content offensive to his company and wanted to make absolutely sure we understood how upset he was before we began our discussions about an important contract Network Systems had with Pac Bell. He did this partially as an effective negotiating tactic—it put us on the defensive right from the beginning—and partially out of genuine frustration.

"Bob, the problem is when our competitors go in to see the RBOCs, they don't have to spend their time this way. They get to spend 100 percent of their limited time with the customer talking about their products and their relationship. We only get to spend about 25 percent of ours that way. And over time, that difference adds up."

This whole conversation took less than ten minutes, but it seemed to be the reason for our meeting. Bob thanked me for coming over and left. A minute later, Bill Marx wandered in. He'd been promoted and was leading the Business Communications Systems and Microelectronics businesses. His office was now in Basking Ridge. "How did it go, Carly?"

I told him about Bob's questions and my answers. He smiled and said, "Good." And that was all.

There was only one other notable thing about that meeting. A couple of weeks earlier, Lori, Tracy and I had been to the mall. I was feeling particularly stodgy and too much like a corporate VP that weekend, so when Lori suggested we both get our ears pierced with a second hole, I agreed. We had great fun, and I thought two earrings in each ear looked great: very noncorporate. Apparently, I was right because all during the meeting with Bob Allen I noticed that he kept staring at my ears. He swayed very slightly back and forth, eyeing one ear and then the other. Bill was less subtle. He just asked, "Why the heck did you pierce your ears again?" Earlier, Joe Mauriello had been the most direct of all. "Carly, the Bell South customers won't go for those earrings. I think you'd better take them out when we visit." Just to make sure, he'd check out my ears before every meeting.

THAT SUMMER, Rich McGinn, who'd become the president of Network Systems, started asking a lot of questions about the work I'd done for Bill for that Board meeting two years earlier. Beyond that, I didn't have any visibility into whatever deliberations were going on. Nevertheless, I was becoming hopeful. Several months later, one afternoon in September, Rich McGinn called a few of us into his conference room. He told us that Bob Allen would announce the trivestiture of AT&T the following day. Network Systems, Business Communcations Systems, Microelectronics and most of Bell Laboratories would become a separate company: Newco. The computer business, which by now had acquired NCR, would also be spun off (later it reverted to the NCR name). And AT&T would be a network services company.

I was elated. I jumped out of my chair and threw my arms over my head the way an umpire signals a touchdown on the football field. "Yes!" I shouted. Everyone told me to lower my voice—this was very hush-hush news. They were right, of course, but I couldn't contain my excitement at the opportunity. We were going to be an independent company, free to make our own way and reach our potential.

When the news broke, I scheduled a conference call with all the employees in my organization. This was huge news, and they would have lots of questions. What I really wanted to communicate, though, was how excited I was about our opportunity. Everyone, including me, constantly complained about how difficult our jobs were because we were a part of AT&T. Now we would be free. How we responded to our customers and our competitors would be our own decision. We'd encounter other problems, of course, but they would be of our own making. These kinds of problems we had the power and the capacity to solve; we had never been able to solve the problem of our ownership by AT&T. We were now masters of our own destiny.

I was disappointed with the response to the call. Almost everyone, including the RVPs, focused on the downside risks. What if this happened? What if that happened? Then they focused on themselves. When will we know how our jobs will change? Will our titles be different? What about our retirement plans? When I reassured them that the programs and pensions would not be touched, many asked whether they could retire from AT&T, not Newco. In fairness, the trivestiture was a huge upheaval in their lives and their careers. Unlike me, they hadn't been prepared for it; they didn't know it was an option that had been on the table for two years. And yet there was something more fundamental behind the difference in our reactions.

Coping with change is like learning anything new—a new workout routine, a new diet, a new golf swing, a new job. At first it's really hard. It feels unnatural and requires lots of effort. Sometimes you give up and go back to the old way of doing things. But if you keep at it, over time what was once new becomes easier and easier until it's almost second nature. I was accustomed to change. I'd been through enough change to know that good can always come out of it, so I could see the opportunity and the possibilities. My colleagues were unaccustomed to change. It seemed too difficult, and they wanted to hang on to their familiar patterns. They were afraid of what change might bring, and we couldn't return to the old way of doing things even if we wanted to—once the split was announced, there was no going back.

I learned something very important that day. I learned that for many people even deep dissatisfaction with the known present can be preferable to the fear of an unknown future. I learned that when people are afraid, they turn inward to protect themselves and those things most personal and important to them. And as I reflected that evening on the entire extraordinary day, I remembered that every time I moved to a new city and a new school, I would be homesick. The place I'd left seemed so much better. The people of Network Systems were going to be homesick too. They were going to miss the way things used to be. I knew I'd have to work hard to keep their energies focused on where we were going because in their minds and in their conversations, they would keep returning to what they were leaving behind. And I knew from my own experience that it would be easier to face our future when everyone understood that we had no way to go "home" again.

15 | The Power of Teamwork

THE CREATION of Lucent Technologies was about much more than an initial public offering (IPO). It was about what can happen when a whole organization's self-image changes. It was about the excitement that can infect people when their frame of reference changes from doing daily work to making history. It's a story of the intense focus and camaraderie that is built through shared passion and common goals. And ultimately it's a story of how the choices of a leader can destroy both.

In December of 1994, Henry Schacht, the new chairman and CEO of Newco, approached me to become executive vice president of Corporate Operations. The job included an unusual mixture of responsibilities from Strategy to Information Systems. In the immediate term it was mostly about leading our efforts to prepare for the IPO in April of 1995 and the full spinoff in September. Newco was at this point a collection of assets that AT&T was getting rid of. It had no name, no identity, no coalescing purpose or direction. And we had a lot of complex, detailed work to do to disentangle ourselves from AT&T around information technology (IT), intellectual property, balance sheets and buildings.

I didn't want the job. I loved my current position, and I was looking forward to working with our customers now that we were soon to be independent and free of the conflicts that had caused us so much trouble in the marketplace. I told Henry as much, but he insisted and said that Bob Allen had told him he needed someone in the job who really knew Network Systems. I reluctantly agreed, although in truth I had no choice; but I said that I really didn't want to stay in corporate headquarters for more than two years. My hesitation was based on the emotional connection I felt with my North American team—I didn't want to leave them. I had known the special joy of believing in a team more than they believed in themselves, and being rewarded by seeing their pride, pleasure and newfound confidence as they achieved more than they thought was possible.

I had never been involved in a spin-off before. I knew very little about Wall Street or the process we were about to undertake. I had never written a prospectus or read one, for that matter. I had never been on the floor of the New York Stock Exchange. There were so many issues involved in going public that needed to be addressed. Nevertheless, I decided that before Newco could do anything else, we needed to agree on our aspirations. We had to choose what we would become. Any path is good enough if you have no destination in mind, and any goal is sufficient if there is no aspiration. Being identified as the castoffs from AT&T was unlikely to inspire people. Inspiration was essential to keep people moving forward rather than longing for the good old days; it was essential to motivate people to learn new ways of operating instead of relying solely on old habits; it was essential to sustain the higher level of performance now required of us as we went public.

For some, the words *aspiration* and *inspiration* are mumbo jumbo; or hype; or soft, nonoperational stuff. These are people who forget that every income statement and balance sheet in the world is produced by the everyday hard work of everyday people. And people achieve more when they're motivated by a purpose worthy of their efforts. They align their individual actions into a more powerful collective effort when they know they strive for a common and commonly understood goal. Nowhere are aspiration and inspiration more important than in a large, complex organization undergoing major change. In large companies myriad actions taken and countless small decisions made must add up to the bottom line. And in a period of change, each employee must break old habits and learn new skills, and every employee's actions and decisions must align in new ways to produce something different.

I read everything I could get my hands on because although I knew Network Systems well, I didn't know the other organizations that together were forming Newco. I read about their histories, their business plans, their accomplishments, their strategies. I studied all the numbers. I read what the AT&T Board had seen when making the decision to spin us off. I talked to the bankers and listened to all their analysts. I asked a lot of questions and when I felt well informed, I argued strenuously that we should aim high, strive for much, and focus on the possibilities. We would have only one opportunity to create this new company.

As it was my role, I brought my point of view to the table when the senior-most executives of the new company gathered under Henry Schacht's leadership to decide together on everything from our strategic intent to the operational details of customer service. Henry knew that everyone would have to own what Lucent would become. He wisely chose to take the time to build consensus on every important aspect of our challenge. Rich McGinn was impatient with these meetings; they were long and messy and frequently frustrating. He was insulting behind Henry's back, just as he'd been behind Bill Marx's back. Henry knew, however, that building the team, and building the vision, and building the plan to deliver that vision all required an expenditure of time and energy. Those meetings welded a collective determination to succeed and a collective decision to lead.

The essential ingredients of our leadership vision were three. We would be a broadly defined communications company rather than the more narrow telecommunications equipment supplier. This distinction was important because Lucent could focus its energies on data as well as voice, on components as well as systems, on consumers and businesses and governments as well as network providers, on diverse technologies. Being a communications company was not only the highest aspiration we could strive for, it also provided common purpose to the collection of assets that made up the company, from microelectronics to consumer products, from network systems to basic research.

We would take full advantage of every aspect of our history and every asset we had. The practical consequence of this was a decision to leverage our capabilities rather than seek to disinvest in some or deemphasize others. We were essentially unknown in the marketplace, and now we would introduce a one-hundred-year history of innovation and accomplishment with pride. Rather than focus solely on the future, we would celebrate our past. Finally, we would be as bold, as nimble, as aggressive as a brand-new company because in many ways that was exactly what we were. This had a direct impact on the goals we set and the choices we made.

The name *Lucent,* which means glowing with light; the choice of the bold, red logo (which I insisted we reconsider after it had been rejected, because it reminded me of my mother's paintings), and the first advertising campaign that featured the introductory "résumé" of a "one-hundred-year-old start-up" were all consequences of these three decisions. The naming, branding and advertising of Lucent were all acclaimed as great marketing. Advertising and marketing are great only if they are authentic—real reflections of a company's aspirations, capabilities and choices. Authentic advertising and marketing are therefore the consequence of specific strategic and operational decisions, not disconnected campaigns or wishful thinking.

Marketing and advertising are, of course, one form of communication. And although there are many forms of communication, there is but one audience. Experts will argue that there are many audiences—there are employees, and customers, and shareholders and communities. I believe that in reality these have all become one. First, technology has now made it so; as we all know, for example, it is simply no longer possible to speak to employees without shareholders hearing about it or vice versa. Second, particularly for a large public company, most people are members of more than one group. An employee is a shareholder. A shareholder is also a customer and lives in a community where the company has a large facility. A customer lives there as well and owns stock. All of these people are influenced by everything they see and hear as well as by their friends and neighbors and colleagues.

Although different types of communication can serve different purposes—a prospectus provides a detailed view of all the risks and uncertainties a company faces, whereas an advertising campaign may provide an abstract view of a company's character—they all find their way to the same audience. And so authentic communications are not simply reality based, they are also consistent among different groups. You cannot say one set of things to stockholders and something completely different to employees and expect authenticity. Different messages may be pleasing for a time, but they will not be authentic, and over time people will reconcile them by choosing which to believe.

Authentic communications are therefore inherently difficult. They require the right balance of risks and aspirations because both are real. They require the right balance of complex detail and simple concepts because both are required for comprehension. They require the ever-present knowledge that any word and any number may matter deeply to anyone who cares. This is true of every public company, whether Hewlett-Packard or Lucent Technologies. I labored over every detail of the presentation we would make to shareholders during the road show, sweated every aspect of our advertising, and spent many, many long nights arguing over every word and every number of the prospectus.

Initially I had not imagined that I would be as involved with the prospectus as I became. The bankers had described this as "something the lawyers and the accountants work on." It quickly became clear to me that this document was much, much more. It was a declaration of who we were and what we chose to become. Beyond that, it was the subject of intense negotiation between our AT&T parent and the fledgling company they were about to set free.

It is the particular nature of American business that negotiations become real when words go to paper. All kinds of things may be said, and agreed to, in advance of the written word. None of it is truly settled until it's committed to writing and the writing sticks. One night around midnight I got a call from Jim Lusk. He had been chief financial officer in my previous job and was now the comptroller of Lucent. He led the finance team working on the prospectus and was in New York with his team and their AT&T counterparts. "Carly, I need some help. We've got lots of issues down here, and I can't get agreement on anything." I trusted Jim. If he said he needed help, he did.

"I'll be there."

We pulled virtual all-nighters for weeks. It was a learning experience; and as all learning is, it was quite fun. That very first night, I asked what the small button by the door of the conference room was. It turned out there was a similar button in every room at these offices where the prospectus was being drafted and printed. I loved it when I was informed that you could push this button at any time of day or night, and someone would appear to take your order for any kind of food or beverage. Any kind! I joked that I needed one of these at home. To lighten the mood, I would frequently test the system. When our discussions hit a roadblock, I would stop them to fantasize about what we should ask for when we pushed the button; usually we'd all conclude our waistlines couldn't take it, especially since M&M's seemed to have become a staple of our diet, but we laughed a lot nonetheless. Everyone got a big kick out of my delight, and soon we were all calling them Carly buttons.

I instituted a process called "the page turning." Usually once a day a very large team of both AT&T and Lucent representatives would gather to argue over the words of the prospectus. This was where all the rubber hit the road. Jim had called for help because agreements that he thought had been made would fall apart when the words were actually on the paper. Or words that had been agreed to previously would be reviewed again, and people would change their minds. Or no one could agree on anything at all, and so they couldn't move forward. So now we needed a process for arguing, for agreeing, and for deciding to let our agreements stand. Thus the page turning was born.

The group's job was to read each and every page of the prospectus. I proposed a process whereby we would fully debate each issue that arose on each page. We would debate the issue until either the group came to agreement or concluded it could not. If no agreement could be reached, I would make the final decision on behalf of Lucent if I felt I had the authority to do so. A representative of AT&T would decide on their behalf—different people were accountable for different issues—if they had sufficient authority. If the decision had to be escalated to someone outside the room, the issue would be logged. Every issue fell into one of these three buckets, so each could be decided or set aside. When we had completed this process for each page, we would turn it. Once turned, a page could not be turned back. We would debate, then we would decide, and we would not revisit.

The physical act of turning the page became a symbol of progress and a victory to be celebrated. After particularly long discussions, the group would spontaneously erupt in good-natured applause when we all, with great fanfare, simultaneously turned the page. At first we would stay on a page for hours. Over time, the group began to recognize who brought up legitimate issues and who wasted the team's time. The peer pressure to spend one another's time wisely kept the group moving forward. After a week or so, we improved on the process by agreeing that issues could be worked ahead of time, and subteams could agree on language to be presented to the whole group.

The group accepted my process because everyone wanted to move forward. They accepted my process because they needed a way to ensure that every valid point was considered and debated and that at the same time decisions were made in a timely manner. Sometimes leaders make decisions for others. Sometimes leaders let others decide. And sometimes leaders build processes that help everyone make decisions and help people choose where they should lead and where they should follow. This insight would later guide me when I arrived at HP.

We used a version of this same process when we built the final road show materials. (A lengthy road show, where we visited as many investors as possible, was necessary to find buyers for Lucent stock.) The cumulative effect of all this group effort and team decision making was a real sense of camaraderie and shared purpose that infused and infected the new leadership team of Lucent. When we began our road show, we split into three teams of three executives each. Our enthusiasm about our new company and our new mission was obvious to anyone who listened to us. Many investors told us they were sold on our passion. When we arrived in New York, the *Wall Street Journal* quipped, "It's the Rolling Stones. It's Barbra Streisand. No, it's the Lucent road show!" And Henry, whose team Jim Lusk and I were on, would joke at the beginning of each meeting by drawing a line down the center of the long tables where we sat across from prospective investors and saying, "Please don't feed our presenters, or they'll climb right over the table to convince you!"

The road show was a mind-numbing three weeks of eight presentations a day. And yet I loved every minute of it—the intense pleasure of the seamless team that Henry, Jim and I became, the thrill of doing something for the very first time, the excitement of talking about something I believed in so deeply, the knowledge that we were building a company right before our very eyes.

Our employees could feel it too. The January day we introduced our new name and logo to them evoked a collective outburst of joy and enthusiasm. Tears were in my eyes while I watched Henry unveil the red, hand-drawn circle and play the first ad as employees rose in a spontaneous ovation. There were many wet eyes in that auditorium that day. And on the September morning we sent a hot-air balloon aloft to symbolize that we had become completely untethered, and I watched our new flag whip in a crisp New Jersey breeze, the tears came again. I loved Lucent.

The contrast to what was happening at AT&T was stark. The people and leadership of AT&T had spent all their energies disentangling themselves and disposing of assets. They had not considered what would remain when they were finished. They didn't seize the opportunity to reimagine themselves because they didn't see it. And this failure of imagination affected everything—their enthusiasm, their teamwork, their aspiration, their performance. Internal politics were intense, which is always what happens when there is no worthy goal to focus people externally. And you could feel the difference between what was happening at Lucent and what was happening at AT&T every time you went from one location to the other. Many of the AT&T friends I'd made while negotiating all night would call me and say something like "Boy, did I make the wrong decision! Everyone thought you guys would be the boring company with no future, but I guess we turned out to be." I would remember this later when I arrived at Hewlett-Packard and faced the de facto decision to spin off what became Agilent Technologies.

The two years I spent in Corporate Operations were an amazing learning experience. Before the IPO, I'd thought of Wall Street as the mysterious, powerful machinery behind the greatest economy in the world. Wall Street was hard to understand or explain, but it had great powers of discernment. Bankers were the high priests of the religion of capitalism, and analysts were their acolytes. As had been the case many times before, though, experience and observation revealed the truth behind the mystery. Wall Street is a collection of many, many people. These people have egos, ambitions, and conflicts of interest. Like any large group of people, they have a wide variety of goals and objectives. Although some are discerning and wise, not all investors are smart and not all bankers add value. Some are driven by emotion and the conventional wisdom more than others. Some are driven by the thrill of a deal, others by the numbers of a deal, still others by the potential of a deal. Wall Street, and the market, works because it is large and liquid.

Over time there are enough people with enough money that common sense will prevail. Time and the law of large numbers have to work, however. In the short term, or when the players are few, emotion, ambition and greed can overwhelm common sense. This was reasonably apparent in 1995, long before the bubble of the late nineties or the growth of hedge funds. Still, in 1995, most investors were really betting on the underlying asset that is represented by a stock certificate. Five years later, more and more bets were being placed not on the asset, but on the value of the certificate itself. Today, for many traders and investors, this currency and its fluctuations have become more important than the company and its capabilities.

I'd learned other things as well. I'd learned a lot about an information systems division and its impact on the operations of a company. I'd negotiated an outsourcing deal with IBM and lived to regret it (and I'd learned a lot about their vulnerabilities, which would help HP compete against them later). I'd benchmarked Hewlett-Packard and found a company of many admirable qualities that was almost impossible to do business with if an agreement between its many different business units was required. I'd witnessed the power of teamwork and a common cause. And once again I'd learned what people can really accomplish when they have the right leadership and support, the right game plan and the will to win.

*My father and mother around the time
of their marriage*

My mother

My father

At age 3

At age 8

With Dean Rudy Lamone at the University of Maryland in 2004

Mike Brunner of AT&T Government Communications

My husband, Frank

Frank, with Lori and Traci, during our first year of marriage

In the tub with Traci and Lori

With Deborah Bowker during our year at MIT

Bill Marx of AT&T Network Systems

Kathy Fitzgerald of Lucent

With Carol Spurrier during our Italian vacation

With an exhausted Kara during her first trip to Disneyland

above: **P**resident-elect George W. Bush with the technology company CEOs in Austin, Texas, January 2001

above: **W**ith Henry Kissinger and Rabbi Schneier, when I received the Appeal of Conscience Award, New York, 2002

With President Thabo Mbeki of South Africa as we visited Mogalakwena

*Our granddaughters,
Kara and Morgan*

Summer 2005 in Lucerne Switzerland

16 | Marching on the Bus

WHEN MY TWO YEARS as executive vice president of Corporate Operations came to an end, Henry was true to his word. He asked me to become the president of Consumer Products. This was the division of Lucent that manufactured and marketed consumer communications equipment—wireless and wireline telephones mostly. After three months of intense immersion in my new organization, I asked to see Henry and Rich alone. I was pessimistic in my assessment of the situation. The people were enthusiastic, but the products weren't competitive. Our manufacturing costs were too high and our volumes too low. The quality, features and design of our products were falling further behind those of our competitors. Consumer markets are dominated by brands, and the investments in the Lucent brand had been directed almost exclusively to the business market. In an increasingly global marketplace where our most formidable competitors were European and Asian, our distribution was far too U.S.-centric.

At the conclusion of a long, exhaustive presentation that laid all this out in more detail, I closed with three options for Henry and Rich to consider. The first was to continue on the current path, making as much improvement as was possible. The outcome of this scenario would be real but incremental improvement in our financial results. It would not yield a turnaround, merely a more respectable outcome. We could be profitable but not at benchmark levels. Option two was to invest for leadership. This would require a large increase in spending for consumer-focused brand building, global distribution agreements, hiring of key design and engineering talent, relocation and retooling of our factories. Option three was to consider divesting Consumer Products in whole or in part.

I recommended option three. I did not believe that Lucent had the patience, the ambition or the resources to build a major consumer company. I said that having a perpetually lagging consumer products business would hurt the whole of Lucent. I recognized that such a decision would take time to make and more time to explore and execute. Therefore, I also presented a plan for option one. I committed the Consumer Products team and myself to making the business profitable and delivering better featured products to the marketplace. We would have to make some management changes to deliver, but it could be done. Rich and Henry were somewhat shaken. They had not expected this assessment. One thing was certain: there was no more money for investment, so market leadership wasn't possible. I knew they were disappointed, certainly in what I'd said, but perhaps in me as well. But candor is the hallmark of the truly loyal, and Lucent—and Henry—had all my loyalty.

I devoted myself to my new organization. People were starved for leadership, so a little went a long way. Although I did not share with them everything I had told Henry and Rich, I was direct about both our challenges and our constraints. We weren't going to get any more money to invest. An Asian competitor like VTech, or a European competitor like Nokia, had some important advantages. Our choices were simple and few: we could choose to do better with what we had—or not.

As is true whenever a new leader issues a challenge, a critical mass of the old-timers must rise to that challenge. If this fails to happen, the new leader is simply ignored. People who've never operated in large, complex companies are often surprised to learn that even a change agent with title and position can be effectively rendered powerless by people's collective decision to maintain the status quo. A boss can hire and fire. A boss can reallocate people and money. A boss can measure and reward. A boss can threaten or inspire. Each of these actions and decisions will be analyzed and interpreted by an organization. Some interpretations will motivate change. Some will discourage change. But no boss, even a president or a CEO, can order people to change. No boss can force people to behave differently. People operate based on their own free will. They make their own decisions, and in big companies those decisions are easy to hide.

People choose to change and people choose to lead. Homa Firouztash ran the wireline business of Consumer Products. He was a handsome Iranian man who'd barely made it out alive when the Shah's government fell. He trusted very few. He had wanted my job and thought his colleague running the wireless business wasn't up to the job (he was right). He had every reason to ignore me. All the resources of product development, manufacturing and distribution reported to him, not me. They trusted and respected him; they didn't know me. And yet Homa chose to lead change.

We had come to the end of a long, difficult meeting of the broader organization where I laid out all the challenges we faced and the choices we needed to make. We had finally arrived at that moment where people really had to choose to go one way or the other. A leader is foolish to think that the choice need not be made; it must be made, and people must acknowledge that they are making it. Real change always starts with such a moment.

Homa had not said much that day, nor for the previous two months. Now he stood. His English was imperfect, and his remarks were disjointed. But Homa spoke with conviction and authenticity, and so he led effectively. And at the end of a long speech in which he essentially said he didn't much like where we were, and he'd much rather we had more money and more time, and he didn't think Lucent appreciated Consumer Products sufficiently, he concluded: "Well, I say, let's get on the bus and start marching. And if you won't march, then get off!"

It was a mixed metaphor, to be sure. Everyone laughed and applauded at the same time. He'd made his point and his mark, and from then on, whenever we wavered, we'd say to each other "Are you marching on the bus?"

Others joined the critical mass and chose to lead. Continuing with the mixed metaphor, Roger Spence jumped in with both feet and redesigned our hiring and evaluation processes so we could make substantial personnel changes in far less time. Roger had been in Consumer Products a long time. He was excited about change; he found it fun to think in new ways. He had a great sense of humor and used it to smooth the sometimes rough road of change. He led by choosing to create something new, by committing himself to the outcome and by influencing others to do the same. Leadership is about making a positive difference, and anyone, from any position, can choose to lead.

We began to perform. We began to hit our goals. And the organization began to feel the momentum and the growing confidence that always accompanies higher performance. People don't want to be mediocre; they're just sometimes afraid they can't be any better, or that it won't make any difference even if they are.

As the excitement of the organization built, Rich and Henry decided to pursue option three. It was the right call for the long-term health of both Lucent and Consumer Products, and so we began to explore possible partnerships. I could only share this knowledge with a very few. That burden separated me from my team and made me feel lonely. It was the right decision and it was necessary for the long-term health of Lucent, but it was hard nonetheless.

We did not want to sell outright immediately because we had existing agreements between Consumer Products and Lucent and its customers that needed to be protected. However, the assets of Consumer Products, which had become more valuable because of everyone's hard work, needed to be majority owned by a company willing to make the necessary investments. That meant a consumer company with ambitions in the communications space. Ultimately we negotiated a joint venture (JV) with Philips Electronics, which was embarking on a major push into the communications field leveraging the strength of their consumer products and distribution. For many weeks I was traveling back and forth from New Jersey to Brussels in secret. It was both physically and emotionally exhausting.

Because Philips would be the majority owner of the new company, the new CEO came from Philips and he got to select his new team. I supported the choice of that CEO and fought hard for the right people from my team to be included in key leadership positions. I would serve on the Board for one year. I was pleased with the balanced team, and I believed the JV was in the best long-term interests of Consumer Products, Philips, Lucent and the new company we were creating together. I liked the new CEO and traveled with him to every major location of Consumer Products to personally introduce him to people, to explain the strategy, to explain why I supported the decision, and to thank them for their dedication and hard work. It was sad work for me, although I did not let my feelings show. I was letting go of people, not just assets, and saying good-bye is always hard for me. Seeing their faces for that last time made it harder still, but I felt I owed them my personal presence and gratitude. I've had a lot of practice at saying good-bye, but it doesn't get any easier.

As the new venture got underway in the next year, it quickly became clear, to my great regret, that the agreement had been a mistake. Strategy is about making choices. Execution is about making those choices work. They are two sides of the same coin. The strategy was sound, but the leadership team could not execute. I was as accountable as anyone for the eventual failure of the JV.

The new CEO for the JV turned out to be the wrong choice. I traveled to New York to meet with executives of Philips, the majority owner, to express my views. The venture would fail unless the CEO we'd all supported was replaced. He was being distracted by personal issues. He wasn't decisive; he couldn't confront and resolve the inevitable disagreements arising between two leadership teams thrown together to create a new company. He was also like a son to the CEO of Philips, who acknowledged my points, knew his own CFO agreed with me, and yet could not make the move. One of the reasons leadership is lonely is that it requires both passion and dispassion. A leader must be part of the team and yet able to step back and see clearly. Enough distance is required to make the tough calls.

WHEN I FINISHED my round of good-byes to the people of Consumer Products, I was out of a job, and there were no clear prospects. Much was changing at Lucent. Henry was retiring—sooner than he wanted, sooner than was wise for the organization, but he was pressured into doing so by the relentless impatience and ambition of the CEO-in-waiting, Rich McGinn. Henry had been unfailingly generous in his partnership with Rich and had made it abundantly clear that he was the next CEO. Rich repaid Henry by mocking him and constantly threatening to quit. When Henry said his long, emotional farewells to the officer team of Lucent Technologies, Rich sat in the audience rolling his eyes and theatrically look-

ing at his watch. And when Henry stepped aside, Rich destroyed the teamwork that Henry had so carefully built.

First, Rich created two Co-COO (cochief operating officer) positions.
Dan Stanzione, who'd been running Network Systems for the previous two
years and had been the president of Bell Laboratories before that, would
share the COO responsibilities with Ben Verwaayen, the former CEO of the
Dutch telephone company, whom Rich had recruited to Lucent with
promises for the future. Both Dan and Ben were committed, principled and
ambitious men who imagined they could be the Lucent CEO someday. To
their credit, both men tried to make it work, and created a reasonable division of labor between them, but it was an arrangement that permitted Rich
to play one off against another by how he chose to share information and by
what he confidentially asked each of them to do for him. It was also an arrangement the organization could take advantage of. If Ben made a decision
people didn't like, they could always go to Dan and vice versa.

Next, Rich took what had been the three businesses of Lucent—
Network Systems, which sold systems to telephone operators; Microelectronics, which sold to equipment manufacturers; and Business Communications
Systems, which sold to corporate customers—and created eleven businesses. Each would be led by a president, and each would have a profit and
loss statement. Rich wanted smaller, "more nimble" businesses. The roles
and responsibilities of these eleven presidents, and the conflicts and over-
laps between them, were left undefined; but most of the resources of the
company reported to them, and they were accountable for delivering the
results.

Finally, Rich created a two-tier management structure. The Operations
Committee would be composed of himself; the two COOs; the CFO and
Pat Russo, the EVP who now had responsibility for Human Resources, Public Relations and Marketing, Strategy, and Public Affairs. The Operations
Committee would meet every two weeks. The Management Committee was
composed of the eleven presidents and the two COOs. The Management
Committee met once a month. The two committees weren't really sure who
was supposed to do what, so the power struggles between them began almost immediately. People observed the confusion and the conflict and ex-
ploited both when it served their purposes.

Rich had created a hub-and-spoke management structure. He was at the hub. His COOs, CFO, EVP and eleven presidents were all spokes. Any structure, even one that's awkward and unwieldy, can work with enough alignment and teamwork, but Rich wasn't interested in building a team. He used information, access to his office, and personal favor to make sure everyone was kept off balance. Beyond that, he didn't really understand how results were delivered. Prior to Lucent, when he'd run Network Systems, he'd usually left the tough operational details to others. When he would gather his immediate subordinates together to demand higher performance, he would routinely leave the meeting after his opening statement. We were left to our own devices to decide how and who should deliver.

I'd worked with Rich for almost five years by this time. He was fast on his feet, facile and charming when he chose but lacking in character. I didn't trust him as a leader, and I didn't like the management structure he'd created. Rich asked me to become the president for the Global Service Providers Business. On paper it was the largest job at Lucent because the income statement represented all of our business with network operators around the world—in essence, the old Network Systems. In reality, I would control very few of the resources that were required to produce that income statement. I managed all of our sales and services resources but none of the product development or manufacturing. I knew that products and manufacturing were the power centers at Lucent and that my fellow presidents would exercise their prerogatives to the fullest extent possible. I would be accountable for the overall performance, but Rich would not give me the responsibility.

I was insulted that Rich hadn't just made me president of Network Systems, replacing Dan Stanzione. I was exhausted just thinking about the complexities of navigating my way through all these new internal structures. I would be reporting to Ben Verwaayen, who had big ideas about all the things we should be doing differently. I was defensive and behaved badly with Ben, telling him I thought Lucent had done all right so far and that maybe he should learn something about the organization before he declared it broken. Frank and I decided to take the first two-week vacation of our lives. We both needed the rest and time to think. I told Rich I'd let him know my decision when we returned.

We traveled to Italy with Carole and Greg Spurrier. We flew to Milan, rented a car and drove to Portofino, Siena, Umbria, Florence, Venice, Lake

Como. It was wonderful being back in Italy, speaking Italian, being with my husband and my friends. Two weeks off felt like an immense luxury. We were all on a gondola in Venice when my cell phone rang. On the line was Rich McGinn. He offered me a raise and a lot of stock options and said he needed to know my decision. I told him he'd know when I returned. I wasn't being coy; I just didn't know my answer yet. And the money didn't help me make up my mind.

Rich never understood my motivation. It wasn't the money and the stock options. I enjoy the things money will buy, and I buy them. I appreciate that money is a symbol of an employee's value to the business, and I believe I should be compensated competitively. But money does not win my heart, and my heart has to be in the job I choose. For me passion sustains the strenuous effort required, and this new job would require especially intense devotion. If I said yes, I would devote everything I had.

In November of 1997 I decided I would give it my all for two years. I could not leave Lucent—I loved it too much. I couldn't leave the people I'd worked with, and I couldn't leave the idea of the one-hundred-year-old start-up. Rich thought he'd persuaded me, but in truth I stayed in spite of him, not because of him. Now I needed to figure out how to drive higher levels of performance across six different organizations. We could only succeed through alignment and collaboration.

Alignment and collaboration need not be fuzzy, ill-defined concepts for "let's just all get along." Effective teamwork is more than good manners and good will, although both help an organization function more effectively. Alignment results from shared goals. Collaboration results from shared measures of success. Both common purpose and common metrics must be clearly defined and clearly agreed upon. People need to know why they are collaborating and when they are successful. They need to know that everyone else is committing to the same things. And they also need to know they can't achieve results any other way. The simple "page-turning" process that we'd used to build the prospectus of Lucent was an example of alignment and collaboration.

Collaboration across organizational boundaries is fundamentally different behavior from command-and-control decision making within an organization's boundaries. Collaboration requires more consultation and agreement among peers. It requires acceptance of accountability while sharing resources. It means trusting others to do their jobs while knowing that others must trust you to do the same. Command-and-control decision making is a vertical movement of information up a chain of command and of decision down that chain. Collaborative decision making is the horizontal movement of information and decisions across and among many chains of command. Command-and-control decision making is defined by the boxes and lines on an organizational chart. Horizontal collaboration is defined by processes and the hand-offs from one group or person to the next. It is perhaps best captured by who communicates with whom—in meetings, in e-mails, in phone calls.

If you thought about the fastest way to get a product to a customer, you would end up drawing a horizontal line of collaboration across many different departments: every department from product development to manufacturing to shipping to sales to installation needs to be involved. Any movement up and down each department's chains of command just prolongs the process from the customer's point of view. The customer suffers if any department misses a step along the process. And yet, inside an organization, collaboration is inherently more difficult to teach and motivate than command and control. We all understand that a boss can tell a subordinate to do something; a request from a peer for cooperation doesn't seem to carry the same clout. It seems faster to "just do it ourselves" rather than rely on others to do it with us. It feels easier to understand coworkers within our own organization. And so people have to be convinced that collaboration is the only answer. And leaders must have the discipline to demand it, measure it and reward it.

I spent the next many months shuttling between my fellow presidents' offices and between Dan and Ben, to whom the presidents reported. We had to agree to goals that were tough but achievable. We had to agree on how to measure success and who was accountable for delivering what. We even had to agree on how to evaluate and reward our people; if those who failed to collaborate were promoted over those who chose to collaborate, people would quickly get the message that we weren't serious.

It was tough, detailed work, but we all wanted the same things. It helped tremendously that most of us had worked together before. I buried the hatchet with Ben, and we became great allies. He remains today a dear friend. All of us knew the challenges inherent in both Rich's leadership style and the structure he'd chosen, and we were collectively committed to making Lucent a success. We came to agreement.

I insisted we have a joint meeting to announce and explain our agreements to our broader, collective teams, and joint presentation materials to codify the details. Rumor and mystery are counterproductive in business—everyone needs to hear the same things in the same way, at the same time if possible, to avoid confusion and second-guessing. Clarity and consistency are necessary to prevent misinterpretations or reinterpretations, so verbal communication must be supported by written materials.

I also wanted us to have some fun along the way. No one knew what we should be calling ourselves anymore. We used to be Network Systems. Now we were six separate organizations that all served the same customers. It was too cumbersome to say every name every time we wanted to talk about our groups. And we couldn't leave groups out; they would misinterpret the exclusion. This problem could become a source of humor for our meeting.

I am fond of saying "If you can't fix it, feature it." In this case we needed a name. We would become the BUFKANS: Business Units Formerly Known as Network Systems. Like The Artist Formerly Known as Prince, our color would be purple. And because it was the Year of the Dragon in the Chinese calendar, our mascot would be the dragon. We introduced this at our meeting with tongue firmly in cheek and gave everyone a purple T-shirt with a dragon on the front and BUFKANS on the back. People loved it because it was silly, because it gave us a theme to rally around, and because it made a serious point in a not-so-serious way—we might not have a good name, but we could be a good team.

And we performed. All the time and care we took to agree on our objectives and measurements, all the tough discussion that we'd endured to clarify our collective and individual roles and responsibilities—all this paid off. Careful planning and discipline and driving for real buy-in always pay off, but they take time and patience.

Our teamwork would be greatly challenged when Lucent acquired Ascend Communications. Rich wanted to be sure Lucent didn't smother this new business, so Ascend would remain a stand-alone business and report to Dan Stanzione. This meant Lucent would have two separate sales forces calling on the same customers; one for Lucent products, one for Ascend products; one which reported to Ben, one which reported to Dan. Despite this structural separation, our telephone company customers were increasingly focused on data and wanted to begin integrating voice and data capability. These two sales forces would have to work together, and that burden would fall on me. I was the leader of the Lucent sales force, and Lucent needed Ascend a whole lot more than Ascend needed Lucent.

Ascend was a $1.4 billion company for which Lucent had paid almost $24 billion. Headquartered in Silicon Valley, they were very much a sales-dominated culture. The leader of their sales force was a hard-drinking charmer who took pride in his irreverence and independence. He told lewd jokes and had lots of sales and customer meetings where women attended to entertain. Although he could dress to the nines, he took great delight in donning gym shorts and flip-flops for meetings where business-casual attire was called for. It was part of his shtick: "I'm tough, I deliver, and I don't give a damn what you think." He was independently wealthy as a result of the acquisition, and he didn't have to do anything he didn't want to.

The Ascend sales force took their cues from their leader. Almost exclusively male, like a great many other Silicon Valley companies at that time, they didn't think much of an old East Coast–based company that sold voice equipment. By this time our sales force was almost half women, with a leadership team that was dominated by women. We were right in the middle of the dot-com boom, and the terms *new economy* and *old economy* had been coined. Ascend was definitely new economy—high growth and high flying with an arrogance to match their stock price. The old rules didn't apply to them. Lucent, in their minds, was definitely old economy. We clearly didn't get the new world order, which is why we'd spent so much money to buy them. They didn't have much to learn from us or much incentive to work with us. We clearly weren't as tough or as smart as they were.

Rich and Dan called a joint meeting between the two sales forces in California. I thought it was a very good idea to kick things off. I also knew that this first encounter between us would be crucial to what followed. How things start has a big impact on how, or whether, they continue. Shortly before the meeting Frank and I took a vacation on St. John, in the Virgin Islands. We rented a big house, and our family and Frank's sisters and brother-in-law came down, and we spent a wonderful week. Every day I would walk to the beach and back for exercise, and every day I would think about this meeting with Ascend. As I trudged up the hill to our house in the heat and the sun I would wonder: How could we earn their respect? How could we put ourselves quickly on an equal footing? How could we demonstrate that we had something to offer?

I felt an obligation to answer these questions for my whole organization. I knew our people were very nervous about this meeting, as was my leadership team. Ascend's reputation had preceded them. When I was packing for the meeting, Frank asked if I'd decided what to do. "Yes, but I won't tell you until I've done it. Can I borrow a couple of your socks?" I didn't tell Frank what I had in mind because I didn't want him to try to talk me out of it.

The meeting would begin with a speech from Rich, then Dan, then my Ascend counterpart. I dressed carefully that morning in a loose-fitting pantsuit and cowboy boots. Rich and Dan talked generally about the opportunities and their excitement about bringing two great sales forces together. True to form, the Ascend sales leader took to the stage in gym shorts and flip-flops. He was flippant and funny and said the right things about a future of teamwork and success. I think he was sincere, although no one was really sure. When it was my turn, I used slides to present quite a lot of data. I talked about the joint prospects that lay before us by customer, geography and product set. I made what I hoped was a serious, fact-based case for cooperation based on available opportunity and competitive realities. I spoke from behind a podium. And then I said: "You know, our cooperation is based on shared opportunity. But our partnership must also be based on mutual respect, and that is earned by telling each other the hard truth. The hard truth is we think you Ascend guys are a bunch of cowboys who don't understand our customers' requirements for quality of service."

This was what our people worried about, among many things, and now, as I said this, the crowd shifted uncomfortably. The "Ascend guys" were taking umbrage.

"Don't get upset. You think worse about us." Now everyone was restless. This didn't seem like the right tone for a team-building session. Rich and Dan looked worried.

"The truth is you think we're a bunch of sissies (I chose the word deliberately). You think we're not tough enough or street smart enough."

Then I moved from behind the podium, and as I did so, I pulled up one pant leg and showed them my cowboy boots. "But I just want you to know that I'm not wearing flip-flops. I'm wearing Tony Lama cowboy boots, and we can kick ass with the best of 'em." People laughed.

I took center stage, turned my back to the audience, unbuttoned my jacket and slowly dropped it to the floor. When I was quite sure I had everyone's attention, I turned back around to face them. The bulge in my pants from Frank's borrowed socks was obvious to anyone in that very big ballroom. "And our balls are as big as anyone's in this room."

Rich literally fell off his chair screaming with laughter. The place erupted in whoops and hollers. After several long minutes of pandemonium, my Ascend colleague came back onstage and said, "I know when I'm beat." And we stood together and answered questions.

It was an outrageous thing to do. I hadn't been sure I'd have the guts to go through with it. Not everyone appreciated the humor—a few people thought it was tasteless and crude—but effective communication means speaking in a language people understand. I'd made my point.

17 | Loneliness

THE FALL OF 1998 was terrible. I became a celebrity and my mother died. While incomparable in so many ways, these two events have this in common: Each would change my life. And both would make me lonelier.

Lucent Technologies was riding high. Kathy Fitzgerald, a dear friend then and now, was the senior vice president for Marketing and Public Relations. Smart, savvy, witty and tough, she was the best in her business. She was plenty busy because Lucent was always in the news. She was in charge of our press relations, and in this regard no one questioned her abilities or her authority—she was that good. I had worked with her in Network Systems, worked side by side with her during the launch of Lucent, and trusted her judgment without reservation. If she asked me to talk to a reporter about Lucent, I did; but otherwise I steered clear of the press. One day she called and said that *Fortune* magazine was inaugurating a feature called "The Fifty Most Powerful Women in Business." They were coming to Lucent because we had so many senior women, and they specifically wanted to interview Pat Russo and me. Kathy was excited about highlighting Lucent's diverse management team—Lucent would probably be the only company with two women on the list. I agreed to the interview, of course, and met with Pattie Sellers, a *Fortune* editor, for about an hour in Kathy's office.

Several weeks later Kathy called to say *Fortune* wanted to come out for a photo shoot. She told me it was possible that both Pat and I would end up in the top ten. (We did.) And several weeks after that I got a call one evening from Pattie to inform me that I had been chosen as the Most Powerful Woman in Business. I was stunned, excited, and immediately called my mother, who was ecstatic.

In that first interview, and for all six years in which I was named the Most Powerful Woman in Business, I said that although I was flattered and honored, the list was a bad idea. It is one thing to highlight successful businesswomen. That can be a wonderful way to encourage other women to enter the business world, or perhaps to stay there, and it can serve to remind everyone that diversity makes business better. But the list sends a different message altogether. It implies that business is like tennis or golf or soccer—there's the women's ladder or team, and the men's. Women have to compete against one another because they can't compete with men. Beyond that, there is no Fifty Most Powerful Men in Business list. Many male colleagues have frequently expressed to me their gratitude for this fact, especially when they've read the descriptions of women who've fallen a few notches. They're all glad they don't have to be subjected to the same level of scrutiny and criticism. "This is what you get when you're successful?"

My reasoning obviously didn't prevail at *Fortune*. They're in business to sell magazines and lists sell. The added benefit of a "surprise winner"—an unknown woman had "beaten" Oprah Winfrey for the top slot—also sold. It was patently ridiculous to say that Carly Fiorina had more power and influence—however you choose to define it—than Oprah Winfrey. No objective analysis would support such a conclusion. But it made a great story.

After that, everyone always asked: "How does it feel to be the most powerful woman in business?" I didn't feel any different from the day before, but somehow that answer never was satisfying to people. Later I would try to deflect the question by saying "I don't know. I've never been a man." Or perhaps a bit more seriously, "I've never thought of myself as a woman in business. I've thought of myself as a person doing business who happens to be a woman."

I always wanted to get off the subject as fast as possible. I didn't want to talk about being a woman in business. I wanted to talk about business. For my entire career I'd been a woman who'd succeeded because I wouldn't let men pigeonhole me. I challenged them when necessary, spoke in language they could understand, and demonstrated my value through actions rather than words. I'd made my mark by getting things done. Along the way I'd changed a few men's minds about what women are capable of and provided encouragement and opportunity for other women. This new label "Woman in Business"—most powerful or not—was going backward.

The cover picture, the story and all the hoopla that surrounded it made me a celebrity. Celebrities are viewed as public property. They're seen as figures, not flesh-and-blood people. They're caricatured and scrutinized and criticized in a way private citizens, even if they're rich and powerful, are not. We love to see celebrities rise; we love even more to see them fall. I didn't understand all of this then as clearly as I do now, but what I did understand immediately is that people began to treat me differently.

When I met people for the first time, they now had a whole new set of preconceived notions about me. In a meeting in Beijing a very important Chinese minister asked whether I was also the richest woman in America. Those I had known before saw me in a new light. They watched me more closely to see whether I would change as a result of this new fame. Some people thought that as a celebrity, I was now different from them, separated from others. Many could no longer see me at all. They could only see "Carly Fiorina, the Most Powerful Woman in Business."

There are Indian tribes who believed that a photograph would steal your soul. It's a useful analogy because the more photographs taken, the more invisible the real person becomes. It is indisputable that fame opened doors for me and for the companies I represented. Open doors mean new opportunities, and for these I am grateful, but being famous is a lonely place to be.

M Y MOTHER WAS ALREADY ILL when she saw me on the cover of *Fortune* magazine. She was much sicker than any of us realized. She was the strongest person I have ever known. She had a zest for life that seemed unquenchable, and so we all assumed she would recover.

Her illness had started in January, when she began complaining of arthritis pain in her knees and wrists. Throughout the spring and summer she seemed weaker and lost her appetite for some of her favorite foods. In August she and my father had planned to stay with us in New Jersey for a few weeks. She instead called tearfully and said she was too ill. I went home, and between trips to the hospital and various specialists, I finally managed to convince her that she needed full-time help at home. And I began going back and forth to California every couple weeks to visit.

My mother was fiercely independent. All her life she had feared being unable to care for herself and becoming a burden to others. She had always resisted medication and now rejected the drug treatments doctors suggested for what everyone thought was rheumatoid arthritis. She was losing weight and strength rapidly. We moved her bed downstairs into the living room so she wouldn't have to climb the stairs. And each time I came home she would tell me I shouldn't have.

When my mother first saw *Fortune*, she could not stop hugging the magazine. I am truly thankful it made her so happy. We sat in the living room and she said, "I wish you lived in California. I miss you so much."

"Mom, I wish I did too in so many ways, but my life and my work are back East. I miss you too, but you know I'm always here when you need me."

"Oh, I know, but it would be so nice to have you closer." And then she got a faraway look in her eyes and said, "Who knows. Maybe someday you'll become the CEO of Hewlett-Packard."

I do not know why she said it. We had never talked about the company. I laughed out loud and said, "Well, that's never going to happen!"

And she responded, "You never know, Carly, you just never know."

By November she was back in the hospital. I told my sister I was going to come out for a week. When Clara told my mother, she insisted that I change my mind. I came anyway and surprised her. After an entire week of tests, she underwent exploratory surgery, and the doctors determined she had acute vasculitis. We were all immensely relieved. She didn't have cancer; her doctors were confident she could be treated; and when I left, we were both optimistic. Ten days later she would be dead.

I called my mother four and five times a day after her surgery. And so I still think I should have heard something in her voice, sensed her growing despair. On the afternoon of November 30 I boarded the Lucent plane with Ben Verwaayen to travel to Europe. I called my mother right before I got on the plane. I told her I was going to Europe and would be back in a few days. When we said good-bye, she said, "I adore you." They were the last words I heard her say.

Four hours into the trip I decided I should call California. It was unusual—I didn't make personal calls from the airplane—but something told me to call. When I reached the hospital, my sister came on the phone and said, "Mom has made a decision. She wants to leave the hospital, she's taking herself off all her medication and she's going to stop eating and drinking."

"Please, please let me talk to her."

"She says she'll talk to you when you get here."

"Then at least tell her to keep drinking until I get there." My mother was determined to control her own death as she had controlled her own life, and so she refused.

My worst nightmare was coming true. My mother was dying, and I couldn't get to her. Over the the Atlantic Ocean, in the middle of the night, I frantically thought about how to reach her. I asked the pilots if they could turn the plane around, but they had insufficient fuel. When we landed at Schiphol airport outside Amsterdam, I booked a seat on the first flight I could find to California, which wasn't scheduled to depart for another six hours. Then the plane had mechanical trouble, and we sat for three more hours. It really was like one of those terrible dreams where you're running and running but you just can't get anywhere.

Throughout those endless hours of waiting and flying, I kept asking myself: "Why wouldn't she talk to me? Why didn't she tell me? Did I say or do something that made her give up?" Perhaps she could not bear to hear me cry. Perhaps she could not bear to listen when I would try to persuade her to change her mind. Perhaps I'd been distracted when she was trying to tell me something important. I still cannot reconcile myself to the answers, nor can I forgive myself for my failure to realize that she had chosen to die. I should have been there.

I maintained my composure until we landed in San Francisco, almost twenty-four hours after I'd called the hospital. As we touched down, a huge and resplendent harvest moon hung low over the horizon. The tears came then, just as they still do whenever I see a full moon. By the time I reached home, she was incoherent. I sat by her bed that night, and at 5:00 A.M. on December 2 she passed on. I hope she knew I was there. I hope she heard me whisper, "I love you, I love you," over and over again. I hope she felt my hand on hers. I will never know; but when she died, a single tear lay on her cheek.

We were all in shock. Not one of us was strong enough to stand and give a eulogy. And so, instead, I asked the organist to play all the stirring, triumphant hymns my mother had loved best. Throughout the funeral, and every night for months afterward, I cried inconsolably. I would come home from work, eat dinner, go to bed and cry. I did not know I could cry so much for so long.

I cannot forget her image as she drew her last breath. Sometimes when I look in the mirror, I see her so clearly it takes my breath away. I miss her every day. I try to make her proud every day. She died too young and too soon, but her life was a blessing. And at the end of her life, as I witnessed her courage, I discovered my own. I saw what she had chosen and endured. I learned that I could survive what I had dreaded since childhood. All my other fears seemed so much smaller now.

18 | The Recruitment

LUCENT WAS A HOT COMPANY, so, especially after the *Fortune* story, recruiters called a lot. I never returned the calls. I'd committed myself to remain in my current job for two years, but late one evening in February of 1999, I was working alone in the office when the phone rang. A voice said, "This is Jeff Christian of Christian & Timbers. Don't hang up. I'm calling about the CEO job at Hewlett-Packard."

I was instantly tantalized. Everything I had read about this company, everything I had personally experienced about this company told me the CEO job would be an extraordinary challenge. Hewlett-Packard was the storied, original start-up that had spawned Silicon Valley from a garage. Then growth and innovation had stalled. The company had become known as the gray lady of Silicon Valley. In articles about technology and the information technology industry, HP was rarely mentioned anymore. As a result, its Board had decided to split the company, separating the original test-and-measurement business from the computing and printing businesses, which would retain the HP name. In some ways the split was similar to what we had done with Lucent and AT&T but with one important difference. The businesses that became Lucent had always been considered noncore to AT&T. The long-distance telephony business was the heart of AT&T and retained the AT&T brand. At HP, in contrast, the test and measurement business had started it all in that famous garage, yet it was being spun off and was losing the HP name. Without knowing any more than this, I knew there were culture wars and identity crises going on at Hewlett-Packard, in addition to all the other complexities of a major corporate restructuring.

Jeff Christian and I agreed to meet for lunch at the Short Hills Hilton. I was nervous about running into Lucent people and having to explain why I was dining with a recruiter. It would be extremely disruptive if rumors began circulating that I was leaving or looking for a job. And HP certainly didn't want their prospective candidates in the media. (Because the search had been made public by the company, there was, of course, discussion in the media about it. Many names were mentioned as candidates, but never, in almost six months, had my name come up.) So Jeff and I picked a quiet, out-of-the-way corner and kept our voices very low. No one paid us any attention.

When I'd heard Jeff say "Hewlett-Packard" over the phone, I'd wondered: "Why would they be calling me?" That was still my reaction, so it was the first question I asked at lunch: "Why me?" It was a question I would ask over and over again before I took the job. Understanding the answer seemed essential. Realistically, I would be a nonconventional choice, even a risky one. I had never been a CEO, and HP was a complex company with lots of challenges in major transition. The fact that the Board was looking outside the company was revolutionary enough. To consider someone from outside the industry, a nonengineer, not to mention a woman, would indeed be controversial.

Jeff had several answers. The Board believed they needed a real change agent; they really were looking for a distinct departure from the past. The industry was moving faster, and the company needed to change in substantial ways to keep up and compete in the Internet age. They thought the Lucent spin-off from AT&T was perhaps useful experience for the very complex split they had just announced and now had to execute. At the same time, they wanted someone who would respect the famous HP Way; they were looking for someone who could bend, not break, the culture. The Board knew the company lacked a strategy and needed someone who could shape one and communicate it. Finally, it turned out that some of the HP people I'd met with during my benchmarking trips and my many attempts to partner with the company had recommended me to the Board.

Jeff described how the Board had undertaken a very rigorous process of defining and prioritizing the key skills they were looking for in a new CEO. They had spent several months in this process and were prepared for several more months of interviews and deliberations. It seemed quite clear, and very reasonable, that this was going to be a long process. Hewlett-Packard was a huge and important company. The choice of a CEO was critical. This was not a decision to be rushed into.

The Search Committee included Lew Platt, the current chairman and CEO; Sam Ginn, chairman of the Nominating and Governance Committee; Dick Hackborn, a former HP executive; and John Fery, the former chairman of International Paper. If HP was interested in moving ahead, my next interview would be with Lew. I'd last seen him in 1995, when we were still trying to partner with his company. Ultimately we'd given up and gone to Sun Microsystems, a fierce rival, simply because HP couldn't make a decision and move. It had cost Hewlett-Packard virtually all of Lucent's business. I left that first meeting with Jeff pretty certain I wouldn't make it to the next one. I knew HP, and Lew, as cautious to a fault, and I wouldn't be a cautious choice. But I was intrigued and challenged, and I must admit I heard my mother's words ringing in my ears: "Maybe you'll be the CEO of Hewlett-Packard someday." It made the hair rise on the back of my neck and persuaded me not to write it off entirely.

I decided that if the process continued, I would do three things: I would be completely open with Rich McGinn. I would ensure that the HP Board knew exactly who I was and how I would operate; there couldn't be any surprises, and they needed to be prepared for whom they might wind up with. And I needed to know what I would be getting myself into. This would be a challenge unlike any other. I was going to have to do a lot of homework if this got serious.

With this tentative plan in mind, I went back to work and quickly became consumed again by the challenges of Lucent. Several weeks passed and then the call came that Lew Platt wanted to see me. The choice of venue was important—neither one of us wanted to be seen in public talking together. So HP sent a company plane to New Jersey and flew me to San Jose's airport, where Lew and I met in the hangar that housed the company fleet.

Lew had just returned from a trip to Japan and was tired and jet-lagged. He nevertheless gave the meeting his full energy and attention. We talked for several hours—far longer, I think, than either of us had predicted. Lew was clearly frustrated and concerned by the company's flagging growth and profitability. After the go-go years of the early nineties, HP's performance had deteriorated. By March of 1999, the company had missed analysts' estimates eight quarters in a row, and they were on their way to missing the ninth. He said no one would set challenging goals at HP. He said he felt almost powerless to drive the company toward higher performance because of its highly decentralized nature and structure. He felt the culture was both a great strength and a source of weakness, and certainly an impediment to change. He thought the upcoming split would be traumatic.

And so we talked about aspirational goals and culture. I talked about how certain values that were important in the culture could perhaps be used to drive higher performance. I remarked on my experience at Lucent and said that the split could potentially release a lot of latent energy in the organization despite the trauma—or maybe because of it.

It didn't feel like an interview. It felt like collaboration—two people, both of whom had great admiration for HP, talking together about how to make it better. I went to a whiteboard and wrote things down as we agreed on them. Innovation, customer loyalty and contribution were all values that could drive higher performance. Goal setting was essential to performance. Set goals too low and people can overachieve the goal and yet still underperform against their competitors and the market; set the bar higher and people may miss the internal goal but still overperform against external targets.

Lew used the term *transformation* a lot. But most of our conversation wasn't about strategy; it was about operational performance and how to improve it. I asked a lot of questions about structure because of my experience with all the various HP business units. I asked a few questions about the Board, but it was clear there was great tension between Lew and several Board members, particularly Dick Hackborn. My impression was that although Lew was frustrated, he wasn't ready to go and his "retirement" was as much the Board's decision as his. (Later I would learn that he told his subordinates after the January 1999 Board meeting that he had been fired, but the public story was always that he had chosen this time to retire and search for a new CEO.)

Lew was both generous with his time and surprisingly candid about his disappointments. He ended the meeting by saying "I haven't been this excited in a long time." I left the hangar liking him tremendously, deeply concerned that the challenge was even greater than I had imagined, and yet encouraged that we might actually be on the same page about how HP could move forward. And it was clear to both of us that I would proceed to the next round of interviews with the other Search Committee members.

My next meeting was with Sam Ginn at the San Francisco Airport. I traveled all the time, and airports were busy, anonymous places. No one would be suspicious if I was seen in one. Sam Ginn, the chairman of Vodafone PLC and former chairman and CEO of AirTouch, was even a customer of Lucent's, and we'd done business together. We had both been through the Bell System and AT&T, so we had some common experiences we could draw upon.

Sam was tough, direct and minced no words. HP lacked a strategy. The culture was stultifying. There was no talent management process—the Board never talked about people in the organization or their development. People, he told me, didn't move around in HP the way they had at AT&T. They just grew up in a single business unit—they were deep in subject-matter expertise but narrow in experience and perspective. Strategy, culture and people were Sam's themes at each and every one of our meetings. This was why the Board had concluded they needed a change agent—a "transformational CEO" was how he chose to describe what they were looking for.

As Jeff had done, Sam also described the thorough, rigorous process the Board had used to define the skill set of the new CEO. As chairman of the Nominating and Governance Committee, he was proud of the questionnaire that Board members had answered and of their thoughtful responses and careful discussion. He felt confident the Board would come to the right conclusion because of its thoroughness, the careful vetting they would do of each candidate, and the amount of time they were spending as a Board to make sure they were in agreement each time they winnowed the list of candidates.

I asked him about the Board members. What were they like? Did they disagree about anything? Sam viewed the upcoming split of the company, and the consequent split of the Board, as an opportunity to change some things about the Board. He didn't elaborate, but I thought it was an important point to come back to if we had another meeting. I did learn that Phil Condit, the chairman and CEO of Boeing, and Sam thought a lot alike on many issues and that Dick Hackborn was going to be a very key player in the CEO search. Walter Hewlett, Susan Packard, Pattie Dunn and Jay Keyworth were never mentioned. They didn't seem to be key players in Sam's mind.

I asked him about what I perceived as an extreme form of decentralization: lots of individual business units acting virtually independently. I told him I had experienced the results of this as a customer of HP's and as a prospective partner. He heartily agreed with my observation and said he thought it was a result of history, lack of strategy and lack of leadership. I asked whether it bothered the Board that HP didn't seem to be a player in the same way that Sun or IBM was. Scott McNealy, the CEO of Sun, had famously remarked that HP was "that nice printer company." Although Scott was famous for his digs and quips, this one struck a little close to home. It turned out that Sam and Scott were golfing buddies. Sam had quite a lot of respect for Scott and thought he was right about HP. Sam joked that the other famous saying about Hewlett-Packard was that they were the only company who could market sushi as "cold, dead fish." "We need better marketing!" he said.

Why, I asked, would they consider someone like me from the telecommunications industry? He answered that networks and networking were key to the Internet age, that communications technology was more and more intertwined with computing, and that the AT&T/Lucent spin-off was relevant. I observed that I wasn't an engineer. We both agreed that this, coupled with my status as an outsider to both the industry and the company, would cause a lot of commentary, angst and skepticism. The fact that I was a woman never came up. I left this first conversation with Sam uncertain about whether I'd make it to the next round.

On another day, in the same airport, John Fery asked in several different ways why I thought I could take on the challenge of the HP CEO job. They were the right questions. Why indeed? I told him that I would not, and could not, take it on alone, that I would need the Board's help and support as well as the management team's. I said that I'd had quite a lot of experience going into brand-new situations where I was an outsider and that I had successfully taken on other challenges that required me to develop new skills when my existing skills were not enough. I was also straightforward in admitting that although I loved new challenges, this one was more than I had ever dealt with before. The Board needed to be very sure about their choice of me, or anyone else for that matter. Transformation was not to be taken lightly. Big companies have a logic all their own. Established hierarchies and bureaucracies can sabotage anyone—including a CEO. Changing HP would be a long and messy journey. The Board needed to be sure that's where they wanted to go, and they needed to be sure about the leader they put in charge of the journey.

As much as the HP Board was interviewing me, I was interviewing them. It was vital that we understand one another. It was essential that I know as much as possible before committing myself. If I left Lucent, it would be a gut-wrenching decision for me as well as a blow to an organization I loved. I thought I had a shot at the top job someday. I was paid well. I had lots of options that were worth a lot of money. Leaving would not only be a big risk, it would also be a big loss. And then there was our home life. Our younger daughter was finally adjusted to New Jersey. Our eldest daughter, who was going through a difficult divorce, and our granddaughter lived in Virginia. All of Frank's family was close by in Pittsburgh. Our friends were all on the East Coast. As I'd told my mother, I never thought I would return to the West Coast to live—we loved the East.

I had started doing research in earnest now. I read Dave Packard's *The HP Way* for the fourth time. (I had read it three other times over the years for various business classes and during my benchmarking visits to HP.) I would read it one more time before I'd been at HP two months. I began looking for references to HP in everything I read about the industry. I visited the HP Web site regularly.

My first meeting with Dick Hackborn wouldn't occur until June. I already knew Dick's views were pivotal to the Board's selection process, but this was also a key meeting for me. Dick had started and run the LaserJet printer business for Bill and Dave. When Dave Packard returned from his stint as deputy defense secretary in 1990 and summarily fired John Young, Dick Hackborn was the man Bill Hewlett and Dave asked to become CEO.

He had to turn them down three times before they looked to Lew Platt. And in that very public CEO succession process a very clear signal had been sent. John Young was changing too many things. Dave said as much. Lew Platt was a distant second choice, and his job was to preserve. To make sure of it, Bill and Dave put their first choice, Dick Hackborn, on the Board. Bill and Dave were getting on in years, so, for the first time, they began to put their children on the Board as well. Who was Dick Hackborn and what did he really think about transformation?

The meeting was also important because HP had just announced a reorganization. Every time I visited the HP Web site I was struck by two things. If I were a customer, I wouldn't be able to figure out how HP was organized or whom to call for sales, service, and so on. Beyond that, I didn't see much of the Hewlett-Packard company or brand. I saw a lot of individual products and businesses, but no coherent whole. The company didn't seem to have an organizing principle or consistent purpose. In other words, without the two founders and the HP Way, there was no HP. What would happen when the company split and that history and those values had to be shared with another company that would be both customer and partner, and, in some cases, competitor? History alone wouldn't be enough to hold the place together and drive performance; the company was already disintegrating and deteriorating. The Board had clearly made a decision to keep the computing and printing businesses together. What would be needed to actually execute that decision?

The reorganization that had just been implemented seemed to make these problems far worse. Instead of one CEO, there were now, in fact, five. Lew Platt was the "corporate" CEO. Four other CEOs had been named for four businesses: the LaserJet printing business (Carolyn Ticknor); the Inkjet printing business (Antonio Perez); the PC and industry-standard server business (Duane Zitzner); and the systems business—mostly UNIX, storage and associated services (Ann Livermore). As implied by their CEO titles, each business had a high degree of autonomy and authority—they owned their strategies, their development and manufacturing resources and separate sales forces. The roles and responsibilities between Lew and the other CEOs were unclear. The company's announcement had explained the change as making HP faster and more responsive.

I thought it was exactly the wrong move at the wrong time. It would continue to tear HP apart at a time when it needed to come together. It would make the job of a new CEO, whoever that person was, much more difficult. If the Board felt this was the right move at the right time, then I was definitely the wrong person to be CEO. I needed to know where Dick Hackborn stood. Dick was in New York and so we met for lunch there. I was surprised by Dick's persona. He was introverted and didn't seem quite prepared for the interview. He didn't ask many questions, so I started asking mine.

"What do you think of the recent reorganization?"

He didn't seem to think it mattered much. "It was just something Lew wanted to do."

I pressed him. "Why would the Board permit a major reorganization right before bringing on a new CEO?"

"Well, the new CEO can change it."

"Isn't that a lot of disruption to put an organization through if you know you're just going to reorganize again?"

Then Dick looked a little sheepish. "Well, to tell you the truth, the Board was so tired of fighting Lew on everything—he really didn't consult us on this—so we just decided it was easier to let it go; and if we have to, we'll fix it later."

I was taken aback by the answer. What kind of CEO would reorganize the business without at least advising the Board, particularly someone who was about to leave? What board would let a major reorganization stand at such a time, unless they fundamentally agreed with it? Why would they let the outgoing CEO make the move at all? So now I needed to level with Dick.

"Dick, I think this is exactly the wrong move. I believe HP needs to define a coherent strategy and structure that binds the company together and makes it easier to do business with. As a customer and potential partner of HP's, I have always believed that the company's unique advantage comes from its broad portfolio of assets. If there aren't real synergies in these businesses, HP needs to split them up further. If you think this reorganization is the right move for HP, then I really don't think I'm the right person for the job."

For the first time, Dick perked up. "You're exactly right, Carly. We need coherence." He talked with genuine frustration, even anger, about his disappointment with HP. HP was falling behind and was now mediocre in both perception and reality. He said, "Radical change is what we need." I told him I'd been dealing with HP people for almost ten years, and in all that time I'd never felt a sense of urgency from anyone. Everyone was extremely pleasant, polite and genuinely nice, but no one seemed to have a competitive spirit or a sense that time mattered. Everyone talked about technology and values—they didn't talk about customers or competitors. I would discover this over and over again once I actually went to HP. But for right now, it was something that Dick Hackborn and I could enthusiastically agree upon.

By the end of our lunch that day, Dick Hackborn and I had agreed on three very important points: that HP lacked, and desperately needed, an external focus on customers and competitors; that time was not on our side, and a sense of urgency was required; and that synergy was the key to unlocking the unique value of the Hewlett-Packard Company. I felt the discussion had gone well, but I remained uneasy about the recent reorganization. It was inconsistent with everything we had agreed upon. It had set the company back, exacerbating both its internal focus and its decentralization. How could a Board member who agreed so enthusiastically with me have so passively permitted a major move like this to occur?

It was my first experience with what I would come to learn was common behavior: people did not confront issues at Hewlett-Packard. Dick could agree with me that it was the wrong move, but he could not confront Lew to prevent it from happening. My entry was made more difficult because the Board had implicitly supported a move by the departing CEO that was precisely the opposite of the moves I would make. It was tough on employees because they were confused and expended lots of energy on both Lew's reorganization and mine. And the management team's credibility was hurt because they had explained their new CEO titles with great conviction and then were forced to explain why they no longer had them.

After a few months at HP, I learned that the values of the HP Way had been corrupted in some important respects. Respect for the Individual had come to mean being courteous and noncombative even when candid, serious disagreement and debate was what the business really required. Highest Standards of Integrity applied to sins of commission—you didn't lie. It didn't apply to sins of omission—you could be silent instead of speaking up; you didn't need to say what you really thought. And just as Dick had at lunch, people said lots of things behind others' backs that they were unprepared to say to their faces. People said one thing in the room, another outside it.

The recruitment process proceeded slowly, but clearly the Board's interest in me was growing. At our second meeting, Sam Ginn started to talk about money. This was a difficult subject because I had tens of thousands of very valuable Lucent options that would vest in October. (Despite the large stock-based package that HP eventually gave me to partially compensate me for these options, I ended up losing more than $85 million by leaving Lucent in July.) Lew Platt said that he and his executive team had gone through an extensive psychological testing process. The Board had decided that all CEO candidates should go through the same process. This seemed sensible if the Board really wanted to know who they were getting, so I agreed. (Later I heard that some CEO candidates were insulted by this suggestion and frustrated by how long the recruitment process was taking, so they took their names out of the running. I don't know if it's true.)

The psychological test consisted of two parts: a Web-based questionnaire, which took me well over three hours to complete, and a face-to-face interview with two psychologists. The interview occurred in Foster City, California, on Father's Day. We talked for more than two hours. The questions were about anything and everything personal. I was asked more about my family relationships than about HP. Later, the two psychologists reported out to the Board on me and the other candidates. Neither the results of this process nor the report was ever shared with me. I don't know the nature of the Board's discussion, but after I'd been hired, several Board members told me I'd clearly surpassed every other candidate by then and that my candor had stood out.

After the interview I drove back to San Francisco, where I was staying with my father. He thought the whole "psychological thing" was insulting and, as he put it, "California silly." He kept saying he didn't want to influence my decision. When I was growing up, he'd always said: "Each of us has to follow our own star." Even so, he was also devastated by my mother's death and desperately wanted me to move back to California. I talked with him carefully and deliberately because I didn't want to build his hopes. He was so lost and lonely, and I didn't want to disappoint him. Now I told him all the reasons HP wouldn't offer me the job: I'd never been a CEO, I wasn't an engineer, I wasn't from the industry, I was an outsider, I was a woman and this would be a first. Later I learned that John Young had used virtually all these same arguments to reassure the Lucent Board, on which he served, that they wouldn't lose me because HP would never offer me the job.

My father said, "But, Carly, you can sell them on why you'd be a great choice. They need to change and you can change them." And so I explained to my father why I wouldn't sell them, why I needed to make this a difficult choice for the Board, not an easy one.

This job would be exceedingly hard, and the Board couldn't get buyer's remorse halfway through the journey. They needed to buy into me as the CEO all the way, and that required them to understand in every possible dimension what a controversial and risky choice I would be and how tough and risky the transformation they said they wanted would also be. And then I also told him why perhaps I didn't want the job at all. I told him that our life was set in New Jersey, and as much as I loved him, this would be a very difficult move on the family. I told him how much money I stood to lose. I gave him every argument I could think of to dash his expectations. I knew I was getting through to him because he seemed to shrink into himself the longer I talked. It hurt me to make him so sad, but I felt I had no choice. That night I wondered whether I was doing the right thing in pursuing the job at all.

IT WAS A MEETING in late June of 1999 that apparently clinched my selection as the new CEO of HP. There would be other meetings both before and after this second conversation with Dick Hackborn, but by all accounts, from the Board's point of view, they made their decision after Dick reported back to them on our second and final meeting.

We met at the Chicago airport out of an abundance of caution. I'd suggested it because while on the Board of the Kellogg Company, I'd learned it was a good place to meet if you didn't want to be found out. The search had been going on now for close to six months. The speculation in the media was intensifying. Articles were being written about the two internal candidates, Ann Livermore and Carolyn Ticknor. I learned later that the Board had never considered them real candidates, but allowed the organization, the outside world and the two women themselves to believe they had a real shot.

Without really knowing anything about the place, we ended up at the

Gaslight Lounge. The waitresses wore short skirts and fishnet stockings. Dick Hackborn seemed uncomfortable and embarrassed—I assured him I'd been in much worse places (one wonders what he thought I meant!). He clearly came prepared to talk as long as was necessary to make up his own mind (we ended up meeting for almost four hours and drinking what seemed like gallons of iced tea). I came full of questions and doubts.

First, we talked about the Board. I wanted to know how they'd come to the decision to split the company, fire a CEO (for clearly that's what had happened in Dick's mind) and look outside for a new one. A CEO had begun a strategic planning process with the thesis that Hewlett-Packard, at about $40 billion in revenues, had become too big to grow and too complex to manage. The Board, along with the help of McKinsey & Company consultants, had agreed that HP needed to be split up (several different split scenarios were evaluated before coming to a final decision) and had, along the way, told Lew that he would lose his job. It was clear that this was an unexpected outcome for Lew and that he felt betrayed by the Board. This explained the resentment I could see every time I met with him. He tried to keep his emotions hidden, but he couldn't disguise his bitterness—which ultimately would boil over at his farewell dinner and would greatly influence his decision to fight the Board publicly on the Compaq acquisition.

I asked him lots of questions about the Board members, particularly the family members. Dick was careful and respectful in his responses, but he was clear that Bill and Dave had never wanted their children involved in the business. He said that the Board wanted to "professionalize" itself over time. He meant by this that membership on the board would be driven more by credentials than family connections. Sam Ginn was driving this professionalization process on behalf of the Board. Walter Hewlett had decided to go to Agilent (the new name of the test and measurement business). Susan Packard Orr, who was clearly liked and respected by everyone, would stay for a while, although she had indicated her desire to leave the Board as soon after the split as possible. David Woodley Packard, Dave's eldest son, had been so upset by the split of the company that he'd resigned from the Board. And Bill Hewlett's son-in-law, Jean-Paul Gimon, had agreed with Sam that he should leave the Board as soon as the new CEO was named. Very soon after I arrived, I learned that Jean-Paul didn't understand that this was the plan. It was a very quick, and unnerving, introduction to family politics.

Looking back, I think one of the most remarkable things about the whole recruitment process was how little the family came up. They simply weren't a big topic of conversation. Family politics did not seem to be a big factor in how the company operated, and family members didn't seem to be influential players in the boardroom. In fact, I never met with any of them during the long recruitment process. I didn't know enough to ask for such a meeting, and they didn't seem to think it was necessary.

We talked a lot about the subjects we'd covered in our last meeting. Time was against the company. There was no competitive focus. I asked a lot about the management team—who they were, how good they were. Dick seemed to have high regard for most of them. "Our biggest issue is leadership and strategy, Carly. The people are capable, the products are good." It was a fun conversation—to think about all the opportunities and to be in agreement about what was needed to take advantage of them.

And then the conversation took an interesting turn. I asked what Lew's plans were. Lew, of course, was both chairman and CEO. Dick indicated that Lew should leave as quickly as possible. I thought a longer transition could be useful. First, the CEO job would be quite enough for a while, and I didn't need to be chairman as well. In fact, I told Dick, I didn't want to be chairman. I would need some help. And the spin-off complicated matters. It would take immense time and effort. Both Agilent and HP would have to quickly move to establish their new, separate identities and their operating plans. There would be a lot of difficult decisions about who got what resources. There would be a lot of arguments, particularly over intellectual property. Someone needed to adjudicate, and that someone couldn't be the new HP CEO or the Agilent CEO. It needed to be someone everyone could trust to be objective and neutral. I thought that person was Lew Platt.

Dick's disdain for Lew suddenly was apparent. He thought it was a terrible idea. He couldn't dismiss the logic of my arguments, though; so now he threw a curveball.

Rick Belluzzo had been the head of the computing business when he'd abruptly left. While he was at HP, he was widely perceived as the heir apparent to Lew. In fact, I had met with Rick several times while I was at Lucent and had even addressed an HP sales conference at his request in San Francisco. Now Dick said, "Rick is a really good guy. I blame Lew for his departure. Why don't we make Rick Belluzzo the chairman?"

What was Dick actually trying to do? It was an unworkable suggestion. Rick and I were virtually the same age. Rick was by then the chairman and CEO of Silicon Graphics, and he clearly had ambitions of his own. Dick would be setting up an impossible situation for both of us: the chairman and CEO, instead of working as a team, would be competing against each other. Besides, I assumed they were interviewing him for the CEO job. If he was good enough to be chairman, why didn't they make him CEO? I said as much. It wouldn't work, and I wouldn't do it.

Dick backed off quickly, but my suggestion to keep Lew on for a while as chairman didn't seem workable to Dick either. So I suggested Dick as chairman. He was surprised but clearly flattered. I needed help from an old-timer who knew where the bodies were buried and knew the HP landscape. By the end of that long lunch, I thought Dick and I had an agreement. If I became CEO, he would serve as chairman.

Later I would ask Lew Platt about Rick Belluzzo. It was one of the rare moments throughout a very long recruitment process, which must have been especially difficult for Lew, when I saw him lose his cool. "I've told this Board that they'll bring Rick back over my dead body! He is not a candidate." Oh, the politics and resentments and disagreements that were suggested by his comments juxtaposed against Dick's! I asked Lew about his transition plans, without sharing with him my conversation with Dick. He said he'd go as quickly as the Board decided was useful. He assumed he'd move on quickly.

Later Lew became so outraged that his nemesis, Dick Hackborn, would become the chairman that he insisted on a longer transition. Sam Ginn, who usually played the role of reasonable man and peacemaker on the Board, sought a compromise: Lew would stay on as chairman until December. Dick Hackborn would become chairman at that point. I wasn't asked for my point of view. When I was finally told about this arrangement, after I had already accepted the job, I told Sam it was going to be a problem. I thought the bad blood between these two was going to make life difficult for everyone, most especially for me.

After almost six months of meetings, I finally met with the full Board in July, for dinner. I arrived early knowing that this was an evening full of meaning. I drove to the parking lot of Marcus & Millichap. I sat in my car and thought about the significance of going from typing and filing to becoming CEO of a Dow 30 company without traveling more than a block. I thought about my mother—about her words that day, about her death, about what she would think and say on this night. More than anything, I wished she were alive.

Prior to this evening I had only met with four members of the Board. I had been told the dress was business casual. The evening began with wine outside on the patio. Everyone was friendly, and it seemed to me they had already made up their minds. I don't think Walter Hewlett was there—if he was, he made no impression. The conversation was light; and as the evening wore on, I was surprised I wasn't getting asked more questions. And so I finally decided I needed to say something.

I talked about my respect for the company. I talked about how long I'd been associated with it. I talked about the opportunity the split of the company represented: an opportunity to inject new energy and speed into HP. And I talked about the HP Way. I said the most important thing I could do was strike the right balance between preservation and reinvention. It was the first time I'd used those words. I said the word *preservation* because the legacy of the company was a powerful symbol and motivator. I chose the term *reinvention* because invention was a core virtue of Bill and Dave's, and I needed to find a word for change that captured their pioneering spirit. The phrase seemed to resonate with the Board, and I would use it over and over again.

Although no one said so, I drove back to my father's house that night knowing the Board had made their decision. And I knew in my heart that I had made mine.

19 | Is That an Armani Suit?

ON FRIDAY AFTERNOON, July 16, 1999, I sat in Rich's office and told him I was leaving. His eyes filled with tears, and he said, "Carly, it will never be the same. You're the soul of Lucent."

I had not expected this reaction. From my very first meeting with Jeff Christian, Rich had known I was talking to Hewlett-Packard. I had owed him the truth. In all that time, he'd only had two conversations with me about it. Neither Henry nor any other Board member ever talked to me about it. I think Rich believed he could keep me with money, and he was betting I'd never be offered the job.

The last week in June, shortly before my dinner with the HP Board, Rich McGinn had held a leadership retreat in the Pocono Mountains. It was disastrous. For the first time in Lucent's four-year history, the executive team thought they couldn't hit the numbers for the next year's plan. Rich was in no mood to listen. His top fifteen executives were trying to tell him he'd lost touch with reality, but he kept ratcheting up the objectives for the organization. He'd been unwilling to accept any input on the agenda topics we should have been covering, and now we had no real opportunity to discuss our challenges openly and objectively. The team that had once been unified was now divided. And Rich either didn't see it or didn't care.

One of a leader's jobs is to assess the capability of the organization. If a leader underestimates the organization, it underperforms. If a leader overestimates its capability, the organization disappoints. A leader's job is to assess accurately and then to increase the capability of the organization by building skills, building teams and building confidence.

Every boss has heard a subordinate say "I can't deliver this performance." A leader makes a judgment about the reasoning behind the words. Sometimes people say "I can't" because they don't know how to do what's being asked of them. In this case, a conversation about alternatives and solutions is necessary. Do we need to build new skills, or examine different opportunities, or think creatively about other approaches? This kind of problem solving requires open and collaborative dialogue. Have we thought about this? Have we tried that? Can someone else help us?

Sometimes people say "I can't" because they want an easy answer for a tough challenge. Lower performance takes less work than higher performance. In this case, a conversation that reconfirms the reality of the opportunity and the validity of the execution plan is in order. Perhaps extra incentive is required to raise people's sights from what's easy to what's possible. Perhaps different motivation must be found to encourage people to reach further.

Sometimes people say "I can't" because the objective they're being asked to achieve is truly out of reach. Then it's vitally important to make sure everyone has the same view of reality. Why do people see the facts differently? And where is common ground? If this objective is unachievable, what should we be striving for?

Whenever a leader hears a team say "We can't," for whatever reason, much more conversation is required. And teams are built through such conversations. Teams are built when people can work together to successfully solve problems and achieve goals. Teams are built through effective collaboration.

At the end of two days we hadn't had a real conversation. We were not collaborating. It was a continuation of an all-too-familiar pattern. My colleagues were distressed. Many of them approached me. One conversation in particular stands out in my mind. Gerry Butters, then the head of the Optical Networking Group, took me aside and said, "Carly, this isn't Rich's company, it's yours. You are our real leader. Lead us."

I have believed all my life that leadership has nothing to do with title or position. Leadership is about making a positive difference for and with others. Leadership is about the integrity of one's character, the caliber of one's capabilities, and the effectiveness of one's collaboration with others. Anyone can lead from anywhere at any time. I have seen people lead from lowly as well as lofty positions. And so Gerry's request tormented me. I loved Lucent—shouldn't I stick it out and lead, despite all the difficulties? And yet the CEO of the company I loved was not a leader, and I did not respect him. As I watched the Pocono meeting unfold, I realized I could no longer be loyal to Rich. I would not undermine him, but I could not follow him. It was time to leave.

M Y LAST WEEK at Lucent was agony. It must have shown on my face because people kept asking me what was wrong. I could not say good-bye. The news that I was going to leave Lucent and join Hewlett-Packard was material information to both firms, and so a public announcement was required. I had a tearful conversation with my longtime secretary and dear friend Maybeth Osmun, and another one with my loyal and capable executive assistant of eight years, Kate Silvieri. I told Kathy Fitzgerald because she would have to prepare the announcement. She said I was as white as a ghost when I entered her office. We sat together and cried. And the last thing I said to Rich as I left him alone in his office was "Rich, take down the numbers. People really can't deliver what you're asking for."

That night Frank and I boarded an HP plane and flew to California. I was emotionally drained and sleep deprived. When I arrived in the hotel at about 2:00 A.M., I wrote a letter to the employees of Lucent Technologies. They wouldn't read it until Monday, but I had to turn the page before I slept. When I woke up, my commitment would be to Hewlett-Packard.

The weekend was a whirlwind of preparation. First, I wanted to talk to Ann Livermore. I knew she was disappointed and that she'd be asked a lot of questions; there had been intense speculation about her in the press and numerous profile pieces published. I wanted to reach out and tell her directly that I looked forward to working with her and that I supported the strategies she'd been articulating in the marketplace. I presented a large retention offer. She was shaken by the events of the last twenty-four hours but nevertheless was gracious, professional and supportive. Both Hewlett-Packard and I were lucky to have her.

Then Lew and I began to prepare for the announcement to the employees. We made a videotape together. In it I spoke of my admiration for Lew, my gratitude for the opportunity, my excitement at joining such a legendary company. I talked about both change and continuity. I spoke of the importance of innovation, of contribution, of customer focus. I talked about speed because I knew time was against us; the market and our competitors were moving much faster than we were.

We prepared intensively for the press conference that was to occur on Monday morning. Since my name had never come up as a possible candidate, everyone would be surprised. There would be many reporters, so we spent a lot of time thinking about how we would answer their questions. "What are your objectives as the new CEO?" "What was the Board's selection process?" "Lew, how will you and Carly work together?" "Do you think it makes a difference that you're not an engineer?" "As an outsider, what do you bring to the table?" "What about your compensation package?" "You're not from the computer industry. What's the relevance of your communications experience?"

Perhaps it was because two of the candidates who'd been speculated about were both women. Perhaps it was because my gender hadn't come up much in the interview process. Perhaps it was because we were all focused on demonstrating my credentials and making the right, very important first impression on that very important first day. Whatever the reason, the one question we didn't prepare for was the question most frequently asked: "What about the glass ceiling? How does it feel to have broken it? Does this mean it no longer exists?" As hard as it may be to believe, we didn't prepare for one question about my gender.

The evening before the news broke on Sunday, Lew and I had dinner with the executive team. I had already made my first decision: I wasn't bringing in a new team with me. I'd already read as much as I could about each of these executives, and I knew some of them might not be able to go the distance. Nevertheless, it was important to give all of them the benefit of the doubt and the opportunity to become change agents. They'd been at HP a long time, and I had to earn their respect and their trust before they could commit themselves to what I would ask.

This was a bureaucratic organization with a deeply rooted culture. Outsiders were rare and usually rejected. Meaningful and sustainable change could only come from within. I could be a catalyst for that change, but if a critical mass of the current leadership team didn't embrace and own it, change wouldn't happen. When the employees of the company were asked to change, they'd look to people they knew. It wouldn't be enough for the new CEO to say "We must change." The employees would have to hear it from others.

I'd been in big companies for twenty years. I knew the organization could ignore me or sabotage me. I'd seen it happen before. I didn't know all the relationships or the history that mattered or what the informal power structures were. Beyond that, I didn't have all the answers. I was a brand-new CEO in a brand-new situation with a company that had prospered for sixty years. These people knew more about the challenges facing HP than I did; I needed their help. If Hewlett-Packard was going to change, the company needed much more than a new CEO. HP needed a whole new mindset about itself, about the nature and pace of the industry, about the demands and requirements of its customers and about the ferocity and skill of its competitors.

The dinner did not go well. The team hadn't been prepped ahead of time, and now they were cool and curious. When we sat down, Lew asked each of them to introduce themselves. I noticed that all of them used their CEO titles. They talked about "my organization" or "my people" with a proprietary air. The message was clear: I'm fine, I own my business and I don't need your help. When they'd made the rounds, Antonio Perez was blunt: "So, Carly, tell us; why you?" I didn't think I should justify the Board's decision or their process, so I said; "Lew, why don't you describe for the team the process the Board has been through during the last six months?" Now that the reality of a new CEO had sunk in, Lew wore his own disappointment about how he'd been treated on his sleeve; no one could miss the resentment as he spoke on behalf of the Board.

The dinner said it all. Neither the Board nor Lew had been upfront with this executive team about their belief that fundamental change was required. No one had shared their selection process or criteria. No one had warned them that their new CEO believed a different strategy and a new structure were required. I wasn't going to get any help from this Board, and the management team had the same skepticism about me that a government bureaucracy has about a new political appointee: "We'll see how long she lasts." This was going to be even tougher than I'd thought.

Before I could start, however, I'd have to survive the first day. In retrospect, our preparation for the press onslaught was laughable, despite the outside experts we'd brought in. I knew every word Lew and I said on that Monday would be scrutinized by employees. We were embarking together on a long and difficult journey of change, and how we began would matter. The words I used to describe the company, my objectives, our challenges and our opportunities would stick. The organization would remember them, and I would have to live with them. As a new leader I wanted to speak to all employees about what we had in common, about what would pull us together. I wanted to talk about Hewlett-Packard—our respect for the legacy of this great enterprise, our desire to build a future together, a recognition that we were not as focused or fast or aggressive as we needed to be in this new Internet era.

I didn't want to talk about my gender or the glass ceiling—these topics were distractions from the mission at hand, and they separated me from the vast majority of my employees. And so I was unprepared and impatient with all of these questions. When I said, "The glass ceiling doesn't exist," it made headlines. I was trying to change the subject. I was trying to say that women could do anything men could do. I was trying to tell women that although there are plenty of obstacles and prejudices, there isn't some invisible barrier that prevents them from achieving their dreams. I was reflecting my own experience that more is achieved by focusing on the possibilities than by fixating on the limitations or the inequities. I didn't succeed in conveying any of this, and from the first day on, I could not escape the categorization of "Carly Fiorina, female CEO." Nor would I ever escape the relentless attention of the media.

I never wanted to draw attention to myself, but once it was focused on me, I wanted to deflect attention to the company. Whenever I agreed to an interview, I'd set ground rules: I won't talk about the glass ceiling, I won't talk about myself, I'll only talk about the company. Over the years that followed I turned down numerous requests from *Glamour*, *People*, *Vogue*, Diane Sawyer, Oprah Winfrey and more. These were great venues and personalities, but they weren't interested in the company; they were interested in me.

From my first until my last day at HP, I was criticized both for being in the press too much and for being unavailable to the press. From the first stories of my hiring until the last of my firing, both the language and the intensity of the coverage were different for me than for any other CEO. It was more personal, with much commentary about my personality and my physical appearance, my dress, my hair or my shoes. That first week, the editor of *BusinessWeek* came to see me with the beat reporter because they'd been working on a story for several months. Hewlett-Packard was going to be the cover story whether we liked it or not, and everyone recommended that I talk with them. Before we'd even sat down, the very first question from the editor was "Is that an Armani suit you're wearing?"

Vanity Fair, despite being warned numerous times that they were writing fiction about me, continued to report that I traveled constantly with a hairdresser and a makeup artist. There was a persistent rumor, bolstered by commentary in the local press, that I'd built a pink marble bathroom in my office. (I had actually moved into my predecessor's office and neither built nor bought anything for it.) There were no private bathrooms or even doors in executive offices. The CEOs of Lucent, Cisco, IBM, Dell, Sun Microsystems, Microsoft, Compaq, Oracle, GE, 3M, Dupont and so on all flew in corporate jets, and HP had owned them for thirty years. Nevertheless, my travel on a company plane was reported as evidence of my disrespect for the HP Way, my "regal" nature, my "distance" from employees.

I was alternatively described as "flashy" or "glamorous" or "diamond studded," which frequently was translated to mean a superficial "marketing" type.

Every speech I gave while I was the CEO—and there were many, forty-seven in 2004 alone—was in response to a request from a customer or an employee of HP. I turned down far more than I accepted. Each of these speaking venues was a great opportunity to meet with, and influence, customers and to represent the capabilities of the company. Other CEOs were also always invited to speak, and yet my attendance was singled out as evidence that I "sought the limelight."

I was usually referred to by my first name. There was much, particularly painful commentary that I'd chosen not to have children because I was "too ambitious." People dismissed Frank's own career and contributions to our family and the community by inaccurately describing him as a "stay-at-home spouse."

In the chat rooms around Silicon Valley, from the time I arrived until long after I left HP, I was routinely referred to as either a "bimbo" or a "bitch"*— too soft or too hard, and presumptuous, besides. Certainly, beyond my gender, I was not a typical Silicon Valley CEO. Where the archetypal leader was an introvert, I was an extrovert. Where the Valley loved to dress down, I loved to dress up. While Valley leaders talked about the bits and bytes of technology, I talked about the human impact of technology. I hadn't grown up in the Valley; I came from the East Coast and I'd grown up in big, brick-and-mortar, old-economy companies, not small, new-economy start-ups.

During the first few months of my tenure, Scott McNealy of Sun Micro-systems decided to kick off his analyst meeting by making fun of me. Sun Microsystems was flying high in the late nineties and so was Scott, so everything he said and did received huge play in the media. He presented a skit featuring an actress with a blond wig and long, red fingernails standing in front of a garage. The garage collapsed on her head, to the great amusement of the assembled audience.

When I finally reached the top, after striving my entire career to be judged by results and accomplishments, the coverage of my gender, my appearance and the perceptions of my personality would vastly outweigh anything else. It disappoints me greatly. I have always believed that actions speak louder than words. Perhaps, in this new era of always-on, always-connected information, where fact, fiction and opinion seem to carry equal weight, that's no longer true. It is undeniable that the words spoken and written about me made my life and my job infinitely more difficult. Perhaps others' words define me more clearly in many minds than my own actions. Perhaps it is part of the reason I wrote this book.

In those first few days as a CEO I was sobered by the commentary of the media, the cool reception from the Valley, the skepticism of the executive

---

*"Industry Wants Girls to Stick to Knitting," by Charles Cooper, CNET, Friday, March 10, 2006, 4:00:19 PST.

team, and the passivity of the Board in this all-important transition. And I was buoyed by the employees of Hewlett-Packard. The first day alone I received hundreds upon hundreds of e-mail messages. Some asked about "e-services" because this had been recently announced as the company's Internet strategy. Some wondered what I thought about the HP Way. The vast majority expressed excitement about the opportunity for change. From that first day onward, I read all the e-mail messages that were sent to me, and answered a great many of them. My courage to do what was required always came from the employees. The company belongs to them—not to the Board, or the founders, or the families of the founders. The people of HP are HP. My job as CEO was to build new skills and capabilities, as well as new confidence and aspiration. I deeply believe that every person has more potential than they realize. I knew that HP had more potential than most people could see. My job was to lead the transformation of a once-great company that now was floundering by unlocking the potential of its people and its assests.

Over the years, I received tens of thousands of messages from employees, and thousands more when I left. I receive them to this day. In that entire time, only one was unsigned. The authors of all of the other e-mails, both those who were supportive and those who were critical, let me know who they were as well as what they thought. I am deeply grateful for the candor and wisdom of the people of HP. They are the guardians of its legacy and the builders of its future.

20 | A Thousand Tribes

I TACKLED MY NEW JOB in the same way I had always approached a new assignment: I met with as many people and asked as many questions as possible. I studied the details of our numbers and our plans. I traveled extensively and met with customers, partners, employees.

All throughout my tenure at HP, I met constantly with customers. I could help open doors and close deals but I also always wanted to know how our customers thought we were performing. If you want to know what has to change inside a company, ask the customers. One of our most important customers at GM said to me: "Carly, you have the best people in the industry; whenever I ask them to solve a specific problem, they always respond with dedication and excellence. But I never know whom to call; and if I can't find them, they never find me." Many customers reiterated this frustration that we were reactive rather than proactive, and difficult to do business with. Every one of them said we were too slow. Whenever I asked them to pick one word to describe HP, they would say "nice" or "engineering driven" or "technically excellent." Not one of them said "focused" or "effective" or "leading edge." All of them said we were being outmarketed by our competitors. All of them said we were too expensive. Our largest customers said we weren't investing enough in new products or features to keep up with our rivals. Many complained that in a networked age, HP products didn't even work with one another. Others said they thought our engineers started from scratch every time they designed a new product; one customer said in exasperation, "Can't you at least put the on/off switch in the same place?"

When I asked our salespeople to describe a typical customer meeting, they all joked about meeting one another for the first time outside the customer's door. They complained that when a customer called an important meeting, either every business unit sent a representative and we overwhelmed the customer with too many people and too much confusion, or no one showed up at all. HP was not a customer-focused company. We didn't collaborate well on behalf of customers. We didn't anticipate customers' needs or competitors' actions; we waited to be called upon. And our customers were calling on us less and less—that was why HP's growth rate was slowing while the rest of the industry's was accelerating.

I have always believed that leading companies must focus on customers. Some will argue that a company should focus on competitors or stockholders. Of course all are vitally important, but only a customer can buy a company's product. Without revenue there is no business, and without revenue growth a business is lagging, not leading. Transformation at HP had to start with how we served customers.

I HAD ALWAYS ADMIRED HP LABS, so I decided my very first "coffee talk" would be with HP Labs employees. Coffee talks had originated with Bill and Dave in the early days, when Lucille Packard would bake cookies for the engineers and Bill and Dave would sit around and drink coffee with their first employees and talk about the business. The term was now used to describe any personal interaction between managers and their employees. I didn't think it was all that remarkable to go first to HP Labs—after all, this was a technology company and innovation was our life's blood. Bill's and Dave's offices, preserved perfectly to this day, are in the HP Labs building. Following in Henry Schacht's footsteps, I'd made it a practice to visit Bell Laboratories once a month while at Lucent, and I knew that such interactions were not only meaningful for the researchers, they also allowed me to keep abreast of the most important technological advances. I intended to visit HP Labs once a month as well.

The people of HP Labs thought my choice was remarkable, however. They were thrilled that I intended to visit on a regular basis. No one came to see them, and no one seemed to care what they were doing. They were viewed mostly as a corporate expense that the businesses didn't need and couldn't control. Innovation was touted as one of the HP values, yet no one measured innovation or invested in it or rewarded for it. The results were clear: HP was one of the few companies with a central research laboratory, yet didn't even qualify as one of the top twenty-five innovators in the world as measured by patent production.

On one of my first visits I was shown something called Cool Town. It was truly impressive. Cool Town later became the centerpiece of my very first public speech about HP and my vision for the company. Cool Town was a lab where every person, place and thing had its own Web presence and identity. This meant that every person, place and thing was connected to, and could interact with, every other. It was the first glimpse of what I later came to call the "digital, mobile, virtual, personal" future—a future in which everything physical and analog can be represented in digital form; where anything can move anywhere because it exists in cyberspace and can be networked; where virtual reality can someday be as compelling as physical reality; and where individuals can control myriad actions, events and information on their own behalf. How HP chose to use its assets at the dawn of the twenty-first century, the first truly digital, mobile, virtual, personal era in human history, would form the foundation of our strategy and our competitive advantage.

I could hardly contain my delight and excitement at seeing Cool Town. This was what HP could do. Cool Town took advantage of every capability we had, and it differentiated us from our competitors. I asked Dick Lampman, the head of HP Labs, how many other executives had seen it. "No one. We can't get anyone to come." I asked what was going to happen to Cool Town. "We're supposed to be shutting it down next month. We can't get any budget for it." Every business manager was focused on his own product lines. Each manager was accountable for sustaining her current business. No one knew how to fund a future that might fall outside his or her defined business boundaries. No one was rewarded for spending money on an uncertain possibility that might not improve present performance, even if it seemed important to the larger company. No one knew how to pool together the considerable resources of HP; everyone managed his or her own profit and loss statement. In essence, the entire management process at HP had become focused on incrementalism. All of a manager's time, and most of our considerable product development resources, were concentrated on the current product lines. If a product improvement required more investment than a particular business could afford in a year, it didn't get done, even if the consequences over the long term were dire. We had lost our leadership positions in UNIX as a result of this management mind-set. We didn't measure new product introductions, or new patent filings. I left Cool Town determined to save the project and change the way we funded and valued our research efforts. And Dick Lampman would become a dedicated and effective change agent in that process.

My first meeting with my new executive team occurred shortly after my arrival. We had about two weeks remaining in the company's third quarter. (Hewlett-Packard's fiscal year extends from November 1 to October 31. The third quarter is May, June and July.) I asked where we stood for the quarter; were we on track to deliver against our plans and the market's expectations? It seemed to me an obvious question they should have expected, but they all seemed surprised. One executive asked me whether we should miss the quarter so that we could blame it on Lew and start fresh in the all-important fourth and final quarter. I answered that we had set goals for the quarter, and we needed to deliver against them—a transition between CEOs was irrelevant. Bob Wayman, whose title was chief financial officer, said that he didn't know where we stood as a company. He explained that the four CEOs each had their own CFOs, who didn't report to Bob and who never shared their numbers with "corporate" until the quarter was over and they'd finalized their own profit and loss statements. When I pressed the line executives for details, they responded that they were "on plan" or "off plan," without any specifics. When I asked how these plans added up to Hewlett-Packard's results and the expectations for our performance in the marketplace, no one could answer the question. When I began a conversation about how we could deliver "above plan" in some divisions to compensate for performance "below plan" elsewhere, the resistance was stiff and immediate. These executives didn't think it was part of their jobs to improve the company's overall results—their jobs were to deliver against their own plans. It was no wonder that the company would miss nine quarters in a row.

Hewlett-Packard was literally the sum of its parts, and no one tallied the sum until everything was over. I knew now why Lew Platt had given CEO titles to the line executives; they were more CEOs than he was. And Bob Wayman didn't really act as the company's CFO; none of the business CFOs reported to him, so Human Resources and Public Relations and something called International did.

Because both Board members and customers had identified our lack of marketing as a major problem, I met with the marketing people. Corporate Marketing reported to the CFO. They were marginalized and demoralized. The business unit marketing teams were proud of their products and their brands. Each team had its own advertising budgets and strategies. Each interacted directly with distribution channels. None of them coordinated with one another. After a week or two of conversations, I put together a single sheet of paper that was covered with various product brands that we promoted in the market; HP had 150 of them. At meetings I began to ask people what they thought when they looked at it. Nine out of ten people would study it carefully and then point out to me which product brands were missing. Only one in ten people would ask "Where's the HP brand?" It was not merely symbolic that the product sub-brands had become more important than the company's brand, both out in the marketplace and inside the business. It was reflective of the reality that the "thousand tribes" had no collective identity. The company was eighty-seven different profit and loss statements.

Duane Zitzner, the CEO for the PC business, was having a two-day meeting with his team and invited me to come. I sat in the room and listened and took notes for two days. Duane talked about "my products" and "my guys." His team talked mostly about their products, far too little about customers and competitors, and not at all about the rest of HP. They could have been a stand-alone company. Each of the eighty-seven product divisions at HP had its own HR team, IT team, finance team, marketing and sales team, and R&D team. They all had their own way of doing things and did most everything on their own.

I knew from reading *The HP Way* so many times that Bill and Dave's strategy had always been to give engineers the tools they needed to invent new products. If a new product was successful in the marketplace, Bill and Dave would create a separate business around it. Engineers would become business managers. Each business was defined by its own profit and loss statement. Each manager was responsible for ensuring the success of his business, and each manager controlled the resources he needed for success. Having that profit and loss statement, and controlling those resources, was the source of people's power and the organization's respect. Products, and the engineering that produced them, were at the core of Bill and Dave's company. And the company had always been Bill and Dave's job—a manager's job was to care for his own business. When Bill and Dave left, no one assumed their role. No one managed the company.

Around this same time, Bill Hewlett's son-in-law came to see me. He complained that Sam Ginn had told him he'd have to leave the Board, but Jean-Paul Gimon was sure I would reconsider. He said Bill Hewlett had put him on the Board. He said the rest of the family was watching carefully. Jean-Paul was sure I would reverse Sam's decision out of respect for the founders and their families.

Sam Ginn felt strongly that Board membership was his job as the chairman of the Nominating and Governance Committee, and not mine as the CEO or Dick's (and later mine) as the chairman of the Board. Sam Ginn was adamant that Jean-Paul wasn't qualified. He'd assured the other Board members that Jean-Paul would go. He suggested a meeting with Walter Hewlett, for whom he had more respect, to explain the situation. Walter said he understood Sam's position but that representatives from both families should remain on the Board. I suggested that Walter, who now served on the Agilent Board, also serve on HP's Board; it seemed a workable compromise that would satisfy both the families' need for representation and Sam's need to change a Board member. Sam was delighted. I couldn't read Walter's reaction, but he agreed. So Jean-Paul was off.

THE DOT-COM BOOM WAS in full force. Every company was spending money on technology, worrying about being left behind, and wondering what Y2K, the impending turn to the new century, meant to the computer systems of the world. I had come into HP with a belief that we were running out of time. During the recruitment process, Board members had often spoken of time being against us. I was in a hurry; every one of our customers and competitors was moving faster than we were. And yet the pace I encountered as I traveled and talked with HP people was slow and stately. While the rest of Silicon Valley seemed perpetually juiced up on too much coffee and not enough sleep, HP people seemed relaxed and calm. The parking lots emptied at 4:30 or 5:00 every afternoon. The most frequently asked question from employees in those first few months was what I thought about work/life balance. Lew had described this as his number one priority for the company.

Early on, Dan Plunkett asked me to describe my reactions when I first arrived. Dan was an organizational behaviorist and a consultant I'd used frequently at Lucent. He would also work with me at HP for my entire tenure. I searched my mind for the right analogy. Finally, I said I felt as if all the buildings I visited were wrapped in layers and layers of gauze bandages. Outside blared a cacophony of sound, the light was bright and dazzling, and thousands of exciting ambitions jostled for attention. Inside HP the sounds were muffled, the light was faded, and the gentle images of Bill and Dave as kindly, older father figures were more visible than the harsh realities of the marketplace. HP, especially at headquarters, which was so close to the original garage, felt like a mausoleum or a cocoon. All success was measured inside this protective environment and internal politics were rampant.

While they were active, Bill and Dave were legendary leaders for the people of HP. Once they had departed, they became epic figures, and over time events became history and history became myth. HP was Bill and Dave's business, and so Bill and Dave made the decisions on behalf of Hewlett-Packard. Jay Keyworth, a long-standing member of the Board who'd been a good friend of Dave's, once said to me: "There was nothing democratic about the way Bill and Dave ran HP. It was more like a benevolent dictatorship." When people were uncertain whether a new product should be launched, Bill and Dave decided. Until my arrival, Bill and Dave had always decided when it was time for a new CEO and who that CEO should be. When the split of the company was announced, Bill's son and Dave's daughter were asked to address the company and tell people what they thought their fathers would say and do. Their message of somewhat tepid support was diluted further by the decision of Dave's eldest son to quit the Board in protest.

Bill and Dave were larger than life. Some who knew them well have told me they diminished those around them. I cannot say; I never met Dave, who was deceased, and when I met Bill for the first and only time, he was virtually incapacitated. What I do know is that when I arrived at the company they founded, I encountered a group of people who could not imagine their future beyond Bill and Dave and the strategy and practices they'd always followed. I saw a company that had no identity or sense of itself beyond the celebration of Bill and Dave's legacy and the values they had preached. The past was comforting and the source of wisdom, so people searched their memories for guidance. People were proud of Bill and Dave. Since their departure, no one had ever measured up and nothing had ever matched "the way things were." People lacked confidence in themselves and in each other. Time had stood still for the people of HP; they did not know how to move forward without their founders. They were afraid of change; what if changing anything meant destroying everything? The organization was brittle and timid.

Despite the fear, however, I knew there were HP people who longed for change. From my travels and my conversations and those many e-mail messages, I concluded that a critical mass of people knew that if the company wasn't moving forward, it was falling behind. People who talked with customers and encountered competitors felt the need for change most keenly. They sought a champion for the change they knew was necessary.

Change always takes great effort. Once begun, change is never exactly what you expected it to be; people sometimes tire of the effort and long for the good old days that now seem better after all, especially when viewed through the mists of time. In every institution the powerful and the decision makers always favor the status quo; continuity preserves their position. As I'd learned over and over, many people prefer even a deeply problematic known to the risks of the unknown. Be careful what you pray for; Don't rock the boat; Don't change horses in the middle of the stream are all cautions about the risks of uncertainty and the consequences of imprudent action. For all these reasons, the natural inclination of any organization or institution is always to maintain, to preserve, to protect the way things are. In many real ways, change is an unnatural act and so requires a sustained disruption of sufficient force.

At HP, however, the past and the status quo were also wrapped in the religion of the HP Way and the mythology of the founders. Bill and Dave had once been radicals and pioneers, but now there were too many instances when a new idea was quickly dismissed with the comment "We don't do it that way. It's not the HP Way." "The HP Way," a phrase Dave intensely disliked because he feared it would come to mean anything anyone wanted it to mean, was being used as a shield against change. New ideas had a hard time surviving at HP. New people did too. Susan Bowick, the vice president for Human Resources, had been around a long time. She knew change was long overdue, and she knew change would be extraordinarily difficult. "Carly, at HP we need more than change agents. We need change warriors." She was right. And she also rightly predicted that as I became a champion of change for some, I would become a dangerous heretic for others.

Before I held my first in-depth management review, I'd made several decisions. Everyone at HP, starting with the executive team, had to learn to think about the company as a whole, not just his or her own business. We needed to be inspired by something beyond the memory of Bill and Dave. We needed to determine our direction by going out into the marketplace and looking ahead, not by staying inside and gazing into the rearview mirror. We had to collaborate more because our customers demanded it, and our competitors were beating us; we needed to acknowledge that each division's independence was wasting resources and diluting our force in the marketplace. We had to aim higher and perform better, for it was already quite clear that the company had vast, untapped potential. HP lacked fundamental performance discipline and for years had failed to harness its collective strength and leverage its unique assets.

We needed more leaders. Managers control resources, but people follow leaders. Managers produce desired results within known boundaries and defined conditions. Leaders take risks, take action, create some excitement and create something new. And we had to demystify and deconstruct the HP Way because what it had become was an impediment.

One night at home I realized I needed to keep the whole picture in mind. The reinvention of HP would take a holistic approach. This was a complex systems problem just like so many I'd studied at MIT. There was so much to do and so much at stake that I could not afford to ignore any of the parameters that affected the organization's performance. So on a piece of paper I drew four lines to form a square. I labeled the square "The HP Leadership Framework." I labeled the top line of the square "Strategy and Aspiration." A company's strategy reflects a decision about how to invest resources; a company's aspiration reflects the reason and the purpose for those investments. Moving clockwise, I labeled the right perpendicular line "Structure and Processes"; these are how a company organizes and operates to get work done. The bottom line I labeled "Rewards and Metrics"; a company values what it measures and measures what it values, and people pay attention to what is rewarded. Rewards drive results. The final line I labeled "Culture and Behavior"; how people act every day and the habits and personality of a company may not be codified in the way formal organizational structures and rules are, but they are at least as powerful.

If I had not joined these four lines to one another, I would not have formed a complete square. Likewise, if Strategy and Aspiration, Structure and Processes, Rewards and Metrics, and Culture and Behavior work at cross-purposes to one another, a company is weaker and less effective. A company is a system, and the transformation of a company requires a systemic approach. For HP to succeed, we needed to change all four parameters of the Leadership Framework. For HP to become a single, powerful company rather than a thousand tribes, we needed a common understanding and commitment to all sides of the frame. When I left HP more than five years later, we were still using the Leadership Framework as our guide.

As we lay in bed together that night, Frank and I talked about all the work that had to be done and everything I had learned in my first two months with the company. "So what do you think?" Frank asked.

"I think this is going to be a high-wire act without a net."

21 | Choosing to Lead

M Y FIRST IN-DEPTH MEETING with the management team took place at Seascape, California, over a three-day period. I had several objectives. The first was to observe my new team closely: Who were they? How did they act and interact? Leaders are defined by three things: character, capability and collaboration. Leaders are candid and courageous; they know their strengths and use them; they bolster their weaknesses by relying on others with complementary skills and by constantly learning and adapting; they know when they need help and seek it; they know when help is required by others, and they provide it. They have strong peer networks and are not afraid to share with others. Leaders come in all shapes and sizes and colors from every walk of life and level in an organization. They can emerge anytime and anywhere, but they are consistent and steady in their actions and approach. Leaders recognize, support and encourage other leaders. I needed to find out how many leaders I had.

In many ways my new executive team had never been asked to lead before. They were all managers who'd grown up in a single business or staff function for their entire HP careers. They knew their own individual units in depth and in detail, but they'd never been asked to think beyond their boundaries. In less than two months I'd seen the breadth and reach of Hewlett-Packard in a way they had not. So my second objective was for my executives to see the whole of the company of which their business was but a part—we would review the entire HP portfolio of products, plans and investments. This had never been done before in the sixty-year history of the business.

Finally, at the beginning of our meeting, I announced that none of these executives would be in their current jobs in three months. I could not tell them what their new jobs would be—we would determine some of that together—but I could guarantee them that their responsibilities would change. I needed to introduce them to the reality that reorganization was necessary. More than that, I said it because I needed to change the context in which they operated. I needed them to see new things about the company from a new perspective. If these executives approached everything from the perspective of protecting their current turf, we would never find common ground. They needed to think more broadly about the whole company and without the baggage of their current job. The best meetings occur when people share a common experience. The most progress is made when people discover things together.

As we completed the portfolio review, it was clear to everyone that our opportunities were enormous. We had great capability and deep resources, but we were spreading them too thin. We were organized around products, and although this had worked in the past, we now competed internally, duplicated effort, and were difficult to do business with. Because LaserJet and Inkjet Printing were separate businesses, engineers in one business were developing platforms that performed the same functions as those also being developed by other engineers. We were doing the same work twice, sometimes more often, although perhaps in slightly different ways, because our engineers thought reuse of someone else's development efforts was a failure. This was the origin of the customers' complaint about the on/off switch being in a different place in every product; HP didn't measure or value reuse and leverage.

At the same time that we were developing the same capability in multiple organizations, everyone complained that they lacked sufficient resources to invest in new businesses. This wasn't just true in printing. We had myriad R&D projects throughout the eighty-seven business units. Some sought to address the same customer need or market segment, and yet every one of the project leaders said we were underfunding their work. Failure to leverage others' work meant we were squandering scarce resources.

Our printing businesses were clearly masters of their universe, but Antonio and Carolyn were smug and so were their leadership teams. They no longer strived for continuous improvement against their own performance. We weren't doing as well as we used to, but when I questioned our deteriorating performance, I was reminded that we were doing better than other struggling competitors.

We were using resources, and yet we could not evaluate their productivity or efficiency. Each of our eighty-seven business units had brands, and channels and HR teams, and IT systems and financial reports. I asked how much money we spent overall on finance, or IT, or HR and how our spending compared to competitive benchmarks. No one could answer the questions. We didn't even know how many employees we had on the payroll.

We were a market laggard, not a market leader. Sun Microsystems was beating us badly in UNIX computing, our largest and most profitable computing segment. Several years earlier Dick Hackborn and Rick Belluzzo had pushed for a major redeployment of resources from UNIX to Microsoft-based industry-standard server (ISS) computing platforms. Dick was on the Microsoft Board, and eventually Rick would join that company's management, although he didn't stay long. Now we had the worst of both worlds; we'd underinvested in UNIX and were also getting beaten badly in ISS by Compaq. Having once been the leader in UNIX, we were now number two or number three, depending on the market; and we were trailing Sun and IBM. We were now number eight in the industry-standard server market.

Our PC business was trailing both Dell's and Compaq's. We were viewed as a product company, while IBM was viewed as a systems company; our services business couldn't compete against IBM's. Our only software product was OpenView; it was successful and generated the highest gross margins in the company, but we had to expand its customer base. Our sales force didn't know how to sell software.

We were a company that had always celebrated invention and yet we no longer invented. Our annual patent production lagged behind others, and we were outgunned by everyone from Siemens to Fujitsu to IBM to Lucent. We didn't measure our innovation, and no one could tell me how many patents we produced. We had no sense of the productivity of our R&D resources. We had too many hardware engineers and too few software engineers.

Throughout the course of these reviews, people talked about their performance against plan, not their performance against our toughest competitors. While others were growing faster, our growth was slowing. We did not know how much money we were spending or how much we were wasting. All these problems spelled opportunity: to cut costs, to deliver value, to grow the business, to perform better. They represented real business reasons for change. Although everyone was excited by the possibilities, we were sobered by the stark reality of our position in the marketplace; in the Internet age the pure product era had come to an end. We were building stand-alone products, but our customers demanded systems and solutions. We needed more collaboration around both technology and customers.

On the one hand, we were encouraged by the embarrassment of riches we saw before us; on the other hand, we knew we'd have to make some choices. I described this discovery process as kicking up rough diamonds as we walked down the street—each glowed with the hint of what they could become, but none had been cut and polished.

I watched my team over the course of these reviews. They were proud professionals, and they saw clearly that we could do better. They also hadn't worked together before. They knew each other well and had been in the same company for years, and yet this wasn't a team at all. They'd never really collaborated before. They were friendly but not collegial. They were polite but not candid. No one would challenge anyone directly, but everyone was passive-aggressive; individuals would give me their opinions about other people privately. When I asked direct questions in this public forum, people were taken aback; I was "coached" that this sort of discussion was better left to a one-on-one meeting. Underperforming bureaucracies always dissolve into politesse. I'd seen it at AT&T, and I saw it now. Real performance takes real candor, and straight talk is required when tough problems exist.

On the final day together, we talked about our aspirations for our company and our role as its executives. I made it clear that Hewlett-Packard was this team's responsibility—not mine alone. I said that we would make the most important decisions about our strategy and structure, about what we'd measure and how we'd behave, together as a team. I said that we needed to establish our aspirations and that once established, we'd not give up on them or one another. When we decided what we wanted to become, we would do what was necessary to achieve our goals. I was determined that HP, as we spun out the original core of our business, not be stunted by the failure of imagination I'd seen at AT&T. I knew that our aspirations had to reflect the real potential of our people and our company and had to be worthy of our sustained efforts. We had to aim high because we were capable of much. Our future had to be as worthy as our heritage.

It was an important day that marked the real beginning of the journey of reinvention. Unlike any other technology company, HP was in both computing and printing, and our customers were both consumers and businesses. After much deliberation, the Board had decided on the collection of assets that would remain in HP and those that would be spun off into Agilent. We would not revisit that decision (although we would later reexamine it twice during my tenure). Instead, we aspired to leadership, and that meant we had to become number one or number two in every market we chose to play in. We would embrace our unique portfolio of products and customers, and we would use it to our advantage.

Soon after the Seascape meeting, the HP Board met. Under Lew Platt the leadership team had attended most Board meetings. I thought it was a useful practice—we'd all hear the same things at the same time. I'd observed the July Board meeting when Lew acted as CEO for the last time. He'd presented the monthly financial results for the company. The committee chairs reported on their meetings. There were no questions and no discussion. The only real interaction came during the breaks. I intended to operate differently. At the September meeting I asked Bob Wayman to present the financials of the company. I asked each executive to talk about their businesses. And I talked about the conclusions of our Seascape meeting and my goals as CEO. There were many questions and lots of interaction. I thought it was a great meeting.

For many years the Board hadn't delved at all into the strategy or operations of the company. Their first real experience in acting as a Board had been their decision to split the company and hire a new CEO. Prior to that, as I'd been told by some of the long-standing Board members, they'd simply acted as a rubber stamp, doing whatever Bill and Dave wanted them to do. Even after Bill and Dave left, nothing much changed. Lew Platt had given them the opportunity to act. He'd concluded that HP had become too big and too complex to manage; this was, he postulated, the underlying reason for HP's deteriorating performance. It was why he'd proposed a split-up of the company.

Based upon what I'd seen so far, HP hadn't been managed with discipline as a company for many years. This was the principal reason for its underperformance. I thought the Agilent split was a mistake; it was the wrong strategic solution for what was essentially an operational problem. We now had spun off some of our most valuable software and networking assets at the very time we needed to invest in them. The split created a nightmare of conflicts around intellectual property. I was asked only once whether I thought the Agilent decision had been the right one. I answered honestly. Nevertheless, my job now was to execute the decision. I said the toughest work would be disentangling information systems and adjudicating intellectual property. We'd fight over both, and both would be complex and costly. Ultimately we didn't fully separate and reconcile these until 2004.

The Board was an interesting collection of individuals. Sam Ginn and Phil Condit were the only Board members who were CEOs of Fortune 50 companies. I would rely on them heavily, and their voices carried great weight in the boardroom; they were the only members who understood from experience the complexities of managing a global company. Dick Hackborn, like many HP executives, was a technologist and engineer. Throughout his HP career he'd been known as a brilliant strategist who'd always relied on a hatchet man to carry out the tough operational work for him. He lived in Boise, Idaho, where the LaserJet printing business was headquartered, and he still interacted with many employees there. Jay Keyworth was a nuclear physicist who'd served as national science adviser during the Reagan administration. This is how he'd met Dave Packard. Patricia Dunn was the CEO, and later vice chairman, of an investment firm, Barclays Global Investors. I was told she had originally favored splitting HP further into separate computing and printing businesses, although her opinions were frequently hard to discern. Walter Hewlett and Susan Packard generally said the least during Board meetings.

In that September meeting, I talked with the Board about how we should spend our time and about my own role. I shared with them the conclusions of our Seascape meeting. Based on these, I needed to focus my efforts on strategy, balance and achieving potential. Under strategy I talked about putting more wood behind our nascent Internet strategy: E-services. We'd received good reaction from the marketplace when an announcement had been made in the spring; but if we were really going to deliver something, we would have to deploy our resources differently. (Over time, for example, we determined that every printer needed to be a networked device and that our computing infrastructure had to deliver the highest levels of availability. Both took real investment and a reorganization of our product development efforts.) I said we had to recapture leadership in the UNIX market and warned that we would return to the Board with a sizable investment proposal. Beyond these immediate decisions, we needed an ongoing process for strategic decision making. Strategy is really about choosing where to invest money, people and time; and over time we needed to make investment choices that were more than merely incremental improvements.

I said that making investment choices was but one side of the coin; the other side was the execution required to deliver on the strategy. We would have to improve our efficiency dramatically; unless we saved a lot of money, we couldn't afford to invest more. And without sharpened operational discipline, none of our investments would pay off.

I commented that both the original Corporate Objectives and the Values that underlay the HP Way represented great balance. The objectives stressed both profit and growth. The values stressed both teamwork and accountability. Balance is the art of leadership—leaders reject the tyranny of either/or and realize that equilibrium among many objectives is key to sustainable performance. And yet despite the wisdom of the founders, the organization was no longer balanced. We accentuated preservation over reinvention, products over customers, independence over interdependence, current profit over future growth, risk aversion over decision, and caution over speed. We needed to regain the appropriate balance, and my role would be to act as a counterweight where necessary, using my position and authority to offset the patterns and routines of the organization.

Finally, achieving our potential meant thinking differently about our expectations for performance and how we measured success. We needed to aim higher and expect more. We could no longer accept mediocrity. We had to measure our success in relative terms and against competitive alternatives. Success had always been defined as achieving plan. We had become an organization that set the bar low enough to walk over, and yet exceeding plan could still mean failure in the marketplace. Each business had its own plan. The only measure of the total company's performance was the semiannual profit-sharing plan. Profit sharing was distributed to employees based upon absolute, total-profit levels. There was no penalty for lack of growth, or inadequate performance relative to competitors, or failure to achieve overall HP objectives. Thus, although HP was missing nine quarters and underperforming, employees were receiving record payments. It was no wonder people believed everything was fine; they were being handsomely rewarded for the subpar performance. If we were to accomplish more, which we clearly had the potential to do, we'd have to both measure and reward success differently.

After we'd finished discussing all these things, someone asked what worried me most about the impending split. I said I'd seen AT&T lose an opportunity to redefine itself when it had spun off the assets of Lucent. Agilent was going through what I knew from experience was a difficult but very exciting process. When they came through on the other side, they'd be stronger and better than before. The people in the remaining Hewlett-Packard had as much tough, difficult work to execute the split as their colleagues in Agilent; yet we couldn't end up as simply the old company with less. We also needed to take an exciting journey and emerge stronger and better. We also needed to use the trauma of the split to reignite our energies and our enthusiasm. We needed to be as new a company as Agilent. We needed to be inspired.

When they asked how long I thought the change process at HP would take, I said at least three years. It seemed a very long time in those go-go days. We could not foresee the technology bust, or the terrorist attack, or the prolonged, four-year, global economic slowdown and stock market malaise that would make our journey even longer and harder than those three years I'd predicted. Still, sustainable change requires the right balance between patience and urgency. A successful transformation of a complex, tradition-bound company would take a long time under the best of circumstances, and yet we had to begin with speed and proceed with determination.

I was glad the executive team had heard the entire discussion. I began to speak to employees about strategy, balance and achieving our potential in coffee talks as I traveled around the company and around the world. If a company is productive, everyone has a role. People needed to know what I thought about my role as CEO. People needed to know the shape of change to come. I talked about my excitement and passion for the company. I reminded them that there was only one name on our paychecks, one name on the stock certificate, and one name our customers relied upon. And over time I'd use the most glaring examples of our disintegration into a thousand tribes. I'd tell them what customers said to me. I'd inform them that we had 150 different brands in the marketplace. The one example that said it all came from Susan Bowick. When we finally took the time to count them all, we discovered 1,500 internal Web sites devoted to employee training. Because every division had its own IT systems and HR staffs, each division had built its own Web sites. Employees could understand this; training was highly valued at HP, and they realized they weren't being served well.

In November the Board approved a historic change in the decades-old profit-sharing plan. We instituted a company performance bonus. Now our goals would be based on external benchmarks and relative performance. We would broaden those goals over time to include measures of growth and customer satisfaction in addition to profit. We would define aspirational, target and threshold levels of performance. We wanted to motivate people to strive for excellence, and aspirational goals were challenging and resulted in the highest rewards. If we fell short of aspirational performance but performed better than target, the rewards were greater than if we'd only achieved target goals. And threshold performance resulted in minimal payout; below this level no additional bonus was received. Bill Hewlett used to say "What gets measured is what gets done." HP had gotten from its employees exactly what it had asked of them. Now we needed employees to reach higher and to think about the outside world.

We would make other changes over time. For example, executives needed to become HP leaders, not simply business unit managers, and so a greater percentage of their pay would be driven by HP results. We included various measures of stock appreciation. After the Compaq acquisition we'd add specific measures of integration progress. Nevertheless, with the first introduction of the company performance bonus, several very important and new principles had been established. Rewards and metrics were used to drive performance and could be changed when different performance was required. The HP Way would not be destroyed because we'd changed the historic profit-sharing plan. We were capable of more, and so we would aspire to more. Winning meant more than delivering what you'd promised; winning meant delivering what was necessary. And excellence wasn't about never falling short; excellence was about always striving for more.

22 | Change Warriors

FROM AUGUST THROUGH NOVEMBER of 1999, my executive team and I discussed and deliberated. We met as the Executive Council, but I told each of these executives that they would come to council meetings wearing two hats. Each executive had always represented his or her own organizations and accountabilities. Now, in addition, they would come to the table with their HP hat on. They were the leadership team of the Hewlett-Packard Company, and together we would make the important strategic, operational and policy decisions of the firm. I was determined to build an aligned team that could make the tough choices necessary to guide the company into the twenty-first century. I had seen how important that kind of teamwork was to Lucent. And because strategy and operations are two sides of the same coin, we needed to talk about both. We would determine our strategy and decide what was necessary to accomplish that strategy. We would monitor our execution and correct course when necessary.

We decided to make major changes to three sides of the Leadership Framework. We had already agreed that leadership was our aspiration. In an Internet age, we'd determined that simply engineering solid, stand-alone products was inadequate as a strategy; instead, we needed to deliver always-on systems, networked devices and appliances, and services. We would return to our heritage of inventiveness and invest in R&D and innovation.

We'd concluded that we had to change our structure to consolidate eighty-seven separate product businesses into seventeen. These were to be managed within two major technology groups to maximize our ability to leverage platforms and R&D spending. We'd decided to bring together all the product development, manufacturing, management and marketing for both LaserJet and Inkjet into one unit. We had to eliminate the internal competition that existed between these two units. Carolyn Ticknor would become the executive vice president (EVP) for Imaging and Printing Systems. Likewise, we'd bring all of the computing-product generation into one organization. Duane Zitzner would become the EVP of Computing Systems. We knew we needed to spend hundreds of millions of incremental dollars to regain our lead in UNIX, but we also knew there was wasted and duplicative effort in R&D. In simple terms, Duane's job was to both spend what was required and save what was possible. We knew we could gain efficiency simply by standardizing how we did things across the company—whether in Finance or R&D.

We would pull together our customer-facing resources because we needed to simplify how we did business with the customer. We also needed to become more adept at selling systems solutions. Our customers were demanding more and more of these systems solutions, and our gross margins were higher when we provided a bundle of products and services rather than simply a stand-alone product. Until we asked a single sales force to focus on systems selling, no one could respond to the customer. We pulled all the sales and services resources that interacted with business customers into one unit, to be led by Ann Livermore; we consolidated the consumer-facing efforts into another unit headed by Antonio Perez. Now it would be our job to bring together the resources of HP on behalf of the customer; it wouldn't be our customers' job to figure out how to navigate through our complexity.

We would change the processes by which we managed the core functions of HR, Finance and IT to dramatically reduce our cost and complexity. We'd identified almost $2 billion in achievable cost reductions by eliminating redundancy and duplication. To achieve these savings, we would align these resources horizontally across the company instead of maintaining separate teams in each business unit. Although the resources would stay within the business units, we would ask the corporate VPs of each function to be accountable for achieving benchmark performance over time. Bob Wayman, for example, would now have CFOs reporting to him, and he would be accountable for delivering the company's financial systems at benchmark cost.

With the Board's approval of the company performance bonus, we'd now established new metrics. With the beginning of the new fiscal year in November, we'd labored over detailed business plans to drive accelerating growth and improved profitability. We'd established operational plans that represented what we were capable of and what was required to be competitive. They had risk associated with them, but without higher aspiration, higher performance doesn't happen.

Any one of these moves represented a major departure from an operating model that had survived virtually unchanged for sixty years. All of these moves together represented a huge amount of change for any company—more than I fully appreciated at the time. Yet each move was a logical response to a real problem and represented a real opportunity to improve our performance. We'd all agreed on the problems and the opportunities and the necessary improvements, and no one could think of a better solution.

We were taking a risk with wholesale change, but we had to start moving with sufficient velocity to actually progress forward. Incremental change is sometimes viewed as safer, but incrementalism often lacks the necessary force to overcome inertia and resistance. If change stalls, it fails. Once change is advanced, retreat is fatal. Sometimes you just have to burn the boats.

BY EARLY DECEMBER I'd shared our conclusions with the Board, and prior to that with Lew. Lew was supportive and made some helpful comments about the various executives' strengths and weaknesses. They'd each gone through the same leadership assessment that I had experienced during my recruitment, and so Lew shared their data with me. Some executives had a fairly accurate self-perception. Others clearly didn't remember their results from the assessment, or had ignored them.

We now scheduled a meeting with the extended leadership team of about three hundred people. We would share our decisions and enlist their support in executing the many changes. I met with my executive team the day before to finalize our agenda and approach. I would open the next day by describing the case for change. Ann, Duane, Carolyn and Antonio would then speak about their new roles, their new titles (for they were no longer to be called CEOs) and their new collaboration and accountability for improved performance. We would then begin to talk about the implementation of our plans.

As the day wore on, the passive-aggressive behavior I'd only caught glimpses of before now broke out into the open. Carolyn and Antonio could no longer agree. Their mutual distrust and dislike were apparently well known to the broader organization, but I now saw it clearly for the first time. Duane, despite the huge new responsibilities he had been given, kept worrying about what he was losing. He kept describing his concern as "coming from my guys," but it was clear he didn't want to relinquish any of his resources or his power. Ann Livermore was supportive, but she was, by nature, cautious. Bob Wayman was usually quiet and analytical. He was a strong supporter of the changes, but he'd let me take the lead in fighting for them. Debra Dunn, who at this point led our Strategy and Business Development efforts, and Susan Bowick were trying hard to help me, but they weren't the power players in the room, and so others ignored them.

What it all boiled down to was a last-ditch effort to back off our agreements and decisions. We covered and recovered the same ground. People stalled for time, trying to run the clock out before we faced the organization in the morning. When the moment of truth arrives, and people really have to commit publicly to a difficult course of action, they may challenge every aspect of it: the process used to make the decisions, the facts employed to support them, the leadership position of those who champion them. If the process is sound, if the facts are agreed upon and accurate to the best of everyone's knowledge and the decisions remain the best available option, a leader cannot blink. To blink when challenged in such circumstances is to lose the ability to choose and decide the next time. If strength is not demonstrated when strength is called for, a leader cannot lead as effectively again. To blink is to lose the support of all who've been supportive. If a leader cannot stand tall in the face of uncertainty, risk and adversity, no one else will either. Delay and indecision are a choice to do nothing. When the status quo is clearly unacceptable, leaders choose to act.

Toward the end of his tenure, John Young had tried to streamline and consolidate a lot of activities, but then Dave Packard had returned from what was by all accounts a frustrating two years at the Department of Defense, declared that John was "centralizing" too much of the company, and summarily fired him. The organization got the message and returned to the traditional productcentric business units and vertical command and control of resources. And in the handoff from John to Lew, people once again got the message that too much change was not what Dave Packard wanted.

By about four o'clock I'd had enough. I'd listened and reasoned and reviewed all that we'd discovered before. Now my team needed a reality check. I said, "Folks, we're not leaving this room until you are prepared to present our decisions and your agreements with one another. Dave Packard is not going to ride back into town on his white horse and save you from these changes." We stayed until eight o'clock that night. It wasn't pretty, but we got it done. And the next day we launched the broader HP management team into the reinvention of the company.

I HAD THOUGHT LONG and hard about how to make the case for change. I knew I couldn't order our people to change and that I would never earn the blind loyalty they reserved for Bill and Dave. But I also knew that people change if they truly want to, and so instead I would appeal to their intellect and to their pride.

First I showed a film of interviews with some of our customers. These customers said to our people what I'd heard: "You're falling behind, you're too difficult to deal with, you're late, you're slow, and you're always reactive. We need you to do better because we depend on you and we respect you." And then I showed them a film of themselves, from a similar meeting with Lew Platt two years ago. They'd said to each other then what I needed to say to them now.

Smart people usually know what needs to change in an organization. These managers had recognized all of the issues and opportunities we were now trying to address. Yet in two years virtually nothing had changed. They were self-conscious as they watched because they realized they had not been the change they sought; they had not led what they knew should be done.

Change takes more than an intellectual understanding of what's required. It takes the support of others, the recognition that retreat is far worse than moving ahead, and the fortitude to keep going. And it takes a decision to lead change. Change doesn't happen naturally. Leadership, on many levels and by many people, is required. This is why a critical mass of change warriors must be called upon. This is why bold action is needed when real change is necessary. This is why a leader cannot blink.

A company is a lot like a computer system. Both have purpose or mission. And both have hardware and software. A company's hardware is its structure, its processes, its plans, its metrics, its results. That hardware can be represented by income statements and balance sheets, by organization charts and job descriptions, by how-to manuals and objectives, by scorecards and reports. A company's software is its culture of values, habits, mind-sets and behaviors. Some may derisively dismiss all these things as "soft stuff" unworthy of a hard-nosed business manager's time. They don't understand how companies actually operate, and they don't appreciate that people are the producers of products and profit. A computer doesn't function without hardware and software, and neither does a company. Like a computer, a company can't perform better unless both hardware and software are upgraded. HP's software had to be upgraded. We had to have new ideas about ourselves and about change itself. We had to learn new habits for deciding things and working together. We had to rediscover what the original HP values actually meant.

On the morning of the second day of our meeting, during our question-and-answer session, one of our managers raised his hand and said, "Carly, you've talked about change. You've talked about taking risks and moving faster. Won't we make mistakes?"

Dave Packard said in *The HP Way*, "To remain static is to lose ground." By 1999, all of Hewlett-Packard's habits and practices were geared toward maintaining stasis. So often the instinct was to stand still until every contingency had been prepared for, until every question had been answered, until every possible risk had been defined. Some in Silicon Valley said that the best way to manage a technology company in fast-moving times was described by "Ready. Fire. Aim, aim, aim, aim." By this they meant that fast action and rapid-fire decision making was critical; and once a decision was made, you expended energy to make the decision right. The joke was that the HP management philosophy had become "Ready. Aim, aim, aim, aim . . ." No one ever fired until absolutely everything was perfect, and so no one ever fired. Susan Bowick used to describe this philosophy as an unwillingness to take the first step in a journey without being fully provisioned for every event that might occur along the way. By the time we had gathered all our provisions, we were too weighed down to move and the moment had passed.

Consensus decision making was celebrated as the ideal. There are, of course, times when consensus is important, and there are other times when an individual or small group decides on behalf of the larger group. At HP, however, a call for consensus was a very effective way of grinding the decision-making process to a halt. Too much time was required to make a decision because consensus meant that everyone had to say yes—and anyone could say no.

I answered the manager: "Yes, we will make mistakes. I will make them and you will make them—if we don't make mistakes, we're not trying anything new. The goal is not perfection; the goal is progress. And in a world that's moving faster all the time, an imperfect decision made in a timely fashion and executed well is better than a perfect decision made too late. We will make mistakes, but our goal should be to learn from them and not make the same mistake twice. When we fail or fall short or make a mistake, we will pick ourselves up, dust ourselves off, learn our lessons and move forward. That's what champions do." I would repeat this many, many times over the next five years.

At Lucent I'd sometimes said, "It's roughly right. Let's decide and move on." That language was much too sloppy for the engineering culture of HP. Now I coined the phrase "perfect enough." I'd say: "Our customers and our competitors will set our pace, and we will move when the decision is perfect enough."

When Bill and Dave had actively managed the company, it achieved $1 billion in revenues. In those days, a coffee talk with the top management could change the course of events. Even after they left active management, Bill's and Dave's words had huge weight and impact because of who they were. Now the new CEO's answer to one question, even with three hundred of the company's top managers listening, would not be sufficient to change people's mind-set or behavior. I didn't take this personally; it's just human nature and the nature of big companies.

I'd spent my whole career in big companies, and I knew that they are fundamentally different in degree and in kind from other organizations and, in particular, from small companies. By way of analogy, both a Jet Ski and an aircraft carrier are motorized, water-going vessels. Driving a Jet Ski takes knowledge and practice, yet even an experienced Jet Ski racer would be unable to captain an aircraft carrier. One can read every manual and take every class to learn how to command an aircraft carrier, but only with experience is the skill mastered. An aircraft carrier has a commander and many executive officers and thousands of people to perform important roles every day in order for the ship to fulfill its mission. It wasn't sufficient for three hundred managers to think differently about decision making and risk taking. Everyone needed to think differently. A software upgrade has to be systematic and systemic.

In particular, everyone needed to think differently about change. I began to quote Charles Darwin to employees: "It is not the strongest of the species who survive, nor the most intelligent, but those who are most adaptive to change." It was a simple, powerful statement to be remembered and repeated by many HP people to many of their colleagues. Change is not bad, change is necessary. Standing still is dangerous. Species that don't adapt become extinct. People who stop learning become old before their time. Companies that stop adapting and learning will fade over time and never regain their former glory.

I told employees about bullfighting. Every bull has his own *carencia*. This is the spot in the ring to which the bull returns when he is threatened. As the fight wears on, and the bull is threatened more frequently, he returns to his *carencia* again and again. And although the bull believes he retreats to safety, in fact he puts himself in graver danger. He becomes easier and easier to attack. We cannot return to our comfort zones. We cannot retreat to the familiarity of how it used to be.

We needed to understand that in a technology company that strived for leadership, change would be with us always. It wasn't once and done. So we began to talk about the journey we were embarking on. We could not rest on our laurels. Our history was not a guarantee of our future. History is something to be built upon as we journey to our future. And we needed to think differently about how decisions were made along the journey in a rapidly changing world. So we talked about sailing. A sailing vessel doesn't proceed in a straight line, although it must achieve forward momentum and sufficient velocity. A destination is determined, a course is set, and then the boat tacks, adjusting its sails to leverage or compensate for the changing winds and tides and weather. Arriving successfully and safely at the end of the journey requires flexibility.

Stories and analogies are powerful communications tools because they are simple and memorable. And change, particularly systemic change of a company's entire framework, requires communication that is authentic, clear, persistent, consistent and ubiquitous. Because people hear competing messages, or resist the message, or just don't hear it at all, my rule of thumb is that real change generally requires ten times the amount of communication you originally plan. And so I would use every forum, every speech and every venue to communicate with the employees of HP. No matter who I was talking to, no matter where I was in the world, I was talking to the employees of HP. People had to hear me, but they also had to believe me; and so my communication had to be authentic, balancing aspirations and risks, optimism and realism, and big ideas with small details. And my communication had to be consistent with other things they'd heard me say over time. And in all that communication, the most important ideas of all were that change was necessary and possible, and we could achieve what we chose.

Even before the acquisition of Compaq, almost eighty thousand HP employees were operating in more than 130 countries. Employees were inundated on a daily basis with messages from their local office, from their immediate boss, from their business unit, from the world around them. There were a thousand things beyond change that competed for their attention. When I first arrived at HP, I'd asked how I could communicate with all our employees at once. I was met with dumbfounded silence. No one had ever asked to do that before. Once a quarter, Lew Platt had made a videotape announcing the profit-sharing payout. The videotapes were mailed around the world, the text was sent out by e-mail (many different systems, not a single global system) and the audio was played in U.S. locations that had overhead loudspeaker systems. Beyond this process, simultaneous communication with everyone wasn't possible.

. . .

A S I HAD in every job before this one, I frequently traveled and visited employees all over the country and all over the world. It was a gesture of respect, and each time I visited a location, particularly one where they'd never seen the CEO before, people were appreciative. I always learned a lot in the process, and they came to know me better. I couldn't see and talk to every employee face-to-face, however. It was impossible to travel everywhere, and even if I could, it would take too long. I had to have other means of communicating effectively, and I had to have them quickly; otherwise, we'd run out of time and gas before the change process had even gotten under way. I needed to send powerful, meaningful signals to the people of HP.

Ultimately we would build one Web site for company information and employee communication, and we would globally integrate our voice-mail and e-mail systems. We would have regular, virtual and physical global senior leadership meetings and consistent materials to help managers pass the communications on to their own organizations. We would have virtual, all-employee meetings twice a year through global videocast. I would regularly send e-mails to every employee around the world on subjects as varied as personnel moves, 9/11, quarterly earnings and tsunami relief. This global communications system was a huge tool in accelerating the integration of Compaq and was vital in keeping everyone on the same page and moving in the same direction. But we couldn't wait until all that was done to start moving. We had to begin the journey, and the message needed to be loud enough and clear enough to cut through all the noise and clutter and resistance and misunderstanding.

W E ALL KNOW that a picture is sometimes worth a thousand words. Likewise, in a company with rich history and lots of mythology, symbols are very important—they're a kind of shorthand that everyone understands. At HP no symbol was more potent than the original garage where it all started, and no picture evoked more pride than the one of young Bill and Dave, in that garage, inventing their first product. Systemic change at HP meant change from within, and that required reaching the change warriors all over the company. They needed to be awakened and called to action.

They needed to hear that we are one company, not a thousand tribes; that our company had been founded by inventors, and inventors build the future; that if we look to where and how it all started, we will find the wisdom and the inspiration to move forward and perform better. Because a leader's motivations and intentions are always scrutinized, employees needed to hear one other thing: that their new CEO celebrated the legacy of HP with pride. She would stand with the change warriors and be held accountable in the journey that lay ahead. She believed it was possible and she believed in them.

To inspire as well as educate, a group of us wrote The Rules of the Garage, which were explicit renditions of how we believed things must have operated in the early days. Those rules were the first step in deconstructing and demystifying the HP Way. We needed to be explicit about the values and behaviors and practices that HP was really all about: for example, "Radical ideas are not bad ideas." Collaboration means sharing and adopting best practices. We described this philosophy as "Share tools, ideas. Keep the tools unlocked." We had to be externally, not internally, focused. "The customer defines a job well done." HP was about excellence, not entitlement: "Make a contribution every day."

We went back to the original HP brand—the one inlaid in the brick of the HP Labs building—and added a single word beneath it: INVENT. We launched the brand with a new ad campaign in November at the annual Comdex show (an IT trade show held in Las Vegas that went defunct with the dot-com bust). At my speech there, I'd talked about my vision for the company and closed with a two-minute film. In those crazy boom days of 1999, we reminded everyone what Bill and Dave had really done. We used lots of old photographs and video footage. I narrated the first ads and stood by the garage at their conclusion. While I had been a reluctant participant in the pose, some employees had come up with the idea, and they as well as others had begged me to do it. "We need to know you're with us for the whole ride, Carly."

I also quietly began negotiations to buy back the original garage, and Dave and Lucille's first home where she'd baked those cookies, from the landlord who'd been renting out the property for twenty-five years. It seemed to me that we should protect and restore the house and the garage so that the men who had invented there would inspire many more generations of HP people. We spent $2.1 million to buy the property and slightly more to restore it. It took quite a while to finish because the responsible manager, who was deeply emotionally attached to the project, became ill with cancer. We could not bear to take the work away from him until after he'd tragically succumbed to the ravages of his illness. The home and garage were finally opened to the public in 2005. (I was sad that I wasn't even asked to attend.)

Before we finalized the new branding and the advertising campaign, I invited the extended Hewlett and Packard families to attend an evening cocktail event outside Bill's and Dave's HP offices. In addition to their children, I invited their grandchildren. We ended up with quite a crowd. Many of the grandchildren were seeing their grandfathers' famous offices for the first time. The children were getting together after some apparent period of separation. Most of them had never been asked to visit HP before. I spoke with them about my respect for their fathers and their families. I shared with them my hopes for the company's return to leadership and excellence. I explained to them the brand launch and the ad campaign. I showed them the two-minute film about Bill and Dave. At its conclusion many wiped their eyes. I was among them, and I still tear up when I see those pictures and hear the music. And Jim Hewlett said quietly, "I haven't been proud of HP for a long time. I want to be proud again."

Some in the media attacked my appearance in the ads as hubris. Maybe Lee Iacocca can do it, or Hank McKinnell or Victor Kiam, but somehow it was different for them. Some old-timers said it was heresy. They whispered that I was trying to replace Bill and Dave. Over time this group would point to my picture hanging beside Bill's and Dave's in company lobbies as more evidence of my designs on the founders' preeminence; it seemed irrelevant that both John Young's and Lew Platt's pictures had hung in the same spot when each was CEO. They wondered why I'd chosen the new logo; was it to excise the names Hewlett and Packard? Perhaps they'd forgotten we'd chosen the logo that Bill and Dave preferred, or perhaps the facts just didn't fit the story. During the proxy battle our opponents fed all these examples of heresy to the media, which dutifully reported them from the true believers' perspective. As is frequently the case, the critics, even when smaller in number, are always louder than the advocates.

Despite the controversy, I knew the change warriors had received the clarion call. I read it in their e-mail, and I saw it in their faces. Yes, customers and partners and competitors had gotten the message too, and that was important. More important, however, inside the company the pace began to quicken, the heads began to lift, the excitement began to build. People began to believe that perhaps HP could reinvent itself. We could reimagine our future and return to our roots of invention. Past and future were not thesis and antithesis; they were the synthesis required for change.

The critics who said I wanted to replace Bill and Dave didn't understand big companies or my motivation. Hewlett-Packard had become too large, too complex and too global to be led through force of personality or dictate or fiat. Hewlett-Packard was clearly bigger than me, but it had also become bigger than Bill and Dave. A complex, global company is managed through a holistic system of strategies and objectives; structures, processes and practices; metrics and rewards; and culture, behavior and mind-set. The system must be coherent and deeply embedded in the organization. Change can only begin if its force is greater than the weight of history and the power of the status quo. And a leader who respects the people and the institution he or she is privileged to lead strives for sustainable performance that will continue long after the leader is gone. "A good leader is he whom men revere. An evil leader is he whom men depise. A great leader is he of whom the people say, 'We did it ourselves.'"

23 | You're Exactly the Same

THAT FIRST AUTUMN, I met about twenty of the old guard who came to view me as a heretic. One day out of the blue, Rosemary Hewlett, Bill's second wife, called the office. She said, "Carly, Bill and I would like to invite you and Frank to lunch at our place." I was truly touched by the invitation. I told her how much I looked forward to meeting them both.

When we arrived, Rosemary, Bill and about twenty other men whom I hadn't expected and didn't know were sitting outside by the pool. It turned out they were all retired HP managers. Bill was in a wheelchair and unable to talk. He was so bent over that I could not meet his eyes. So I knelt down on the cement by his chair and told him how much I respected him and how honored and humbled I was to be leading the company that bore his name. And then, to lighten the mood somewhat, I told him what a handsome fellow he'd been and how the ladies of HP still swooned over the pictures of him as a mountain climber (Bill had had quite a reputation as a ladies' man). He mouthed something unintelligible and shortly thereafter his attendant wheeled him out for his lunch, which he habitually ate in private. The rest of us adjourned to the dining room.

Rosemary sat at one end of the table and instructed me to sit at the other. My inquisitors, for that is what they turned out to be, arrayed themselves along either side of the table. And for the next three hours they asked every question they could think of. At the end of it all, one of them said, "Well, Carly, I think you get an A plus." Rosemary was gracious and flattering. The rest said nothing. Much later this group would become the core of the resistance to the merger and to my leadership.

I'm sorry I never got to meet Bill Hewlett when he was more vigorous. I'm sorry I never met Dave Packard. Jay Keyworth had once said to me, "I wish you could have met Dave."

"I wish it too. We are such different people, but I feel I understand him."

"You're not different; you're exactly the same. Maybe Dave was a little taller, but you both have a broad, humanistic perspective. Like Dave, you're bold, uncompromising and focused on excellence."

It was one of the nicest things anyone had ever said to me. Later he would describe me as "the son Dave Packard never had." While it was a cruel thing for him to say about his friend David, Jay meant that I both understood and had passion for the business Dave had built.

In November, and without warning, Lew called for an executive session at the November Board meeting and requested that I be excused. He talked to the Board for more than an hour. When the meeting broke, Dick Hackborn, who would take over from Lew as chairman the next month, came to see me. We sat in the conference room where I met with the Executive Council.

"Carly, the Board has asked me to talk with you. Lew says you're moving too fast and making too many changes. He believes you haven't consulted him adequately. He says he's shared his concerns with you, and you've ignored him."

I was caught off guard. It seemed very early to be getting cold feet, and the Board in general, and Dick in particular, had frequently conveyed to me their frustration and impatience with Lew. My heart was pounding because I knew, suddenly, that we were at an important moment of truth for this Board.

"What did the Board say?"

"Well, frankly, we were all stunned into silence until finally Sam Ginn said, 'Well, what did we expect when we hired her?' Carly, has Lew talked to you about this?"

"Dick, Lew and I haven't ever had this kind of conversation. In fact, he seemed quite supportive of the organizational changes we're planning. But what the Board thinks now is more important than what Lew thinks. I can't be on probation with this Board. We're either in this change process together, or it won't happen. It's too tough. We must be aligned."

"You're right. We're with you."

I was troubled. Was Dick being straight with me or not? Later that same day, Jay came to see me. He said, "Do you mind if I give you some advice? Woo Dick. Woo Dick." It seemed a very odd choice of words. It seemed to discount the opinions of the other Board members. Over time I would learn that Jay didn't have much use for most of the other Board members. Although he respected Sam and Phil as successful CEOs, he dismissed the rest, and he clearly thought he and Dick were the guardians of Bill and Dave's flame.

I had already decided that I would be much more open and conversational in meetings than Lew had been with the Board. They seemed to appreciate the more informal, informative dialogue, and I truly wanted them to know everything I was doing and thinking. They'd recruited me for a change effort that was clearly even more difficult than they'd described, and we needed to have a common point of view about what was necessary.

This Board and I were embarking on a challenging process together. We needed to be on the same page, and that meant we had to have a common understanding of both our strategic choices and our operational issues. I'd served on the Boards of several large companies, and I knew that the role of a Board member is inherently difficult. The management team's job is to manage the company and produce results. A board meets six or eight times a year and cannot possibly know enough of the details of a business to manage it. And yet a Board must represent the company's owners, and this means knowing enough to ask the right questions. A Board member must determine whether a company is on track or off track. A company can go off track on matters of ethics, or because of poor strategic choices, or because of inadequate performance discipline. A company can go off track if its leadership is no longer willing to make the right moves or decisions. I concluded that the HP Board could do its job only if it had a full understanding of our leadership framework and all the choices we were making about that framework. In addition to the regular review of our current results and our upcoming financial plans, in practical terms this meant we would also discuss strategic choices, organizational structures, performance measurement, our ethics programs, our cultural reinvention and our senior personnel. I also decided that this Board needed to have as much information and access to what was going on in the company as possible. My actions and decisions had to be totally transparent to them. I began inviting them regularly to management meetings such as the one we had in December. I encouraged them to meet with employees and managers without me, which became a regular occurrence for Dick and Jay. I encouraged ongoing conversations with the executive team. And over time we upgraded our Board Web site to permit Board members access to the same information available to any employee. I knew from my service on other Boards that this kind of interaction between all levels of company management and a Board outside of Board meetings was unusual; so was their access to such a large amount of detailed information. Over time, some of my management team would complain about just how much interaction there was; there were times when Board members could distract people from their important daily work. After the merger, many of the Compaq Board members expressed real surprise at the nature of Board interactions with employees and managers.

There were other downsides to my approach. Board members sometimes failed to exercise restraint and ignored where their job stopped and a manager's job started. Board members usually only delved into areas that interested them, so they were getting a limited view of the company and lacked perspective. Dick and Jay, being technologists, loved to meet with the technical teams. Because they lacked operational grounding, they failed to appreciate the consequences of their suggestions. They sometimes tried to redirect R&D spending on the fly. Board members would propose all kinds of ideas—sometimes in Board meetings, sometimes in their own meetings with employees.

Some of these ideas were bad ones; I was told early on to fire Bob Wayman, for example. They thought he had been a weak CFO prior to my arrival. In truth, he had been, but he'd also never been given a real chance to do the job. I argued we should give him a chance, and with his new responsibilities, Bob Wayman developed into a world-class CFO. Some of these ideas were good ones; Dick and Jay came to me with the idea of the Compaq merger. I, and others on the management team, spent a lot of time trying to sort out the good ideas from the bad ones.

More ideas are always better than fewer, however, and the benefits of an open, informal approach outweighed the risks. I knew I should not try to control the information flow. I didn't want to risk misunderstandings and miscommunications. Alignment and trust are achieved through transparency, common information, and candid and ongoing dialogue. The management team had to be aligned, and so did the Board. What we were attempting in the reinvention of HP was too risky and too difficult to operate any other way. I also encouraged the Board to engage in regular executive sessions without me. I didn't want frustrations building up, as I'd seen happen on other Boards. Communications from these sessions would come from Dick, as the chairman, and later, after he'd stepped down, from the chairman of Nominating, Sam Ginn, or the chairman of Compensation, Phil Condit.

In January of 2000 we held a three-day off-site strategy meeting for the Board and the senior management team. We talked about our evolving strategy, our plans for the coming year and our challenges. All the members of my Executive Council attended. I'd asked John Chambers, of Cisco, to come and address the Board. He knew HP well; he knew me well because we'd competed fiercely against each other when I was at Lucent, and I thought the Board could use an outsider's perspective. He bluntly gave us no more than a fifty-fifty chance of success.

At the end of those three days, the Board convened one of their regular executive sessions. When they asked me to rejoin them, we talked about our various strategy choices and how useful we'd all found the intensive, detailed nature of the meeting. Finally, I said, "I must be candid with this Board and tell you that I've been very troubled since your last executive session. I was taken aback by Lew's comments, and I need to know whether I have your support for the program we've laid out here." I would make it a habit for my entire tenure to continually ask Board members for feedback on what they'd heard at a meeting, to express my own concerns and to solicit theirs.

The Board's support was unanimous. Susan Packard spoke up. "Carly, I feel bad that we've caused you distress. Your approach to the CEO job is so different. It's so refreshing to be talking about ideas and not just looking at pages of numbers. We didn't really understand Lew's motivation at the time. I think he was bitter."

Much to my regret, and as she had planned for some time, Susan Packard would leave the Board in 2000, and she and I would later end up on opposite sides during the proxy battle. Always, however, Susan was candid, empathetic and a class act. She carries on the David and Lucille Packard legacy with dignity and competence.

WHEN I GAVE THE COMMENCEMENT ADDRESS at Stanford University, my alma mater, in June 2001, I described my arrival at Hewlett-Packard as the discovery of a place where my values and my character were at home. It was why I had accepted the position, despite all the challenges; I believed HP was a company of "unique values and character . . . a company capable of making technology and its benefits accessible to all."

One of Hewlett-Packard's original corporate objectives reads: "The betterment of our society is not a job to be left to a few. It is a responsibility to be shared by all." Dave Packard once said: "People wrongly assume that our proper end is profit. Profit is what makes all the other ends possible." Bill and Dave challenged their engineers not simply to invent, but to invent things that were both useful and significant—useful in that the invention would serve a real purpose, significant in that it had a real impact on people. HP was to be a company that invented for the many, not simply for the privileged few.

At the dawn of the twenty-first century, the ferment of networked information technology seems to me to be the modern equivalent of the Renaissance. I had studied medieval history because I was fascinated by how humanity progressed from a period of darkness and fear to one of optimism and profound belief in the power of human potential. The Renaissance was fundamentally about the liberation of individual imagination. Today the Internet has created a new form of communication that is open, democratic, immediate, and nonhierarchical. The digital, mobile, virtual, personal world is one in which the traditional barriers of time, geography, access, wealth, power and position begin to fall. Individual potential can be unleashed. We are living in an era that's defined by the power of ideas and the power of connections to knowledge, information and each other. Smart people with all kinds of wonderful ideas live everywhere in the world.

A powerful corporation has global reach and therefore global responsibility. Of the one hundred largest economies on earth, corporations represent fifty-two of them. A corporation can and must make a positive difference in the world. And technology can help unlock people's potential as never before in human history.

My profound belief in these tenets made Hewlett-Packard a deeply satisfying place to be. The company had the right character, as reflected in its values. The company had the right capability with its focus on open systems and standards-based technologies to serve consumers as well as businesses and governments. The company had a history of collaboration with governments, schools and community leaders. And nothing made me prouder than to encourage, galvanize, celebrate and support the intrinsic goodness and desire of HP people everywhere to make a contribution to their communities.

In early 2000 Debra Dunn and I began a conversation about how to focus HP's philanthropic efforts more effectively. Like everything else in the company, philanthropy had become an overlarge collection of good but incoherent, discrete and underfunded projects. Although HP employees had a lot of passion, all these projects were disconnected from the rest of the business and weren't a high priority for anyone on the executive team. As CEO, I felt it was my job to set the tone at the top. Exercising our responsibilities as a corporate citizen of the world wasn't just a nice thing to do; it was an integral part of how our company would do business. We would do well and do good.

For the first time we looked at all our community-based projects across the company and around the world. We established our priorities as education and community development. Each of our approved programs would receive enough funding and management attention to actually make a sustainable difference. If a program had insufficient impact, or was not among our priorities, we would, after an appropriate transition, discontinue our efforts there.

In education we concentrated on identifying and mentoring high school students from disadvantaged communities to achieve competence in math and science. We provided scholarships and internships to these students, and we worked closely with high schools and universities. These kinds of efforts certainly made a difference in young people's lives, and they became core programs for many schools. They also helped our company do well over the long term: the IT industry will not have enough talented engineers and scientists unless we reach and educate those who are today underaccessed and underserved.

At the same time, we focused on community development through access to technology, training, entrepreneurship and partnership. Whether in Houston or South Africa, San Diego or India, every community touched by the people of HP is better for it. We committed management time, attention and money in these communities for a period of three years. We focused on building sustainable programs and capabilities and did much good. Over time, however, community development also means business development, and we needed to create new markets and new customers for our products. The developing nations of the world represent the fastest-growing markets for IT products. In the United States, all our research told us that the HP brand was well known among white, middle-aged men; women, youth and minorities didn't know us or buy us. We would, of course, reposition our brand and redesign our products to address this issue, but our community development activities also resonated deeply. They were substantive proof of our claims for the brand. We wanted to make a difference as well as make a sale.

Our efforts to make a positive impact in the world and in people's lives were not acts of charity, but rather of enlightened self-interest. These programs, therefore, would be reviewed with the Executive Council and the Board just as every other business priority was. Philanthropy had always captured the passion of HP people. Now we would approach it with operational discipline as well. We would measure the impact of our efforts, and we would require professionalism from our partners as well as from ourselves.

Debra would eventually manage these programs worldwide. She, and the people she worked with all over the world, made a real and positive difference. They did good, they helped the company do well, and they were leaders.

24 | Big Ideas and Small Details

AT HP WE NEEDED to learn how to think and act horizontally for basic reasons of efficiency and effectiveness. We were a multibillion-dollar company that procured literally billions of dollars of components and supplies, and yet we negotiated with our suppliers as eighty-seven separate entities. We didn't get the best deals as a result. We vastly overspent on technology because no one shared resources. Our spending on payroll and financial processes alone was worth billions of dollars of savings.

And we couldn't think as our customers did. While they thought everyone at HP worked for the same company, we knew nothing about them as HP customers. We didn't know how much they bought from us in total, and we didn't know what they thought about us as a company. We lacked the knowledge, information and inclination to serve them as HP. When customers bought systems composed of multiple products, they ended up putting those products together themselves; each organization developed and delivered its products, but no one thought it was the organization's responsibility to manage the entire process on behalf of the customers.

All my experience from Lucent told me that nothing would be more difficult at HP than learning the new skill of process-based horizontal collaboration. People worked together within a management unit organized around a product. A team was defined by an organization chart, not by an opportunity, or a problem to be solved or even a customer requirement. Unless we learned how to define, manage and control horizontal processes with efficiency and discipline, we could not lower our costs, improve our profitability or accelerate our growth.

HP's history made horizontal collaboration particularly difficult, but building horizontal processes is a management challenge faced by leaders in every kind of institution. The twentieth century was an era in which problems were solved and knowledge was advanced within vertical chains of command. Alfred P. Sloan gave us the organization chart of the modern business and advanced the practice of modern management. In universities, specialized departments formed the organizing principle for learning and the advancement of knowledge. In government, whether state, local or national, a mission has always been performed within a silo; as citizens we all know how frustrating it is when those silos don't communicate with one another.

In the increasingly complex, global world of the twenty-first century, where networked technology and communications dominate commerce, science and government, vertical chains of command are no longer sufficient to solve our problems or capture our opportunities. We see the most exciting advances in science occurring at the intersections of disciplines like biology and engineering; that was the revelation of my study of neural networks at MIT, for example, and it is the basis of the science of nanotechnology. We see disaster recovery efforts hampered by organizations' inability to work across the traditional boundaries between governmental departments and between state, local and federal governments. We see that potential pandemics like bird flu require horizontal collaboration among many entities and many nations. Perhaps the most dramatic example is occurring before our eyes in the intelligence community. Whereas the CIA and FBI used to operate on the basis of compartmentalized information and a need to know, now the challenge is to share information across a vast, horizontal network of allies in other departments and in other countries in a fast, effective manner.

Horizontal collaboration is fundamentally different behavior from the vertical command and control of resources. It requires accepting account-ability and yet sharing responsibility and information. It requires an appre-ciation of the important role played by others. For example, a product developer must appreciate the role of an installer; products can be designed so they are excessively difficult to install in a customer's location, or they can be designed differently. Each organization must also accept its impact on others and on the outcome of the whole process. HP had to adapt by learn-ing new habits of collaboration across organizational boundaries rather than simply teaming within boundaries. A leader's job is to build capability and confidence, and so very often a leader's job is to provide the opportunity for people to learn new skills.

Part of our strategy to regain leadership in UNIX was to release a very high-end UNIX server we called Superdome. It would be the largest and most complex computing platform the company had ever released. We would be competing for the very first time with IBM's largest computers. We intended to introduce it to the market in September of 2000. A successful launch of Superdome required a great product that performed to complex and exacting specifications. It required identifying the right set of first cus-tomers who could benefit from the product's capabilities and then persuad-ing them to buy the product. We would need to develop new, effective customer training. HP would need to accept responsibility for the successful installation of the entire system; customers wouldn't be able to put this one together on their own. In short, to get it right, virtually every department would have to work together, and we'd have to think about this from the cus-tomer's point of view. We had to get a product from the research lab to the customer's premises; this was a horizontal process that cut across multiple departments and multiple chains of command. We needed to learn how to define, execute, measure and manage this process.

Just as strategy and execution are two sides of the same coin, so change occurs through both big ideas and small details. I gathered teams of HP peo-ple from every organization that would be involved in the launch of Super-dome, from R&D to sales, from market research to technical support to installation. Because this wasn't about bosses ordering people to do things, but rather people learning new skills, we gathered managers from all levels. And for months we met and agreed upon the details of software releases, installation techniques, how trouble reporting would occur, who our first customers might be.

The organization learned many things in the course of these meetings, and I learned a lot about the organization. People were exposed to other disciplines within the business; engineers figured out that maybe marketers had a role after all, and salespeople learned that not every feature is worth developing. Product developers began to think about manufacturing and installation. We developed a way to measure how a customer actually might define success; we called it Total Customer Experience (TCE). If the product was developed on time and to specification, but the installation failed, the Total Customer Experience would suffer. It was insufficient for each player to do his or her part; all the players had to do their parts well and in concert to create a complete process and experience that satisfied the customer.

Today Total Customer Experience is a metric and a set of programs that are deeply embedded in the fabric of HP. TCE is measured regularly, goals for constant improvement are established, and people are paid based on the TCE results. TCE cannot be improved upon without horizontal collaboration across every organization that touches or affects a customer.

Superdome is one of HP's most profitable and successful products, and its rollout to customers was hailed as one of our best introductions of a new product in the company's history. (Some in the ever-skeptical media called it a Superbomb in September of 2000, but eventually they had to admit they were wrong.) HP people saw real, tangible benefit from cooperating across boundaries; and over time this new way of working became more habitual. The practice of bringing together the people who really needed to do the work, regardless of level, rather than bringing managers of the same level together who would then "cascade" directions to their teams, also became a new habit. For example, we would use this same practice to drive the extremely successful integration of Compaq and HP as well as to launch the company into digital entertainment.

Over time we would extend our learning into every process within the company. Ultimately we would require managers to define process maps and metrics so that our horizontal collaboration had the same operational rigor and discipline as any other aspect of our business. We expected continual improvement in the efficiency of every process. Even after the integration of Compaq was complete, for example, we still knew we could save one billion dollars every year in our supply-chain processes.

Horizontal is not the same as *centralized*. Centralized decision making is traditional, vertical, command-and-control behavior where decisions are made in a single central location. Horizontal decision making is distributed across many organizations and locations. Each decision maker knows his or her role by virtue of the process map. Each individual decision can be measured, but the efficacy of the whole process must also be measured.

People frequently confuse horizontal and centralized decision making. Sometimes at HP this confusion was genuine, and sometimes it was an effective resistance technique because it was built into the culture: centralization was bad. Bill and Dave had always lauded the virtues of decentralized units. The heads of the various business units wanted to control power rather than share it. Although they expected to be trusted and respected, they were not prepared to accord the same to others. And some people simply lack the experience to appreciate that well-designed processes can drive behavior as effectively as commands.

HP people had traditionally been promoted within a single business or function on the basis of subject-matter expertise. This deep and narrow experience could be an important ingredient in a manager's capabilities, but it wasn't sufficient preparation for a leader. In fact, subject-matter expertise became an impediment to leadership for some HP people. Managers at very high levels in the organization would spend most of their time on details that their subordinates could, and were eager to, handle. As a result, top managers weren't spending enough time on leadership development or strategic thinking. Very senior people sometimes couldn't see the forest for the trees. They couldn't see the big picture or focus on the essence of the situation.

In June 2000 we formally introduced the Leadership Framework to the senior managers of HP. And with that introduction I quoted from Chinese philosophy, "The great leader is he of whom the people say, 'We did it ourselves.' " Our leaders needed to focus on setting the right framework for the organization. Are we allocating our resources consistent with our strategy? Is our strategy sound? Are we organized and operating efficiently and effectively? Are we measuring the right things, and are our results acceptable? If not, what must we do to improve the performance of the organization? And are we as role models portraying the values and behavior we need? Are we exhibiting the right mind-sets and attitudes? Are we teaching our people new skills and capabilities? These are the proper questions for leaders in the twenty-first century. Command-and-control is no longer adequate to the task, so we coined the phrase "Set the frame and set people free." A leader's job is to set the frame so that the people a leader serves can do the right jobs in the right way to the best of their abilities. A leader's job is to build lasting capability into the organization he or she serves.

These management meetings were serious events where attendance and participation were mandatory, but we also needed to have some fun as a team. From our first senior leaders' meeting through the last I would attend, skits and contests always played an important part in the team building. At one meeting we asked teams to create videos of the "old HP" and the "new HP." At another we asked teams to pick, and sing, theme songs for the company. We always discovered wonderful hidden talent on the management team. All of this was harmless fun and helped people blow off steam and get to know one another better. And poking fun at the boss was always an important and frequently hilarious part of these events; you can bet that the alleged hairdresser on the airplane was always good for a laugh!

Bob Knowling was an operational executive I'd known for some time. He'd led many massive change efforts in his career at large companies, and he had also been the CEO of several smaller technology companies. I asked Bob to speak to our senior leaders at this meeting. I wanted them to hear from an experienced outsider how difficult change was and why their personal commitment to leading change was required. Jay Keyworth and Sam Ginn heard his presentation. They were deeply impressed and would later enthusiastically endorse Bob's nomination to the Board. He was unanimously approved.

All my experience taught me that leaders are made, not born. Leadership doesn't just happen; leadership can be taught and developed. A vital part of HP's reinvention was to build leaders from managers. And so, over multiple years, we redesigned all of our management training curricula. We benchmarked multiple companies and industries and designed a unique set of leadership development courses and experiences that came to be known as Winning-Edge Leadership. We made the fundamental decision that talent was a company asset, not a single division's asset, and we began to expect rotation of senior managers among different businesses and departments in order to broaden the managers' experience and perspective. We reviewed the leadership potential of our senior managers with the Board on an annual basis. The Executive Council conducted regular talent reviews in which we would sit together and decide how to develop the most promising managers into leaders.

Leaders can be made, but not every manager can become a leader. Leaders are defined by character, capability and collaboration. It became clear that Antonio and Carolyn could not collaborate effectively. Both would leave. Others would follow. It is never easy to ask someone to leave a business, but a leader must sometimes hurt the few to protect the many. Both before and especially after the merger, each time someone left HP at a senior level, there would be reports in the media that they had left because of me. I was too difficult, too controlling, taking the company in the wrong direction, and so on. There are many competent people, fewer who combine competence and character, and fewer still who are also able to partner effectively with others. A few left of their own accord when it became obvious they would not get the positions they thought they deserved. I watched with interest as male CEOs fired people and were hailed as "decisive." I was labeled "vindictive." I watched with interest as well when six female vice presidents left HP after my departure, and no one thought the pattern was worth commenting on.

By September of 2000, all the obvious metrics seemed to be moving in the right direction. The stock was up strongly, our revenues were growing faster and profits were improving. Dick Hackborn insisted on stepping down as chairman (much to my great surprise he began talking to me about it in February and would not stay past September), and I was named to the additional post. The Board announced a two-for-one stock split. After a somewhat rocky analysts meeting in December of 1999, we had a big success in June, and the stock rose $13 in a single day.

We held our first all-employee meeting via global videocast. The energy and excitement was exhilarating. These virtual "town hall" meetings became an important opportunity to review accomplishments, talk about upcoming events and plans, and get everyone in the company to share a common vocabulary and a common vision. We would regularly update employees about our decisions regarding each facet of the Leadership Framework. The global videocasts were also opportunities for employees to learn something about their own company. In my many meetings with employees around the world, I was always startled by how little people knew about HP. Perhaps I shouldn't have been surprised. Employees spend their days working on their own challenges, and for many, many years the only companywide issues of importance were the Profit Sharing Plan, the HP Way and the founders. I thought it was important to broaden our employees' perspectives by sharing with them the work of their colleagues around the company and the world. HP people everywhere made a difference every day for customers, for communities and for each other, and we needed to acknowledge, celebrate and understand that. I truly loved talking with the people of HP about the people of HP. I took intense pleasure in seeing their pride when they realized they'd accomplished more than they thought was possible.

Dan Plunkett would regularly visit me and ask a single, all-important question: "What are you worried about?" Now I answered: "It's been too easy. We haven't even started, and people think we're finished. This first year is only the end of the beginning. We have a long, long way to go."

W HEN I ARRIVED at HP, I was keenly aware that I was leading more than a company; I was leading an institution of special significance. HP had pioneered technologies as well as work practices. Hewlett and Packard had demonstrated how much difference a company's leadership could make in the community, and they personally helped build the ecosystem of collaboration and innovation that formed the special milieu of Silicon Valley.

Any CEO embarking on a major change program must think beyond a ninety-day time horizon. Institutional reinvention always takes years, not quarters. Because this was HP, I felt a special burden. Once begun on our journey, we could not falter and we could not fail. We were risking much, but failure to follow through on our plans would risk much more. The role of a CEO is to think about years, not quarters. Quarterly results are a measure of past decisions and actions, and a CEO must always face forward. Sustainable performance and operational excellence must be achieved and choices must be made for the long-term health of the business. I do not believe a CEO should manage quarterly earnings or manage the stock price (they are frequently the same thing). A CEO's job is to manage the company and to do so with discipline by making the right choices, building the required capability, setting appropriate goals and creating a culture of excellence, accountability and integrity. The stock price has to take care of itself, and over time it will.

A company's stock price is important, but in my opinion, a company's stock price has become too important. For many, the stock price has become a proxy for everything from the company's competitive position to the competence and accomplishment of the CEO. And although many pundits will say it isn't so, or shouldn't be true, the reality is that nothing is more important to the stock price than a company's quarterly performance against analysts' estimates. When a company misses these estimates, it's never good for the stock or the CEO.

In a large, complex company undergoing massive change, people cannot and will not execute perfectly every ninety days. When people are learning new things, they will make mistakes. Every mistake reveals where additional work is necessary. Each shortfall is an opportunity to make progress. During my twenty-three quarters as CEO, HP missed three quarters of significance: the fourth quarter of 2000, the third quarter of 2003 and the third quarter of 2004. Each of these misses revealed real problems in the organization that needed to be fixed.

In the fourth quarter of 2000 we were still compensating our sales force based on orders rather than revenues. This had been the practice at HP for many, many years because it was easier to track orders rather than revenue to a particular salesperson or team. In a period of relatively slow growth, this system worked adequately because orders and revenues grew at approximately the same rates. We nevertheless were in the process of changing the system because we wanted salespeople to appreciate that a sale isn't truly made until the customer is satisfied.

By the fourth quarter of 2000, we'd ratcheted up our growth rate to 17 percent. This was good news; we were asking the organization to aspire to more, and people were responding. By the fourth quarter, however, the orders were coming in much faster than systems could be installed and revenue booked. We were paying for higher sales expense in one quarter, while the higher revenues weren't recognized until subsequent quarters. This mismatch was large enough to cause us to miss analyst estimates in the fourth quarter. We would have changed the compensation programs sooner if we could have, but the modifications took time and investment. We didn't yet have the IT systems in place to track revenues by salesperson or team, and we couldn't pay people accurately unless we could measure them accurately.

In 2003 and 2004 our misses occurred in the sales organization as well. Our miss in 2003 revealed that the sales force was inappropriately paying multiple teams for the same sale. Both systems and personnel changes were made. In 2004 we uncovered more systems issues related to products sold and revenues booked by our channel partners. Once again, systems and personnel changes were made.

Every one of these misses revealed real operational issues that were buried too deep in the organization. We fixed the problems each time, and we did not make the same mistakes twice. We were a stronger and better organization for the lessons we learned. Although many people were responsible for both the mistakes and their resolution, as CEO, I was ultimately and appropriately accountable.

Every quarter we missed was painful. Each time we did so, the change warriors would lose courage. Each time, those who resisted change gained strength. Each time, I had to recommit the organization to the path we were on, reassure people that we could accomplish what we attempted, and reiterate my passion and enthusiasm for our aspirations and our potential. When I spoke to the people of HP, I spoke to everyone who observed and was interested in us: in our always-on world, every communication finds its way to everyone. Many took my words as naïveté or a failure to understand the details of the business. I was, in fact, clear eyed about those details as well as the difficulties and the pitfalls. I knew that progress, not perfection, was the goal, and I knew the greatest danger of all was that we'd quit along the way. "When we make a mistake or fall short, we will pick ourselves up, dust ourselves off, learn our lessons and move on."

Missing analysts' estimates in a quarter wasn't fatal. Turning away from change and aspiration would have been.

25 | Chainsaw Carly

THE ECONOMY FELT as if it were in free fall in late 2000 and in 2001. In that period the analysts for the tech sector kept ratcheting down their numbers, and tech companies kept revising their plans lower as well. In mid-December of 2000 it felt as if the whole economy had suddenly ground to a halt. In trying to describe what we were seeing in the marketplace, I said on a conference call with analysts that "it feels as if someone just turned the lights out." (Scott McNealy famously retorted, "All the lights are on over here.")

In fact, the downturn was so swift and dramatic that the Federal Reserve behaved in an extraordinary way by lowering the federal funds rate by fifty basis points, not once but twice in January of 2001. The first move caught the markets by surprise because it occurred without a regularly scheduled meeting. The resulting bear market was one of the worst in history, eclipsing the 1973–74 bear market in terms of both the decline in price (48 percent as measured by the broad market index of the S&P 500 from the peak of March 2000 to the trough in October 2003) and in length (more than two and a half years).

No one on Wall Street wanted the dot-com boom to come to an end.

Everyone had made too much money. And so the marketplace engaged in wholesale denial for many quarters. Even as the downturn wore on, both before and after the terrorist attacks of September 11, many well-regarded analysts kept predicting that a recovery in tech spending was just around the corner. By June of 2001, the conventional wisdom was that the second half of the year would mark a return to normal spending patterns.

The reality would be far different. Corporate spending on technology came to a halt, and the huge capital spending overhang caused by the investment bubble in telecommunications and technology of the late nineties would take more than four years to completely clear. Old-timers in Silicon Valley described the period as the worst technology recession in twenty-five years. A global economic slowdown would drag on for four years. At the end of 2004 the economy's health was still a matter of great discussion and debate. Only in 2005 did sustained and respectable growth begin to return to all the major economies around the world.

There is no question that the economic downturn and the bear market made every aspect of my job more difficult, even if it made the requirement to cut costs more obvious. Fear became the prevailing emotion and replaced the optimism of the nineties. It became more difficult for both investors and employees to see any progress or positive changes when the stock price was depressed. As the corporate scandals at Enron, Tyco, Adelphia, WorldCom and many others were revealed, a climate of distrust and doubt emerged. Change requires moving forward, but emotionally, people wanted to hunker down. Operationally everything was tougher as well. Customers weren't buying and hard work became harder.

By early 2001, I knew we were seeing something beyond an economic downturn. This wasn't just cyclical change occurring in our industry; this was structural change. Our customers were behaving differently. As they tightened their own belts, they realized they'd spent too much money on technology, had frequently invested in the wrong things, and hadn't gotten the return they'd expected. They weren't willing to throw money at technology anymore, and when they did spend, they expected more. The technologies in which HP competed had become the backbone and the core of virtually every business. Our technology was becoming more deeply woven into every aspect of life.

As an industry becomes more and more indispensable, that industry will consolidate. As customers continue to demand more and more for less, competitors align to bolster their strength. This has happened in every industry from cereal to automobiles, from energy to banking, from telecommunications to airlines. Nevertheless, it was viewed as foolishness to suggest it might also happen in technology. Although I'd been saying since 2001 that the industry had to consolidate, the idea wasn't treated seriously until Larry Ellison, the CEO of Oracle, who was beginning a consolidation strategy of his own, began to say it in 2003.

Toward the end of 2000, Jay Keyworth came to see me. "Dick [Hackborn] and I have been talking, and we agree we should buy Compaq." He went through all the reasons such a combination made sense. He was enthusiastic and wanted me to call the CEO right away. Later, Dick endorsed the idea.

Of course, any acquisition, particularly one of such magnitude, can't be undertaken so cavalierly. There was the small matter of the rest of the Board's involvement. There was the matter of determining whether such a move made any strategic sense at all. There was integration to consider. And then there was just the basic issue of negotiating tactics—who makes the first move matters in important ways.

I was alarmed by Jay's casual approach. I wanted to throw cold water on the idea immediately; Jay could get carried away with his own ideas and talked carelessly with too many people when he got fired up about something. We had recently withdrawn from negotiations to buy the consulting arm of Price Waterhouse Coopers (PWC). Our discussions had been leaked to the press, and we were forced to discuss our acquisition logic in the public marketplace. As usual, there was a great deal of misinformation swirling about, particularly concerning the price we were willing to pay. I would walk away from the discussions again and again as the price dropped from $16 billion to $3 billion. Although PWC management was keen to do the deal, and the opportunity to add consulting capability was theoretically attractive, detailed examination revealed that we couldn't effectively retain and integrate the people assets of PWC. Beyond that, their financial performance was deteriorating, and I believed the consulting industry was now poised to go through major structural change. Prices would plummet and sales cycles would become longer and consulting engagements shorter as customers demanded more tangible returns for their consulting investment.

The whole experience convinced me that we could never again negotiate in public. If we were going to make a major acquisition, we would have to conduct our discussions in absolute secrecy for months. I told Jay all the reasons why such a deal didn't make sense. I wanted to sober him up about just how difficult this could be. He pushed back hard and gave me all the reasons he and Dick thought this was the right move. By the end of a heated conversation, we'd agreed to three things: we could not consider Compaq in isolation—we needed to evaluate such a move against a broad set of strategic alternatives; Compaq was too big to approach casually—we'd need detailed Board conversations about everything from price to integration, and we might well conclude at any point in these deliberations that Compaq was the wrong move; and we would wait for Compaq to approach us. I told Jay we wouldn't have to make the first move, nor should we. I was convinced the Compaq CEO would come to us.

I had been watching Compaq for a year. In December of 1999, after the first analysts' meeting where we'd declared the pure product era over and announced our intentions to deliver always-on infrastructure, connected appliances and services, I'd watched Compaq adopt virtually the same language and strategy. I knew that although they were struggling against Dell in their PC business, Compaq was doing better than we were in the commercial market; and they were beating us soundly in the fastest-growing part of the server market. They had acquired Tandem and DEC, which gave them valuable high-end computing and services assets. I knew both the cyclical economic downturn and the structural changes in the technology industry would stress their organization even more than ours because their portfolio wasn't as broad as HP's, and so their market position, their financial performance and their stock price would weaken more quickly than ours. They needed us more than we needed them, so we should wait for their call. I had met Michael Capellas several times and felt we could work together. And although I had argued strenuously with Jay, I knew very well why a combination with Compaq made sense. I'd thought so for a year. I also knew the organization wasn't yet capable of executing such a move.

In January 2001 I went to the Board and said that the entire tech sector would experience intense pressure. This represented an opportunity for HP, and one we needed to be prepared for. We would enlist the strategic counsel of McKinsey & Company, and we would consider a broad range of strategic options, including both acquisitions in printing, services and computing as well as a split-up of the company. We would begin our deliberations immediately because we needed to be ready when the inevitable phone call from Compaq came. I was clear from the outset: I would not talk the Board into a particular course of action. The Board needed to come to consensus on two issues. Did we have the assets necessary to achieve our ambitions? If not, what was the appropriate alternative? I was clear about two other things as well. The absolute secrecy of our deliberations was paramount. And doing a deal—even a big one—is easy compared with making a deal work. Lots of people get deal fever—the excitement, adrenaline rush and egos involved in negotiations can overwhelm judgment and common sense. Deal fever causes otherwise sensible people to pay too much and plan too little. I therefore insisted that before we called any bankers to the table, we would have to know clearly how to execute our decision and have a detailed plan to integrate, or disassemble, the assets.

As predicted, Michael Capellas called. He and Shane Robison, his chief technology officer, wanted to visit and discuss a research and product development cooperation. As tech spending continued to crumble, everyone was looking for ways to shrink R&D spending without sacrificing market position. At the end of a cordial meeting, Michael asked to speak with me privately. Without much preamble, he said, "Carly, we think HP should acquire Compaq. HP would be the surviving brand, Palo Alto would be the headquarters, and you would be the CEO." It was a stunning way to open a negotiation. He'd just given away a great deal of leverage.

Without commenting on the specifics, I asked instead, "Michael, does your Board know you're here and that you've made this suggestion?" He assured me his Board was in agreement. Several years earlier, while I was still at Lucent, the Compaq Board had recruited me for a Board seat. I knew that one of their Board members, Larry Babbio of Verizon, had made the initial recommendation. Now I wondered why they would permit their CEO to give up so much in the very first conversation.

From January until September 4, 2001 (the day we announced the Compaq deal to the world), three things were going on simultaneously. First, the Board was engaged in detailed deliberations about Hewlett-Packard's next moves. Second, select members of the management team and I were engaged in discussions and negotiations with our counterparts at Compaq. And third, I was preparing the organization to weather the storm of an economic downturn. While there was much chatter in the marketplace that the upturn was just around the corner, I knew we needed to be prepared to ride out a longer slowdown. HP had never lost money in a quarter. To prevent losses now, we'd have to cut our cost structure dramatically once again. We'd have to lay off a lot of people.

One of the great myths of HP was that employees never lost their jobs. The truth was Bill and Dave fired people when they thought it was deserved. Some, who remembered the facts rather than the legends, knew that Dave was famous for saying, "If you can't do the job, I'll find someone who can." Factories were closed and relocated when necessary. The employee evaluation system that had been in place for many, many years had five possible gradations of performance, including Superior, Excellent, Satisfactory, Needs Improvement and Unsatisfactory. When it was introduced, there were clear expectations that a certain percentage of the workforce would always fall in the bottom two categories.

The hard-nosed focus on merit, excellence and performance somehow became lost in the mists of time. The acceptable way of dealing with softening economic conditions was for everyone to agree to an across-the-board pay cut or fewer hours in the factory. Although these methods have their place, and are tools that I also used, the fundamental issues of productivity and overall cost structure also have to be confronted, and at HP those questions hadn't been asked in a very long time. The employee evaluation system no longer produced a bell-shaped curve of performance. The vast majority of employees always ended up in the top two categories; there were very few Satisfactory performers, and virtually no one whose performance rated a Needs Improvement or an Unsatisfactory. Even when businesses struggled during the good times of the nineties, the vast majority of managers were doing Superior or Excellent work. This kind of disconnect signals one of two issues around performance management: either people aren't performing the right work, or the performance criteria have become too lenient.

Employees knew this was a problem. When I arrived, we continued to regularly conduct the employee survey that had become a time-honored management tool. In 2000, 82 percent of our people said management failed to deal with poor performance. This percentage hadn't varied much in a decade, and yet the organization kept rating everyone as above average. Managers and employees who really weren't performing up to standard (and despite the ratings, everyone in an organization always knows who these people are) were moved from one organization to another, if possible, or were otherwise simply tolerated. In fact, if a particular business was looking for new employees and new skills, the accepted practice was to hire from within first. Frequently this meant that poorer-performing or underqualified employees were moved into these positions. It wasn't acceptable to fire someone for poor performance and hire someone else from the outside at the same time. This was the institutionalization of the inability to confront tough issues directly. Everyone was nice, everyone was supportive, and performance issues weren't dealt with. Everyone had a secure job, but no one questioned whether some shouldn't.

In tough economic times, when the tide recedes, all the frailties in a company are exposed. In that sense, a downturn can be a useful management tool. Issues that were once hidden can no longer be ignored. Now, for HP, "nice" wasn't enough. We had to be candid. I talked with the management team and the broader organization about the necessity for truth telling. I spoke frequently of the need to look in the mirror, see the truth, speak the truth and act on the truth. I said that respect for the individual meant telling the truth: if someone's performance wasn't up to par, we should say so. We had an obligation to give people an opportunity to improve, but if improvement wasn't achieved, we had to act. Failure to confront the truth and act was a disservice to employees who were making a real contribution.

Building an environment where people can tell the truth takes work, especially if confrontation isn't the norm. That work had to start with me, and how I interacted with my management team and the broader employee population. At that very first management meeting at Seascape, it was clear that I interacted and processed information differently from longtime HP managers. I'd grown up debating at the dinner table with my father. I'd spent ten years in the hard-core, combative culture of Network Systems and Lucent. I need debate and dialogue with others to test my own thinking and to make a decision. I test others' convictions or opinions by pushing on their arguments and seeing how strongly they will defend them. When challenged, do people shrink away from their own views, or do they stand behind them? When pressed, do people offer more data to support their position, or do they simply repeat the same things in a louder voice?

I quickly learned that this wasn't how people did things at HP. I adopted several techniques to teach the skill of honest debate and candid dialogue, which we needed to learn both for management meetings and Board meetings. I'd try to remember to tell people how I operated. "I need a lot of debate to process and decide. If I push back on you, or make a statement that contradicts you, or ask a question in response to one of yours, I'm not necessarily disagreeing or deciding. I'm thinking out loud. I'm trying to make sure we've talked through all the angles of the problem." I know I can be formidable in debate, and in management meetings I had more position power than anyone else in the room, so these reminders were important so that people would be challenged to engage rather than intimidated into silence. I also always tried to clarify when we were still in discussion mode so that people wouldn't assume we were nearing a decision before it was timely.

I'm sure there were times when I intimidated people without intending to. Senior executives, and certainly Board members, are paid to be knowledgeable, form sensible opinions and defend them, but not everyone expresses themselves well in debate. Fortunately, problem solving and decision making require an understanding of where people agree as well as where they disagree. I always made sure we summarized our points of agreement, our questions, as well as our next steps, at the conclusion of every meeting. Frequently this summarization occurred in writing, either on an easel we kept in all our meeting rooms or electronically on a PC. If a discussion is to lead to decision and action, then clarity is important, but frequently this process also prompts comments and participation from those who will not engage in debate.

Whenever possible, after all the facts have been heard and a full discussion has occurred, a consensus decision is always preferable. In both management and Board meetings, I would always ask each person to state his or her opinion and the decision they would make. Everyone should be given the opportunity to speak and be heard, and people who have earned the right to sit at a decision-making table should not remain silent. If everyone agrees, the decision is clear.

On the other hand, a failure to achieve consensus can't derail progress when a decision has to be made. Responsible executives who respect the decision-making process will then stand behind that decision and support and execute it.

There are thousands upon thousands of decisions in a business that are made every day in which the CEO isn't, and shouldn't be, involved. However, the decisions that came to the Executive Council came there for a reason. We were explicit about the kinds of decisions that needed to be made by the council: the Leadership Framework issues for the corporation. What is our strategy? How do we organize the company? What do we measure and how do we reward? What kind of culture and behavior are we building? Sometimes, for their own reasons, people would ask me to make a decision outside of the agreed-upon decision-making process, but I brought virtually all these decisions to the council. After all, I was trying to teach executives to wear their HP hat. I was trying to build leaders from business managers. Usually we reached consensus. Where we could not, which sometimes happened when we got into the nitty-gritty of structural redesign or the annual budgeting process, I would ask for everyone's point of view and then I would decide. In the boardroom, with the exception of my very last Board meeting in February of 2005, every decision we made was unanimous.

Sometimes issues came to the Executive Council because they were just too difficult for others to make on their own. How many people we had to lay off in that summer of 2001 was one of those agonizing decisions that people lower in the organization simply weren't prepared to handle. In late 2000 we'd begun the tough work of asking managers to actually use the performance evaluation system as it had been originally designed. We would force a bell-shaped distribution curve so that we identified, and dealt with, those employees who'd been rated as Unsatisfactory or Needs Improvement. We would reward Superior employees appropriately. We would move away from the peanut-butter approach of spreading ratings and merit pay evenly across the organization. Managers were expected to evaluate employee performance honestly and stand behind their decisions. Step by step we would learn to become, once again, a meritocracy.

We didn't redesign anything; we just began using the existing system rigorously and as originally intended. Nonetheless, this was controversial. While many managers, as well as Board members, were delighted that we were finally tackling what had become creeping mediocrity, for many others

this was evidence that I lacked compassion for employees and was destroying the HP Way. And because it was controversial, some managers would
not stand and defend the decision. Knowing that I would not back down,
they instead explained things with "Carly says . . ." And some in the media
reported that I had "imported" a new performance evaluation system to HP
and lacked respect for the founders. I was cold.

The controversy would grow, of course, when it became clear that many
of our lower-performing employees would have to leave the company. By the
late spring of 2001, we concluded that we had to cut thousands of employees from the payroll. Ultimately, six thousand were laid off in August. We'd
had early retirement programs the year before to trim the workforce, but this
was different. This was a major trauma for the organization. Not only were
we asking managers to confront poor performance for the first time in many
years, we were also asking them to take jobs away from people. Both things
are always difficult, even for the most seasoned managers. It is never easy to
alter someone's life and livelihood. In HP's case, most managers literally
didn't know how to approach the situation. Their inexperience was com-
pounded by emotion; in most cases, work groups had been together for
many years. Managers and employees were friends and neighbors as well as
business colleagues. People had worked side by side for a very long time,
and saw each other regularly outside of work. This was why people favored
cordiality over candor—it made everyone's life easier, even if it hindered the
company's performance.

Perhaps it would have been easier to postpone the layoffs until after
we'd made the Compaq announcement. After all, there was so much controversy about the deal that laying off twenty-one thousand people instead of
fifteen thousand probably wouldn't have changed the dynamics much. I
didn't have the luxury of waiting, however. First, in that summer of 2001, it
wasn't yet clear that we should or could do the deal at all. Second, failure to
take swift action would have resulted in losses for HP, and I was adamant that
I wouldn't be the first CEO to post a loss for the company in sixty years. Finally, this was behavior the organization had to learn sooner rather than later.
Whatever happened with the economy or a deal, the management team of
Hewlett-Packard had to learn how to manage performance and productivity.
We had to build new skills, and among the most important was the ability to
look people in the eye and tell them that they weren't performing or that

they were being terminated. It's just a necessary part of running a business effectively.

I don't believe in prolonging pain for an organization. If you have to lay people off, let them know as quickly as possible; don't let the rumor mill run rampant for months while people worry and wonder whether they're on the list. I also don't believe in humiliating people. You don't have to hand people a pink slip and walk them out the door. Everyone deserves dignity. Everyone deserves a human touch. Everyone, even those who must leave, has made a contribution, even if that contribution is no longer necessary or up to par.

Everyone should be treated with respect, and part of that respect is telling the truth in a compassionate way, person to person, rather than relying on a piece of paper to deliver the bad news. Another part of respect is giving people the tools and the time they need to take the next step in their lives. That summer I concluded we needed professional help to accomplish the layoffs with both speed and dignity. We brought in an outside firm to help prepare our managers to face their employees as well as to provide personal counseling and career assistance to those who would leave the company. We gave people time to say good-bye to their colleagues and reach closure before they left. We provided generous severance packages—far more generous than most of the rest of the industry, and more generous than our colleagues at Agilent. I received many, many e-mail messages from employees who had lost their jobs and yet took the time to thank me for the quality assistance we provided. I received that kind of e-mail throughout my entire tenure because we kept the assistance programs in place for anyone who lost a job from that point forward.

That painful summer, when we were asking people to sacrifice, and cutting jobs and contemplating a major merger in the background, also represented an opportunity to demonstrate that employees could ask tough questions of the CEO and get direct answers. This was another very important part of teaching the organization to see the truth and speak the truth. I always encouraged lots of questions in my employee coffee talks. I thanked people when they asked the tough ones that were really on everyone's mind. When people see that difficult issues can be raised without penalty, it sends an important message. And a leader has to tell the truth, even if it's not what people want to hear.

Taking the heat that comes with that truth is part of a CEO's job. There are things I should have done differently. I probably should have taken an extra several weeks and allowed managers a little more time to identify the people who would leave the business. Perhaps in my quest for speed I sacrificed broader-based acceptance of the decision. Perhaps I underestimated people's ability to step up to what had to be done. Nevertheless, it is also true that for many it was just easier to blame the new CEO and bestow a new nickname: Chainsaw Carly. This moniker stuck when the founders' sons began to wage their battle against the Compaq merger; my willingness to sacrifice jobs was a clear indicator of my disdain for their fathers' legacy. Ironically, much later some said I'd been fired because I couldn't cut heads and cut costs. It seems I was too tough for some and too soft for others.

It will always be a CEO's job to raise people's sights and focus them on what's necessary and what's possible. A leader's job is to sense, ahead of others, danger as well as opportunity and to lead the organization to adapt itself to both. Over time the organization would toughen and mature. By 2002, managers knew that achieving best-in-class cost structures was an ongoing part of their jobs, and so there were more job cuts in 2002, 2003, 2004, and planned (and later executed) for 2005.

In the summer of 2001 we had our regularly scheduled strategy sessions with the broader management team. It was clear to everyone that our PC business wasn't on a path to leadership, nor was our industry-standard server business. We were far too dependent on Microsoft and Intel, yet we negotiated with them from a position of weakness because our volumes weren't sufficient to give us the same clout as either Compaq or Dell. Our services business still lacked credibility and scale, even though we'd focused more management attention on it by asking Ann Livermore to lead our efforts. At the end of the session I stood and reiterated these observations, as well as the others we'd reached during our two days of meetings. And then I concluded by saying "The industry we're competing in is getting tougher. Only the strongest will survive and prevail. We're fighting too many battles on too many fronts alone. We need either more allies or fewer fights." Although I couldn't yet say anything specific, I was trying to prepare the organization for what might come.

I wish I had known better how to prepare the organization for the merger when it came. Perhaps I should have been more explicit about all the potential dangers we faced, and our ongoing vulnerabilities, so that when we announced the Compaq merger, people would have viewed it with relief, not shock. But what if we hadn't done the deal at all? And what would our investors and customers have concluded if we had highlighted problems and provided no solutions? How would our competitors have taken advantage of our exposure? And how could employees continue to move foward if they were told by their leader that we didn't know how to reach our destination?

B Y THE MAY 2001 MEETING, the Board had reached consensus that we wouldn't split the company into a computing and an imaging business. They'd concluded further that if we were to make a major acquisition, which was by no means yet clear, it would probably be in computing technology (as opposed to imaging or services, for example). The acquisition of Compaq was an alternative we should continue to examine in detail, although there was no agreement yet on whether it made sense. From then on, the Board would talk about both sides of the Compaq coin: the strategy and the execution. If we couldn't integrate product lines successfully, we couldn't mine the value out of the deal, no matter how sound the strategic logic. So we scheduled many special sessions of the Board, and they debated the details of product roadmaps and organizational structure with the same rigor they debated the economics of the PC industry. Board members asked tough questions about the probability of achieving the cost synergies that could result from the combination as well as tough questions about the character of the executives we would acquire from Compaq. By the time we made the final decision and announced it, the Board had engaged in detailed debate on every subject, from which executives would sit in which chairs to how much market share we would lose in the industry-standard server market in Europe. Every voice was heard, and every vote on every decision, including the final one to consummate the deal, was unanimous and was taken one person at a time. It was the only responsible way to approach a choice that would change the face of both the company and the industry forever.

The preparation for our meetings was rigorous, attendance was mandatory, and full attention and participation was required. The members of the Hewlett-Packard Board had their own particular concerns. Pattie Dunn wanted to be sure we had thoroughly examined the option of splitting the company into imaging and computing. Later on she remarked that she hoped we'd use the Compaq deal as an opportunity to "quit talking about the HP Way once and for all." Sam Ginn and Bob Knowling were the most skeptical, and they were very concerned about the PC business. Jay Keyworth didn't say much in the meetings, but his bias had been clear to everyone from the beginning. Dick was very focused on the details of the product roadmaps and the market share losses we'd experience as we brought product lines together. Phil Condit was concerned about cultural integration and saw a great opportunity for leadership development.

Bob Wayman was surprisingly enthusiastic almost from the beginning. The first time he and I met with Jeff Clarke, the Compaq CFO, and Michael Capellas, they'd presented their views of the numbers we could achieve through the combination. Bob declared the numbers "compelling" and never looked back. In August, Walter Hewlett expressed concern that the combined company would be too big to grow. (This was the original premise that had led to the spin-off of Agilent. Lew Platt had postulated that HP was too big to manage and to grow.) By then we'd brought the bankers on board, so we asked them to do a study correlating size with revenue growth and stock price appreciation. It turned out that with the exception of the period during the dot-com boom, larger companies like GE and IBM actually performed better over time than many smaller companies. A broad portfolio of capabilities, combined with a global footprint, permitted companies to weather economic downturns and prevail in strong markets. Good cash flow and a strong capital structure gave large companies the heft and resources to invest for the long term. When the study was presented, Walter said he'd found it enlightening and that his concerns had been alleviated. Throughout our nine months of deliberations, the quietest person in the room was always Walter Hewlett. He was also the only member of the Board who missed meetings.

During those many months my greatest concern was with execution. I knew a broader and more complete product portfolio, favorable economies of scale, leadership market share positions and the size to both serve our largest customers better and negotiate as equals with our largest partners, particularly Microsoft and Intel, all combined to create a persuasive strategic case. I also knew that strategy would count for nothing if we could not integrate the two companies successfully. And so we began building the detailed integration plan in May, and on the day we announced the deal, we knew exactly who would lead our integration efforts, how we'd approach them, and how much value we would capture. By late July, I was convinced we could, in fact, integrate the companies, even though nothing of that magnitude had ever been attempted in the technology industry. However, other industries, such as pharmaceuticals, energy, aerospace, telecommunications and banking, had all seen their share of massive mergers and successful integrations, and there were lessons we could draw upon. When Compaq had acquired DEC and Tandem, they'd learned a lot about what works and especially what doesn't, and we drew upon those lessons as well. Beyond that, we'd exercised and examined the assumptions and details of our integration plan so carefully, and been conservative enough in our expectations, that I felt we were clear-eyed about the pitfalls and prepared for the risks.

As the Board came closer and closer to its ultimate decision and the bankers became involved, I concluded that realism was what we needed most. Our Board needed to understand how tough this would really be. It was clear the market didn't understand what was actually happening in the technology space. In the summer of 2001 none of the Wall Street analysts were talking about structural change in the industry. No one was focused on consolidation as the obvious next step in an industry that would never again grow at five times GDP. (When I first said publicly that the technology industry had to consolidate and would likely be a two-times-GDP growth industry going forward, my comments were generally dismissed as justification for an ill-conceived deal.) So I told the bankers to be brutal with the Board in their assessment of the market's reaction to an HP/Compaq combination. They predicted a 20 percent drop in the stock price (it turned out to be 23 percent the day of the announcement).

When I met with the Compaq Board in New York in August, I was equally concerned with realism. I had joined the meeting immediately following a presentation by their bankers. Some of the booklets used during their presentation were still lying open on the table, and it was clear from what I could see that the Compaq Board had been told to expect a large increase in the stock price when the deal was announced. I began my presentation by sharing with them the nature of the deliberations the HP Board had been engaged in. I spoke of our thinking about both strategy and execution. I shared our views on product road maps and market share loss, on customer retention and competitive response. And then I said, "I want to be clear. The market will hate this deal. They won't understand it, and they won't reward us for it. Both of our stocks will drop. We will have to convince them that we've done the right thing, and it will take time to do so. Wall Street doesn't yet understand what's going on in this industry." I think most of the Board assumed I was negotiating. By then they were clearly enthusiastic about making a deal. Whatever they thought, my job was to be sober and realistic, and I knew the market reaction would be ugly. I said so in every way I knew how.

This was my first introduction to the Board members who would ultimately join the HP Board upon completion of the merger. Tom Perkins had worked at Hewlett-Packard before he'd left to form Kleiner Perkins, a venture capital firm. He was hugely wealthy as a result of his success. He loved technology but was bored by the other complexities of the business. Larry Babbio was a no-nonsense, hands-on manager with deep operational experience. Like Sam Ginn, Larry had grown up in the telecom industry. Lucy Salhany came from the entertainment industry and now ran a consulting firm, JH Media. Sandy Litvack, a practicing attorney, had served as the general counsel at Disney. There were other Compaq Board members, but these four, in addition to Michael Capellas, would eventually join the HP Board.

After examining all the details of execution and integration, after ensuring we were as realistic as possible about every aspect of the challenge, I was satisfied that we had exercised a high-quality decision-making process and would ultimately choose with all the facts and risks clearly in mind. The only wild cards left were the people. I was nervous about Peter Blackmore, a Compaq executive who'd once been promised a new chief operating officer job. Compaq had insisted on a major role for Peter, but I was doubtful that he could handle the job. I'd expressed these reservations to the Compaq Board (and later several times to the HP Board), but they'd insisted he was qualified; Tom Perkins was Peter's most adamant defender. The wildest card of all, however, was Michael Capellas.

Michael was moody and inconsistent. He could agree to something on one day and object strenuously the next. He could be charming and focused. He could be depressed and disengaged. He could be rude and abusive. Despite his proactive offer to step away from the CEO job in our very first meeting, he seemed more interested in his own title and position than virtually everything else. We spent hours and hours on this topic, and he cut

off negotiations several times when he wasn't satisfied with the reporting relationships. I understood that his job was very important to him, but he
seemed obsessed with it and frequently changed his mind about what he
really wanted. I told the HP Board in midsummer that our biggest problem
with integration would be Michael. I said that I would work hard to make
him successful, but that we'd need to be prepared to move him out of the
company within a year. I asked Bob Wayman and our outside counsel, Larry
Sonsini, who'd been deeply involved with Michael in the negotiations, to
share their views with the Board. They were equally direct in saying he
would be a big issue. We spent a lot of time talking about this as a Board because there couldn't be any illusions about the executive we were throwing
in with. I finally concluded one of those conversations by saying "Michael is
like the little girl who had a little curl right in the middle of her forehead.
When he's good, he's very, very good, and when he's bad, he's horrid."
I would learn later that the Compaq executives knew his patterns well and
would let each other know whether "good" Michael or "bad" Michael was
at work that day.

By the end of July, I knew I would have to soon declare my own point of
view. Was I for this deal or not? One night, flying home from a long trip, I
talked with Frank about my decision process. I knew the strategic logic was
sound, I knew we could execute, and I knew the numbers were real. Yet I
hesitated to fully embrace the deal. Frank asked me, "Can you do it?"

"Yes."

"Should you do it?"

"Yes."

"Does the Board want to do it?"

"Yes."

"Then why aren't you excited about doing it?"

"Because it will be incredibly ugly. It will be a huge shock, and it will be
a fight from start to finish. We'll have a battle out in the marketplace because people won't understand why it's necessary. We'll have a battle inside
the company because we'll have to lay off tens of thousands of people."

I knew accomplishing this merger would require incredible skill, energy,
commitment and will. The integration would be hard; selling the deal would
be hard; dealing with people's emotions, as they fully comprehended what it
all meant, would be hard. Even after we'd announced the deal, we wouldn't

get immediate approval from the necessary authorities to move ahead, so we'd also have to keep executing as a stand-alone company. That would be hard because people would be distracted by what they knew was coming and because our competitors would declare us weak and too busy with integration problems to serve customers.

Even in the best of circumstances, people were going to falter and question and second-guess. Some would oppose us directly. I'd already seen how people can fight change, and the change we were now talking about made everything else pale in comparison. Once the Board made its decision, I would not have the luxury of hesitation or doubt or weakness. I would have to stand strong and remind people that we had chosen our destiny and that we could achieve our aims. I knew I'd call upon many people to help achieve what was necessary. I also knew that when times are tough, people look to, and follow, the leader. And I knew that we were surely heading into very tough times.

When I finally made up my own mind, I wasn't excited about the big deal or a bigger company or job. I was calm because I trusted the process we'd used and my own judgment. Yet I steeled myself for what lay ahead. Once again I began saying the Lord's Prayer every night, over and over again, just as I had as a little girl. As tough as I thought it would be, however, I never expected a fight with the families.

26 | A Down and Dirty Fight

ON SEPTEMBER 4, 2001, we announced the deal. The day started out badly. Someone had leaked the whole story to the *New York Times* and the *Wall Street Journal* the night before. I will never know where the leak came from, but it was obviously from well-informed inside sources. Perhaps whoever did it thought they were helping, but as predicted, everyone hated the deal. Now we'd lost the element of surprise and faced a hostile reaction before we'd even had an opportunity to provide the context of how and why we'd made the decision. We were on the defensive from the very beginning.

The press conference was packed. It felt as if the flashbulbs would never stop going off. Michael and I went through our presentations. Although we were upbeat about our growth opportunities going forward, we did not sugarcoat the necessity for deep cuts in the workforce. We were open about the detailed integration planning that would be necessary. And when the first question was asked, it was clear we hadn't changed any minds. Many people had walked into the room with their opinion already formed by the articles they'd read that morning. Besides, the deal was a complete surprise, and many analysts felt foolish that they hadn't seen it coming. By the end of the day, only one analyst, George Elling at Deutsche Bank, had written a positive note.

As Michael and I left the stage, I knew the fight was just beginning. We were staying in New York that week to meet with as many investors as we could. Still, I felt relief that we had finally started. The last nine months of analysis, negotiation and secrecy had been difficult. Now at least everything was out in the open. We'd made our decision, and we could get on with making the decision work. Despite how difficult the press conference had been, I was upbeat. Michael was distraught. He kept checking the stock prices on his handheld. As I'd predicted, they were both plummeting. He was shocked; he really had thought the Compaq stock would appreciate. Beyond that, he thought he'd be described as a selfless hero, the rare CEO who'd sacrificed his job for the greater good of his company. It was not to be. As the week wore on, I spent more and more time trying to keep him focused and positive. He was obviously angry in our investor meetings. He seemed less and less convinced we'd made the right decision, and less convincing in his arguments as well.

We got a rare bit of positive reinforcement on that first day as we walked to yet another meeting full of hostile investors. We ran into a bunch of HP salespeople. "Great deal, Carly! This is fantastic! We're so excited!" I asked them why they liked this when the whole rest of the world seemed to hate it. "Because we have more to sell. Because our customers like it. Because it gives us the strength we need to compete and win." The salespeople got it right away because they were out talking to customers every day. They knew what our competitive position was better than anyone else. And from that very first week, the salespeople from both companies understood what was at stake and what was to be gained. I thanked these four for their support and told them to share their enthusiasm with everyone they could. It was always the people of HP who gave me the strength to do what had to be done.

After a couple days we all needed a break. We'd been under bone-grinding pressure for months, and the last few days had been truly difficult. People needed to blow off a little steam. The following day was my birthday, so it seemed like a good excuse to gather in the bar on Wednesday night and have some fun. We toasted our deal and had a lot of laughs about the various people we'd met during the week, and how many times everyone asked the same questions over and over as if they were the only ones who'd ever thought of them. There is always something to laugh about, even in the most difficult of times. It's especially important to find the humor in the tough times because laughter helps people manage stress. And when people find something they can laugh about together, they begin to bond. That night was the beginning of building a single team.

Unfortunately, Michael refused to join us, and around midnight he called Jeff Clarke and demanded that he leave the party and come to Michael's hotel room. Jeff left the party on edge. On Thursday, Michael unexpectedly asked me to fly to Texas that evening on my way back to California, where I had yet another speech to give the next morning. I was exhausted, and the detour would add five or six hours to an already very long day; but I thought it was important to acknowledge Michael's gesture. I met with his management team over a lovely and lavish dinner. Michael toasted my birthday with good humor and said all the right things to his team about a great, new beginning.

THE TRUTH IS we'd acquired Compaq. HP was the majority owner of the new combined company; we had more Board seats, and we had more management positions. And yet from the very first day we'd called it a merger. The goal was not for Hewlett-Packard to take over Compaq, as Compaq had done with DEC and Tandem. The goal was to use the best of both companies to build something stronger and better. We would use the best of both product lines, both management teams, and both cultures. We needed the DNA of both companies to form a new company that could compete and win in the twenty-first century. We needed two strands of DNA to adapt to the changing industry landscape. And from the beginning, forming a new culture was as important a part of our integration efforts as technology road maps or IT systems or customer care. We needed the fighting spirit, the speed and the can-do attitude of Compaq. We needed the HP focus on quality and integrity. We needed to celebrate the histories of two great companies and build a future together.

Maybe this dilution of HP history is what set off Walter Hewlett. Although we'd talked a lot about it during our Board deliberations, maybe he just hadn't paid enough attention to realize that after this move there really would be no going back to the past. Maybe he thought the memory of his recently deceased father would fade too quickly in the new company, especially since the Compaq employees would have no historical connection to Bill and Dave at all. Or maybe he was just taken advantage of by lawyers and bankers who saw what looked like an easy opportunity to stop an unpopular deal and enhance their own personal wealth in the process.

We knew from the beginning that the merger would be a very tough sell. The fall of 2001 turned out to be the worst time to try and sell it. The week after we announced the merger, the horrific terrorist attacks of September 11 occurred. The market tanked and fear and pessimism reigned supreme. Then Enron collapsed. Suddenly the company that bankers and academics and media pundits had all called the model for twenty-first-century innovation and success was revealed as an empty shell. Suddenly the Board that had once been declared the best in corporate America looked asleep at the switch. Why hadn't one Enron director raised his hand and said, "Stop"? Their CEO, who'd been crowned king of the hill over and over again, now looked corrupt or incompetent. On top of this, the AOL/Time Warner merger, which had initially been embraced by the market as a harbinger of things to come, was now decried as an example of a big deal gone bad. The integration wasn't working.

Despite this environment, after five or six weeks of relentless communication and incessant meetings with investors, customers and employees, we were making real progress. The stock prices of both companies were starting to recover. Our integration team was rolling ahead. I was surprised late one morning when my secretary said Walter Hewlett was on the phone. He had never called me before. I was staggered when he informed me in a cold voice with a minimum of words that as an HP shareholder, he intended to announce his opposition to the merger and vote his and the Hewlett Foundation's shares against the deal. I'm sure I was stammering when I asked him why. I desperately asked for a meeting where we could discuss and perhaps alleviate his newfound concerns. This request was summarily denied. Then I asked him to take some time to reconsider his decision. I said that a shareholder didn't need to publicly declare his position ahead of time at all. The shareholder vote wasn't expected for a couple of months, and Walter could vote his shares at that time. Walter just said, "I wanted to let you know before we released the announcement. We're going to make it in about half an hour." I had the presence of mind to persuade him to wait until the market had closed.

I give Walter credit for calling me himself. Our public response was calm and measured. We still didn't know we had a proxy battle on our hands. One of Walter's advisers met privately with Sam Ginn to persuade him to reverse his vote. Then Walter actually came to a Board meeting and asked the Board to "change our minds." "Can't we just undo the deal?" he asked almost plaintively. Responsible directors and reasonable people do not reverse in a few days a decision that has taken nine months to reach. Beyond the obvious insult to the Board's deliberations implied by his request, Walter seemed oblivious to the reality that we'd made a tender offer for another company's stock. We were legally committed to a course of action; to undo it would be expensive, time consuming, and damaging to both companies. We were also intellectually and emotionally committed.

I don't know exactly when Walter cut a deal with all his bankers and lawyers, and I don't know when precisely they decided to launch a proxy battle. What I do know is that the advisers were paid to kill the deal. They didn't have to propose an alternative, and they didn't have to manage the aftermath. All they had to do was get a majority of shareholders to vote against the merger. If they could do that, they'd each be richer by several million dollars. If they failed, they'd lose the money, although they would have been paid handsomely for their efforts in the meantime.

I'm sure they thought they were placing a safe bet. Walter had that magic last name, and he would convince all the Hewlett and Packard family members, as well as their foundations, to vote against the deal. David Woodley Packard aligned himself with his childhood friend. (CNBC actually confused David Packard with the senior Dave Packard.) Virtually all of the media and analyst community had already lined up in opposition to the company. Now all these commentators would become willing allies to Walter. Suddenly they looked even smarter. An inside Board member thought it was a bad idea too!

The story line became that the HP Board was like the Enron Board—lazy and inattentive—and that they'd been duped by a willful CEO who, like Ken Lay, was more interested in personal wealth than in the employees of the company. Walter was that sole director who everyone wished had existed at Enron—willing to bravely protest and stand alone against the peer pressure of his weaker colleagues. Like AOL/Time Warner's, the integration of HP/Compaq would never work. Like AOL/Time Warner's, the synergies wouldn't materialize, and the resulting company would be too big and sluggish to grow. And as the press reported on all the economic difficulties and the layoffs of the times, Walter and David would repeat the myth that Bill and Dave had never believed in taking jobs away from people. Walter and David would say that the HP Way was going to be trampled by the deal, and a great and good management philosophy would be lost just when we needed it most.

The HP Board began to be described as "handpicked" or "railroaded." The fact that every Board member save one had been on the Board longer than I'd been at the company wasn't mentioned much. One shareholder lawsuit described the Board as "bewitched" by me. That fall the Board was deliberating on retention and severance programs for the HP and Compaq executives. The Compaq Board had previously approved change-in-control severance provisions, and the HP Board had used retention programs during the Agilent spin. Now highly sensitive and confidential Board documents of various proposed compensation programs had been given to Walter's advisers and leaked to the press. The media seized on these drafts as evidence of yet another CEO's greed. The fact that ultimately more than six thousand managers were covered by these agreements didn't seem to matter much. The fact that the CEO refused to accept her proposed retention payment, just as she had refused to accept her contractually guaranteed bonus the year before, didn't get much press.

Sometime past midnight one morning, I was awakened out of a dead sleep by the ringing phone. At that hour you always expect the worst, so I answered the phone with great anxiety. Michael was screaming into the phone. Apparently, he had learned that I was refusing to accept my retention payment, and he thought I would make him look bad. I tried to be rational, to explain that my decision had nothing to do with him. Compaq had previously existing arrangements. My case was different; and given the controversy, I wanted no confusion about my motivations for pursuing the merger.

Michael was abusive and incoherent; there was no reasoning with him. I was concerned that he'd been on the phone this way for quite a while with others. I asked him who else he'd talked to. When he rattled off four other names, I felt instantly protective. Michael's behavior must have been terrifying to these people who barely knew him and who were all relatively junior. Now I sat up in bed and said, "Michael, you will stop this now. It's the middle of the night. I will not continue this conversation, and you will not call anyone else. We will talk about this in the morning." There was a long silence and he agreed. Ultimately, he would also agree to give up his own retention payment. I was shaken and remained haunted by that conversation. Over time it became clear that this was a pattern, not an aberration.

ALL THE HP EMPLOYEES who'd ever resisted change suddenly had a champion in Walter Hewlett. The retirees who'd been true believers had a patron saint. Walter and David began to solicit e-mails of support from employees. They shared these e-mails with the Packard Foundation Board as they were conducting their own deliberations about the merger. Eventually, Walter and David would commission "employee surveys" at four company locations in the Pacific Northwest where tradition ran deep. Employees were called at home. While the methodology was flawed and the results were not statistically reliable, the results of these surveys were of course presented to the press with great fanfare and as evidence that the "majority" of employees opposed the deal. In fact, we knew from our own ongoing surveys that the majority of employees supported the deal.

David took out several full-page ads in the *Wall Street Journal* and wrote long diatribes about why I was incompetent, unethical and unfit. I would not read them, but Jay Keyworth described them as "misogynist manifestos that sound like they were written by the Unabomber."

When I accurately described Walter as an "academic and a musician," I was excoriated for personal attacks. I explained that I meant no disrespect— my father was an academic, and I'd once contemplated being a musician— but neither profession made Walter qualified to countermand the decision of an entire board.

The themes of greed, incompetence, the callous disregard of management, and the deeply felt resistance of employees all played out over many months. The story got huge play. It was a made-for-television drama complete with a reluctant, slightly rumpled good guy battling valiantly to save his father's legacy and protect the little people from a possibly wicked, definitely ego-driven, controlling woman determined to have her own way. Other themes emerged: I wasn't an engineer, so I didn't understand R&D and innovation. I was throwing away the high-end, really innovative HP products for the low-end, commoditized Compaq products. Maybe we should split the company and "focus and execute." Lots and lots of money was at stake as Wall Street started betting on which side would prevail in this fight. Some hedge funds starting buying HP stock so they could vote against the deal and force a split-up of the company. They thought this was the fastest way to make money.

The notes played by Walter's camp in that very well-orchestrated campaign resonated intensely, given the tenor of the times. The same themes continued to be heard throughout my tenure. In 2005 I was still being described as greedy and arrogant, or a marketing type who didn't understand technology. Reporters still talked about a "handpicked Board" and erroneous reports were filed that employees "cheered" when I left HP. (I know this because employees wrote me and told me they were wrong, and at least one story had to be rescinded.) And even after we'd won the proxy battle, many who had opposed us would remember all the things that Walter had said might go wrong. Their doubts would never completely disappear. Others kept hoping for the split-up they thought would come had Walter prevailed. A lot of people who'd bet on Walter lost a lot of money, and they were always looking for ways to make it back.

Our bankers wanted us to launch into our proxy defense the moment Walter actually declared his intentions to fight us. We held back, though; we naïvely thought that the Packard Foundation might vote with the HP Board. Susan Packard, the foundation's chair, knew the HP Board members. She knew me. So we concluded we wouldn't really wage the proxy fight until after the Packard Board had made its decision. I'm not sure it was ever possible for the two families to split apart over the future of the company. Beyond that, the foundation was a philanthropic entity, and uncertainty wasn't good for their endowment. Their financial interests were best served by stability and predictability in the HP stock. Finally, Lew Platt was a member of the foundation's Board, and from the very first meeting we had with them, it was clear that Lew opposed the decision of his former HP colleagues. During the proxy battle Lew would meet with investors. He would enter HP buildings and meet with employees. He even spoke with Walter about becoming the HP CEO again once the merger was defeated.

Still, I continued to hope for a different outcome up until the moment I got the call from Susan Packard on Friday, December 7, 2001. She informed me that the Packard Foundation and family would oppose the company. They had completed their own "independent" assessment and now substituted their own judgment for the judgment of the company's Board. I believe she was sincere when she told me it was "the hardest phone call [she'd] ever had to make." I am grateful she had the courage and the courtesy to tell me herself. I told her that the people of HP would be devastated now that the families and their Board would have to fight one another. My blood ran cold when I heard the tone in her voice as she replied, "Well, I'm not worried about our employees. We've always been able to count on them." She sounded so proprietary.

Now I felt the full weight of what we were up against. I immediately called Michael to inform him. I conducted a teleconference with the Board. And then I gathered together the core team of managers who'd been in the trenches with me. Each time I delivered the news I felt more demoralized. I was too tired to think of what we should do next. I simply could not comprehend how we'd arrived here, given all the careful deliberation and preparation. I could not fathom why the families didn't at least believe our intentions were honorable.

As I sat alone in my office late that Friday evening, after all the meetings were over, I felt numb. Allison Johnson, who battled alongside me every day, came in and asked if I was all right. "Sure. How about you? Go home and get some rest." It was Charles Charnas who gave me the push I needed. He was one of the old-timers, a lawyer with a wicked sense of humor during off-hours who was usually pretty quiet in the office. I didn't know him very well then, although I knew he was a consummate professional and good at his job. Now he stuck his head in the office. "Carly, I know you're disappointed. We all are. I want you to know that I believe in you, and I believe in this deal and I know you will prevail." I tried to express my gratitude, but I'm not sure he really knew how important his gesture was.

When I finally got home, Frank had mixed a pitcher of martinis. We hardly ever drank them, but I guess he thought I'd need one that night. I told him, with a smile on my face, that I was fine. I meant it.

"I can't believe it. I thought you'd be a complete mess!"

"I was, but now I'm okay. I know what this fight is about."

That night, for the first time in almost a year, I slept long and deep. I knew now that the fight was between the past and the future, between special interests and broader interests, between the few and the many. I knew now that if we fought well, we could win.

On Sunday morning we had another Board conference call. I wanted to give all the Board members (except, of course, for Walter, who no longer attended meetings) an opportunity to voice their views of what we should do next. Given that both families, both foundations and a former CEO were lining up to oppose us, the decision to continue the fight, like the original decision to acquire Compaq, could not be one I took alone, nor could it be one the Board took lightly. Each Board member would have to weigh in. I began the call by summarizing our alternatives: "We can choose to abandon the merger, and begin the process of disengagement. We can choose to restructure the deal. I have asked for recommendations on alternate deal structures from a different banking team, and they have proposed a spin-off of the combined PC businesses, either before or after the merger is approved. Finally, we can continue on our current course and wage what will be a difficult and costly proxy battle. I'd like to hear each of your views." I had not yet weighed in or given any indication of my own opinions.

Several Board members asked about the alternate deal structure. I'd asked for another bank's views on this a few weeks earlier. Despite my own belief that we could prevail, one should always consider the alternatives. It's wise to plan for victory and prepare for every contingency. The numbers of an alternate deal structure were certainly not compelling; we would destroy more value than we would create by attempting to spin off the PC businesses, and it would be a complex distraction. Nevertheless, there was a group of analysts who had suggested that we'd gain some credibility by jettisoning the most controversial part of the deal. After some discussion, I asked each Board member to state his or her point of view. They all declared their determination to proceed. None voiced doubt about their decision, but all were sobered by the reality of what lay ahead. Now I was asked what I wanted to do. I responded, "I believe we should go forward. I believe we will prevail."

A proxy contest is traditionally a down and dirty fight. There is a whole industry of proxy solicitors, lawyers, and PR firms that have expertise in negative campaigning. We needed to decide how we would fight. How things are done is as important as what gets done. This is the essence of character, and although victory was important, the ends would not justify any means. Throughout the proxy I was asked to approve a variety of tactics. I rejected many because they were not consistent with the character of the company we were fighting for.

An authentic, powerful brand is more than a logo or a marketing slogan. Market share cannot be achieved without mind share, so a brand must be invested in and built over time. But that investment will be wasted if the behavior of a company does not match the promise of its brand. The cosmetics of a brand are not the same as the values of a brand. An authentic, powerful brand is a promise and a reminder that a company will be as it says it will be. Among the core values of the HP brand that I now fought for were trust, respect and integrity. Those values mean doing the right thing when no one is looking and even when the consequences are difficult. Our brand meant we would focus always on the positive case for the merger. We would fight fair and we would not sling mud.

The special shareholder meeting, in which all the votes were to be cast and counted to decide the fate of the merger, was pandemonium. It was held in the same auditorium in which we'd always held our annual shareholder meetings, and because Silicon Valley was the epicenter of support for Walter and David, the auditorium was packed with merger opponents. They wore green shirts to match the color of Walter's proxy ballot. When I walked to the podium to open the meeting, I was greeted with resounding boos, catcalls and shouting. Although I was under no legal or procedural obligation to allow Walter to speak, I nonetheless gave him the floor early on in the proceedings. He received a tumultuous ovation. I thanked him for his comments and then I answered every question I was asked. The questions were legitimate, and I think perhaps I even changed a mind or two. However, when I observed that the whole world did not necessarily feel the way the people in Silicon Valley did, I was booed again. I actually don't remember how long the meeting lasted, but it felt like a very long time.

When we adjourned backstage to wait for the results of the voting, Sam Ginn came to me and asked whether I would be amenable to allowing Walter back on the Board. Sam was shaken by what he'd just witnessed. I thought for a minute and said, "Anything that heals the wounds from this fight is worth doing. Go have a conversation with him." By then we were almost certain we had won the vote. I announced that we'd prevailed by a "slim but sufficient margin."

Several days later Sam reported back to the Board that Walter would rejoin if we wanted him. Although Sam was a strong advocate, everyone else was hesitant. No one knew if we could trust Walter again. Jay was the most vocal and the most opposed. He thought anyone who had leaked confidential Board conversations to the press shouldn't be allowed in the boardroom. Besides, Jay opined, Walter hadn't ever been really qualified in the first place, and he didn't contribute much in meetings. Ultimately I convinced Jay that we should set the past aside and focus on the future. We decided to release an announcement the following morning. Instead, Walter sued us, which I learned from the radio while driving to work. In a hastily arranged conference call, the Board unanimously rescinded its decision.

The suit appeared to be based on nothing more than the text of one of my investor speeches and a single, incomplete page from one of the integration teams' reports that indicated a gap still existed between our value-capture goals and the operational understanding of how to achieve them. Later, a recording of a private voice mail I'd sent to Bob Wayman was delivered to a reporter with the local paper. We never learned how this happened. During the trial an unauthorized recording of one of our investor meetings mysteriously appeared in Walter's lawyer's hands. Apparently, one of Walter's advisers, who stood to gain a couple of million dollars by sinking the deal, had persuaded his good friend who sat in the meeting to record our remarks.

While the suit was progressing, the proxy election was being certified. Walter's team began to examine each ballot as if they were in Florida looking for hanging chads in the 2000 presidential election. They were purposely dragging out the vote-tallying process as long as possible, hoping in the intervening time to find some new, damaging detail they could use against us. Eventually they were ordered by the judge to wrap things up.

I spent almost two full days on the stand, in essence being publicly accused of lying and cheating to steal the vote for the merger. Once again Walter's advisers took full advantage of the climate they were operating in. After all, weren't there more and more corporate scandals being discovered every day in which the CEO was in fact lying and cheating? Tyco, WorldCom, Qwest, Adelphia—these were all examples of corruption in the corporate office. The press coverage was breathless and unrelenting. People were trading stock on every tidbit of information that emerged from the courtroom. The spread between the prices of HP and Compaq stock began to represent the current betting on who would win in court. Las Vegas bookies were taking odds.

My first day on the stand I was patient and respectful. Sitting there, it occurred to me that most people don't understand how business operates. That revelation was one of the original inspirations for this book. Most people don't understand that setting targets is how you determine priorities and direct performance in business. Developing iteration after iteration of an operational plan is how you figure out how to achieve business goals. And from the day a target is set until the day the results are produced, there are usually lots of gaps between what people know how to do and what they eventually figure out how to do.

By the second day I was angry. The case was completely without merit. It began to emerge in court that Walter hadn't even read the charges before they were filed. During his earlier deposition he'd been confronted by evidence that he had not told the truth. He said that sometimes lying was justified, and he used lying to Nazis about the location of hidden Jewish families as an example. During the trial, he repeated on the stand that he thought sometimes the ends justified the means. His team was wasting incredible amounts of time and money hoping to find something—anything—that would stop the merger.

None of them were fighting fair. They never had, but they were hoping to take home a couple million dollars apiece. I was being portrayed as the villain, but it was they who were abusing the company, its people, and the entire legal system for their own personal and pecuniary aims. I felt enormous gratitude and relief when the judge in the case not only ruled resoundingly in our favor, but also went out of his way to comment on the "credibility of management."

.   .   .

T HE SPEECH THAT we had been sued over was my most complete and passionate defense of the merger. I delivered it on February 4, 2002. By that time, the conventional wisdom was that we would never get the necessary votes to approve the deal. I had labored over every word because I wanted to declare what was really at stake. I wanted to say what the fight was really all about. This is part of what I said.

In light of all the adversity we've faced since announcing our plans to merge with Compaq last September, why do we remain so steadfast in our commitment to pursuing this merger? . . . We all know that the technology industry is in the midst of transformation. We are entering a period of [technology] which defies all limits and crosses all borders, in which everything works with everything else, everywhere, all the time. . . . The pure product era is over. . . . The Internet changes everything. . . . The dot-com bubble may have burst, but the effect of the Internet on business and daily life is immutable.

Nearly three years ago we set out on a process to preserve what was best about HP and reinvent the rest. . . . Essential as it was, restructuring and refocusing the organization was not designed to be the end point; it was designed to lay the foundation for market leadership. We recognized that leadership in this new marketplace would require the scale to operate globally, to drive standards and to attract partners. We saw that it would require a better market position in key growth categories, such as networked storage, Windows and Linux servers, in managed services and support, in new categories of devices, in new markets. Leadership would require a stronger, more profitable, more balanced operating model across our businesses because as Bill Hewlett and Dave Packard often preached, profitability is still the key to job preservation, and investment in R&D and innovation, and contribution to community. And we understood that achieving a leadership position would require us to address the fact that the rise of industry-standard platforms, open-source communities and trend toward consolidation are inevitable; inevitable because customers demand ever-improving returns on their IT dollars, and greater flexibility, and faster time-to-market and globally deployed capabilities. We knew we could either lead this trend or be swallowed up by it. . . .

First, in enterprise computing, it is critically important that we are successful in all three operating systems used by the industry today—UNIX, NT and Linux. . . . Then there is our services and support organization. . . . While we have the talent to compete with anyone, we don't have the scale. . . . For far too long, our imaging and printing business has accounted for too much of the profitability of the company. We have to invest in imaging and printing to lead, which means our other businesses have to pay their own way. . . . We looked at focusing solely on our imaging and printing franchise, but the consequences were unacceptable. Continued growth, . . . and profitability, requires us to capture more and more of the printed-page opportunities . . . which requires servers and storage and network management software and professional services.

We had choices in our PC business. We could shut it down, which would damage our imaging and printing franchise and mean significant loss of jobs. We could spin it off, . . . but our PC business is not a viable entity in its own right and would not create sufficient value for shareowners. Or, alternatively, we could fix it by adding volume and direct distribution capabilities. . . .

The legacy of HP—the people of HP—are capable of doing and achieving and being so much more than a stripped-down shell of what we are now. For all the gaps we have to fill, we also have huge capabilities. . . . One of the things that Dave Packard says in his book, *The HP Way*, is that he never forgot, and I quote, that "continuous growth was essential for us to achieve our other objectives and remain competitive. Since we participate in the fields of advanced and rapidly changing technologies, to remain static is to lose ground."

Now, some of our critics say bigger doesn't necessarily mean better. And I agree. But it doesn't follow that bigger can't be better, especially in an industry that's . . . consolidating. . . .

This merger isn't just my judgment of how best to secure this company's future. This represents the collective judgment of a talented team of people who have spent the last few years preparing for this transaction. . . . These are people who attended the meetings where we asked the hard questions. . . . These same people have looked at the alternatives. . . . True, there is one dissenter on our board. I am disappointed that Walter Hewlett has come out against this merger. Walter is a good and decent man. And he has a right to disagree. But we have every right to disagree with him too.

Frankly, my problem isn't that our opposition is saying no to the merger. The problem is that they are giving us nothing to say yes to because they haven't proposed any solutions to the challenges we face. . . . We are being asked to simply disregard two and a half years of planning and thought and strategy, in which every option was considered and rejected, . . . in favor of retreating and starting over. . . . The only thing we would lose is time. . . . It's the one thing we can never get back. . . .

To simply say no without offering an alternative plan is to ask the people of HP to give up their vision, to put their ambitions aside, and to settle for less than this company is capable of achieving. The people of HP don't want to rest on the legacy of this company. They are determined to build on it. . . . This is a choice between taking the hill and charging ahead or retreating and starting over. This is a choice between embracing the revolution that is changing our industry or attempting in vain to preserve the status quo. This is a choice between leading and following.

During another time and place, at the dawn of another era in computing, a woman named Grace Murray Hopper offered a piece of wisdom that applies to us today. Grace Murray Hopper was not only one of the first women software engineers in America, she was also a rear admiral in the U.S. Navy. One day she was asked why she liked to be in the middle of the action at sea rather than docked in safe waters at home. She replied. "A ship in port is safe. But that is not what ships are built for."

HP can sit idly in its port and watch the rest of the world go by. It can choose the still waters of inaction over the rough waves of competition. But that is not what Hewlett-Packard was built for.

Many months after the battle was over, people asked me what had prepared me for it. I answered, "Nothing and everything." I was faced with pressures I had never imagined I could endure. I was learning new things on the fly when the stakes were enormous. And yet I would rely on things I knew: how to build teams and keep them together, how to sustain effort and maintain humor, how to focus people on the essential. I would trust my internal compass, that navigational instrument that never fails even when the wind is howling and the sky is dark. I knew I was doing what I believed were the right things for the right reasons in the best way I knew how. And I would draw strength from my faith in people. Most people are good and sensible, and given enough time and enough information, they will make good and sensible choices.

The force of progress will always triumph over the fear of change. And the march of history demonstrates that the many can prevail over the few. HP belongs to the many people who care about its future, not to the few who strive to protect their own positions or line their own pockets or preserve the past. This is what I'd fought for. This is why I knew we would prevail.

27 | Adopt and Go

FROM SEPTEMBER 4, 2001, until May 6, 2002, when we finally consummated the merger and traded our new stock on the New York Stock Exchange for the first time, the people of HP and Compaq performed brilliantly. Despite all the distractions, both companies continued to serve customers, develop products and deliver the numbers. While a relatively small team of us met with investors, going sometimes to eight or ten meetings a day, we were also engaged, along with everyone else, in the business of reassuring customers, answering employee questions and going about the day-to-day business of making the company run. At the same time, on the day we announced the deal, we had named the executives who would lead integration planning, Webb McKinney and Jeff Clarke, and every week, no matter what else was going on, the other members of the Executive Steering Committee and I would meet with the integration team to check our progress and make the necessary decisions and adjustments.

The merger of HP and Compaq has been called one of the most successful ever. Even our critics acknowledge that we accomplished it twelve months ahead of schedule and delivered $3.5 billion of cost synergies—far above the $2.5 billion we'd promised (and been accused in court of overestimating). Michael and I had disagreed about integration from the beginning. He thought we were spending too much time and dedicating too many people. I knew that integration is all about the details and that we could take nothing for granted. I insisted that we dedicate people to the task. I insisted that we hire professional program managers to drive our schedules and monitor our deliverables, just as we had back in the days of the huge and complex FTS2000 program. And I insisted that I be updated on integration progress every single week, no matter what. The Executive Steering Committee would become the final stop in the decision-making process for integration.

We immediately created a dedicated team of people that ultimately numbered more than two thousand employees. By May, we had more than one million hours invested. This integration team worked full-time; we decided early on that people couldn't plan something this massive and complex on a part-time basis. We began by studying data from hundreds of mergers across dozens of industries. Ours was the largest merger ever attempted in the IT industry, so there weren't a lot of examples of success there. However, we studied integrations from every industry—the good, the bad and the ugly—so we could learn the lessons that would help us be successful. From this study we extracted important principles and practices that were used to guide our integration.

Early on, a customer said to me during a meeting: "Remember, Carly, this is your merger, not ours." He was politely reminding me that since the whole point of this deal was to serve customers better, we shouldn't get so internally focused that we forgot them, or made them suffer because of our decision. So we began with the principle that the customer comes first. We would not distract people whose job it was to serve customers every day. It was one of the important reasons we decided we couldn't ask people to plan integration part-time. Starting with the customer also gave us a way to make the really difficult trade-offs, particularly those that are politically charged and involve picking one group or executive over another. The customer became our tiebreaker for the really tough decisions. Who is more effective with this customer? Which product is more successful in the marketplace? We even asked customers for their preferences in terms of both people and product plans. And the integration issues that mattered most to customers became our highest priorities.

Our second principle was what we called adopt and go. This was particularly important in an engineering culture that liked to strive for perfection. Adopt and go meant we had to be decisive, and we had to mean it. We didn't get to invent new products or processes; we chose from what already existed, and we adopted one for the whole new company. We looked at every practice, process, product or person for a particular job that HP and Compaq had. We picked the best, we decided, and we moved on.

Third, we had a relentless value-capture focus. In the summer of 2001, when we'd developed our first integration plan, we'd identified the principal areas where value could be created by the merger, and we quantified that value. Now we asked our integration team not only to verify these opportunities but to identify any others that existed to create more value—whether on the top line or the bottom line—for our customers, our shareowners or our employees. From this exhaustive list of quantified opportunities, we created integration plans of record. These were detailed road maps to determining how to capture the value and identifying who has to do what and when certain decisions and actions have to occur. Ultimately these integration plans of record would become the basis of ongoing operational reviews, and we would tie employee and executive bonuses to their achievement.

We focused on both short- and long-term planning. We set tough goals for ourselves on what we would accomplish as the new company on the first day of business, the first thirty days, the first sixty days, the first ninety days. We also had clear goals for the first year, second year and third year. Once we set these goals, we did not blink. We did what was necessary to achieve them. For example, when we said all our employees needed to be able to communicate with one another via an integrated e-mail system on day one, we meant it, and people stepped up to deliver it.

We always knew exactly where we were in meeting our goals and completing our tasks. Each week others and I would look at a dashboard of goals, metrics, facts, milestones and key decisions.

We integrated both vertical organizations and horizontal processes. We created specific teams around each of these businesses and processes. Both vertical and horizontal activities had specific goals, metrics and time lines.

We found that in many cases the largest value-capture opportunities occurred along the horizontal dimension, as, for example, with our supply chain processes.

Each of our project teams was responsible for conducting regular issue management meetings and documenting decisions. Project managers would raise cross-project issues in regular meetings. Resolution owners were identified, and decisions were documented. Program managers would raise cross-program issues in weekly calls, and these issues would be raised to the relevant steering committee where decisions could be made quickly. We had a very clearly defined escalation path that did not permit issues to linger. If a decision could not be made adequately in the group, it was escalated until one was made. If an issue made it all the way to the Executive Steering Committee, we would make the decision. Usually we agreed, but if necessary, I would decide.

We accomplished the largest integration ever attempted in the industry through rigorous attention to detail, disciplined processes and collaboration, and an expectation for both speed and precision. We accomplished it because of the enormous dedication of the people of both companies.

Technology was the skeletal structure of the company that allowed us to actually make all these decisions, communicate all the actions and enable people to work together across separate companies and around the world. We created "e-rooms," electronic gathering places for every team and every committee. And the integration of 229,000 e-mail boxes, 232,632 accounts, 220,000 desktops, 1,093 network sites and more than 7,000 applications was as heroic an undertaking as any other aspect of the integration.

Integration, like any other operational challenge in a complicated, rapidly changing global business, reminded me a lot of those philosophy papers I used to write in college. You could understand and extract the essence, but only if you first understood all the details. A good teacher can explain the general principle because he or she deeply understands the specifics. A leader can effectively communicate what must be done because he or she understands how people will actually operate and perform.

The integration of the two companies would happen one product, one process, one plan and, most of all, one person at a time. All our employees were looking to their leaders to address what we came to call the *me* in merger as quickly as possible. People couldn't completely move on to the new reality until they understood what it meant to them personally. So we had to start with honest and frequent communication. We told people how many jobs would be lost. We told them why. We told them how long it would be before they knew whether they would retain their job in the new company. Later we told them the process we would use to select people, and the assistance they could expect if they lost their job. In times of great turmoil, people don't take anything for granted. They don't know what will stay the same, so unless they're told otherwise, they fear everything will change.

Our explicit goal was to use two strands of DNA to create a stronger, better company. These two companies had different habits, personalities and values. We pioneered something we called cultural due diligence. Financial or technical due diligence is common in a merger, but we believed we also needed to examine in detail how these two cultures differed. We conducted in-depth interviews with more than 100 executives and 2,000 employees from both companies, and we ran 138 focus groups in 22 countries. We asked two basic questions: "What's it really like to work around here?" "What would you like the values of the new company to be?"

The results were fascinating and useful. There were real differences between the two companies—ten substantive differences, in fact. We didn't paper them over; we talked about them. For example, Compaq focused on fast decision making, while HP focused on thorough decision making. Sometimes Compaq people had to revisit the decision again and again because they hadn't taken all the relevant facts into account. Sometimes HP people lost the opportunity because they decided too slowly. Now we had an opportunity to begin developing fast, thorough decision making. We illustrated just this kind of decision making through our integration efforts. The phrase "perfect enough" evolved to "fast enough"—not too fast, not too slow, just fast enough.

On the question of values there was amazing alignment. When we gathered up all the input, it was clear that people everywhere aspired to the same things. Values are signposts to guide people's behavior when the rules aren't clear and the supervisor isn't present. Goals and metrics are what get done; Values are how those things get done. After all the research, we ended up with the same core values that had always been part of the HP Way: trust, respect, integrity, passion for customers, teamwork and collaboration, innovation, contribution—and one new addition; speed and agility.

Building a new company required education, conversation and the development of common standards and common language. We asked new teams to spend time together talking about the "hardware," the nuts and bolts of integration, as well as the "software" of culture. For example, people had different views on what respect meant—how should men treat women; how should executives treat rank-and-file employees? Why were some employees fearful in certain businesses or locations and not in others? How could we train managers to encourage and embrace open dialogue and diversity? We conducted employee surveys semiannually to gauge our progress on these important issues.

Values are aspirational; not everyone in the organization lives up to them every day. Yet there's a difference between falling short of an aspiration for speed and agility and willful violation of bedrock principles like trust, respect and integrity.

A N EXECUTIVE CANNOT be permitted to do what an employee would be fired for. One of the newest members of my executive council was a talented young executive from Compaq. He had a great future, and I liked his energy, his spirit and his intellect. Asking him to leave was the hardest personnel decision I've ever made. He was having a relationship with another HP executive; while this in itself wasn't a business problem, the abuse of his position and the company's resources to further this relationship was. When a whistle-blower brought these executives' actions to the attention of Bob Wayman, we had no choice. I informed the Board of their behavior, and they were unanimous that both individuals would have to leave. It was the only time I was tearful in the boardroom. It was the right decision, but I was deeply distressed nonetheless.

Michael's behavior had become counterproductive. He set the wrong example for the organization. I had truly hoped for a different outcome, but over time it became clear to the entire Board that a change had to be made. Once again, the decision was unanimous and painful.

In the outside world, I was usually portrayed as the problem behind these executives' departures. Inside the company, people understood that values matter and character counts—as much for the senior staff as for anyone else.

28 | Everything Is Possible

O N MAY 6, 2002, the stock symbol HPQ crossed the New York Stock Exchange ticker for the first time. Some people who still couldn't believe the merger had actually happened once again whispered that we'd abandoned the old HWP because I was mad at the Hewlett and Packard families. It had nothing to do with them. The equation was obvious: HWP + CPQ = HPQ. All the employees understood the simple math that meant one company plus another company was more than two separate companies. Our destinies were now one.

On May 9, I returned to the same auditorium where less than two months earlier I'd been booed during the proxy vote. We were holding our first all-employee meeting of the new company, which was broadcast in live video around the world. While I waited backstage, the thousands of employees gathered in that auditorium cheered and stomped their feet and shouted my name. When I walked out to greet them, they erupted in elation.

I had insisted that the first Rule of the Garage read "Believe you can change the world." The last one reads "Believe that together we can do anything." Some had challenged them by saying they were too corny, but I believe them with all my heart. And as I stood together with the people who'd worked so hard to create the opportunity that so many had bet against, I felt validated in my belief that everything is possible. Not everything is easy, and not everything happens right away. Not everything happens exactly as you think it will, but when people work together, focused on a common goal and inspired by a worthy purpose, then truly everything is possible.

"Everything is possible" became the rallying cry of the new HP. It was a statement we used in our internal communications as well as in our external advertising. It signified our aspirations and responsibilities as a global company, our belief that technology enabled and empowered more people in more places than ever before in history, and our confidence that through continued dedication and collaboration we could achieve our objectives and help others achieve theirs.

I have seen firsthand the marvels of the twenty-first century, a time in humanity's journey that is different from all the history that has come before. We are now operating in a truly global economy for the first time. Of course many people, too many, are still on the outside looking in, denied the basic human dignities of clean water and adequate food or shelter. Too many people still cannot participate in the global economy because they lack peace and safety, education, work, basic medical care or enlightened leadership. Despite these real tragedies and challenges, three billion people have joined the world's trading system in the last decade. China, India, Russia, Brazil, Poland, Lithuania and many more are all nations and peoples who now are eager and active participants and drivers of the global market. Many of these nations have a rich history of achievement in science and education. If just one out of every ten citizens among these three billion people has the preparation and motivation to make a positive difference in the world, then three hundred million individuals, more than the entire population of the United States, can compete and lead in the twenty-first century.

On one of my many trips to China, I was asked to give a lecture at Tsinghua University, the university in Beijing where most of the government leaders have been educated for many decades. The first question I received was from a young woman who asked how I balanced work and family. The second student asked if I had ever thought of starting my own business, and if so, how should she think about starting her own business. A young man said he really didn't like his major and that he'd heard I had quit law school. His parents didn't want him to change his field of studies, but he wondered if I thought it might be a good idea. I laughed and said, "Do you want to go home and tell your parents that Carly Fiorina said it was okay?" He laughed and so did hundreds of the other students. These were questions that I might receive on any American college campus. Every question was asked in perfect English. And when I returned home, I received touching thank-you letters from students like Mei Hongming, and Xiao Chen Xi and Tracy Guo.

IN THE TWENTY-FIRST CENTURY, technology is transforming every aspect of our lives. Just think about the changes that have taken place in photography over the last decade. Photography used to be a physical, chemical, analog process. You took a picture; something physical happened in your camera; you took your film to a photo developer, and once again a physical, chemical process transformed images on film to images on paper; you picked up your photos; you sorted them, and when you had the time, you mailed them to family and friends or put them in a photo album. Today a digital camera or a camera phone creates digital content. That content can be networked and sent anywhere in the world wirelessly; and it can be edited, stored and shared. A virtual experience has been created; others can enjoy exactly the same images at the same time from a million miles away. And it's personal because individuals are in control of every step in the process, including, if they wish, creating professional photos, suitable for framing, in their own homes.

There are thousands of more sophisticated examples of transformation from physical and analog to digital, mobile, virtual and personal. Online gaming, blogging, personal banking, music, entertainment—the list goes on and on, and the changes are occurring at a faster and faster rate. What will it mean when people all over the world have access to any information on any device at any time? The twenty-first century is bringing about the complete democratization of information, the breakdown of traditional barriers of time, distance and wealth, and the onset of complete transparency. The digital, mobile, virtual, personal age puts individuals, not institutions, more and more in charge, wherever or whoever they happen to be.

There was a time in history when we could assume that because someone lacked opportunity, they lacked potential. We now know this is not true. Every single person has potential inside them, and the right leadership, the right technology and the right collaboration can unlock that potential.

. . .

TWO YOUNG WOMEN named Saraswati and Gowri live in a rural community called Kuppam, in India. In their village one in three citizens is illiterate, more than half of the households have no electricity, and most of the able-bodied adults are HIV positive. These young women were forced to leave school after the fifth and seventh grades because their families could not afford their schooling. A number of HP people, working with this community, invented a solar-powered digital camera and a solar-powered printer that fit into a backpack. Saraswati and Gowri were among ten young women chosen to be trained as village photographers and given this equipment.

Knowing how people love to have their pictures taken, these two women seized upon a business opportunity. They decided to follow the region's chief minister as he traveled on his rounds and sell inexpensive photo ops to the village people. In less than a week they had earned the equivalent of a month's income. And today they have built a business for themselves and have started a fund in their village to help other young women start their own businesses.

As part of our e-inclusion efforts, we committed ourselves to the development of a rural community called Mogalakwena in South Africa. I saw people without running water or electricity in their homes confidently using technology accessible in more than twenty locations from libraries to health clinics to schools. I met with many of the three thousand people who had graduated from PC literacy courses and community computer camps. They ranged in age from thirteen to seventy-four, and they were applying their newfound skills in all kinds of exciting ways, from distance learning to better medical care to making their voices heard in decisions that affect their daily lives.

I met Sali George Missinga, an uneducated, impoverished young man from the village. HP people had hired him to move boxes of equipment into the community center, but Sali George had a curious mind. After three weeks of observing what was going on, he asked some of our HP technicians to teach him something about this technology. One year later Sali George was the technical expert HP would send from that community to do computer installations at a local university.

As I talked with Sali George, I said, "You know, Sali, I think I might mention you to your president." And this young man, with his newfound self-confidence, looked me straight in the eye and said, "Good, I think you should. I think I deserve it." When I gave a speech later that day, I introduced Sali to the crowd, and then I introduced President Thabo Mbeki. The president asked Sali George to come onstage and give a speech. He spoke with great eloquence about how his life had been transformed by people who had taken a chance on him and by a technology that had given him the tools to make a difference in his own and others' lives. And at the end of Sali's speech, President Mbeki said, "Young man, I'm going to send you to college."

In the twenty-first century, for the first time in human history, anyone can lead. Of course injustice and prejudice and inequity are still realities. Nevertheless, today leadership has nothing to do with title or money or power. Leadership is not about gender or the color of one's skin; it is not about physical gifts or national origin. With the right support and the right opportunities, anyone can lead from anywhere at any time. Leadership is a choice about character and a choice to make a positive contribution. Leaders can see and then harness the leadership potential in others through the power of collaboration and the tool of technology.

A S WE CAME to the end of our integration efforts, I asked employees to lift their heads to see how far we had come together on our journey of transformation and where that journey would now take us. Phase I had been about aspiration and unification. We had chosen to aspire to leadership and we had unified a thousand tribes to bolster our strength. Our aspirations had consequences, so recognizing that we could not achieve our objectives alone, we had chosen to ally ourselves with the people of Compaq. Phase II was about consolidation and integration. We had consolidated the industry through our acquisition and had integrated the new company.

Phase III, which we entered in earnest in the second half of 2003 and which characterized our efforts throughout 2004, was about leverage and leadership. Now we could leverage all of our assets to shape the new era in technology. We had built a unique portfolio, and now we could leverage it to respond to customers' growing requirements for solutions. Customers didn't want to buy pieces of technology anymore; the era of hot boxes and killer apps was definitely over. As technology became more deeply woven into the fabric of business and life, customers increasingly looked to companies that could pull it all together for them.

Now our business customers demanded technology solutions that were manageable and cost effective, and helped them adapt more quickly and effectively to the changes in their own environment. Our strategy was to help our customers build the adaptive enterprise and to deliver the best return on information technology (ROIT). In practical terms this meant providing a lower cost of ownership, improved manageability, interoperability, reliability and security as well as reduced complexity. Our efforts in software would be focused on management and systems interoperability. Our computing platforms would be flexible, standards-based and high-performance. We could bring together printing, computing and services assets to deliver document management solutions.

Consumers also were demanding more integrated technology offerings. Our strategy was to deliver simple, rewarding experiences: technology and solutions that were simple to own, to buy and to operate, and that made our customers' lives more productive, more fun, more valuable.

We had economies of scale, great innovative capacity, and increasingly effective discipline around customer satisfaction. Our unique value proposition was therefore high-tech, low-cost, best total customer experience (TCE): reliable, relevant innovation at a price our customers could afford, with an experience that set us apart.

Turning Phase III into business reality required a detailed operational plan. We used the same program management governance that we'd relied on in Phase II to focus the organization around Profitable Growth, Achieving Benchmark Cost Structures, Improving Performance Discipline, and Accelerating Go-To-Market Effectiveness. Each of these programs had specific goals, plans and metrics, and every organization had a committed role to play.

Our Profitable Growth programs were focused on improving our gross margins by, for example, accelerating our use of direct distribution, growing our software business more rapidly, selling more bundled solutions and moving to margin-based sales compensation. Achieving Benchmark Cost Structures recognized that we had to continually strive for improved efficiency and a lower cost base. This meant, for instance, constantly evaluating how many people we had, where they were located, how we managed contingent labor, as well as how we managed labor-intensive processes like warranty and repair. Improving Performance Discipline was focused on using program management processes throughout the company to drive consistent, reliable execution.

Finally, Accelerating Go-To-Market Effectiveness was a set of programs focused on our sales force. Our selling resources had to be qualified to sell technology solutions. We had to deploy these highly trained salespeople efficiently. We had to leverage effectively the vast network of channel partners we worked with. We could not complete the transition from a company that sold products to a technology powerhouse that sold systems and integrated solutions without a transition in our selling capabilities as well.

The Leadership Framework became the common language we used to keep 150,000 employees operating in more than 150 countries on the same page. Constancy and consistency are necessary to achieve coherence in a company, and without coherence a company might as well be broken apart. We invested in training and communications programs to ensure our employees understood our strategy. Our operating model delineated our structures and processes. Each vertical business and horizontal process had its own specific goals and metrics. We measured and paid for results through a balanced scorecard that focused the organization on financial performance metrics like revenue growth and profit improvement; on operational efficiency metrics like inventory turns and cash generation; on programs that bolstered total customer experience; and on specific programs to address the issues that affected employees, which we identified and measured through our Voice of the Workforce surveys. Every manager had a balanced scorecard. Along with this balanced scorecard, every employee and every executive was also evaluated against our core values and our leadership behaviors. How things get done is as important as what gets done, and there was rigor, discipline and a systematic approach to both.

The years 2003 and 2004 were not perfect. The global economic weakness continued, and our execution was sometimes inconsistent. We missed our targets for the third quarter of each year. Despite this, the growing momentum of the organization was unmistakable. Each of our four main businesses was now profitable. We had regained leadership in UNIX. We were number one in industry standard servers and Linux-based servers. Our printing business was growing faster and generating more profit than at any time in its history. Our PC business was now number two in the world and had achieved sustainable profitability. We now commanded more shelf space for our consumer products around the world than HP and Compaq had as separate companies, and we had leading, profitable positions in both consumer PCs and consumer printing. Our services business competed head to head with IBM and was both more profitable and growing faster. We'd acquired and integrated seven software companies, and our software business was reaching critical mass. We'd completely revamped the online shopping and servicing capabilities we offered our business and consumer customers. We had revitalized and repositioned the HP brand in both the consumer and business markets. Our market research told us that the brand was now viewed as not only high quality, but also relevant and forward looking.

In those two years we outperformed analyst estimates for revenue by $2 billion and achieved $73 billion in revenues in 2003 and $80 billion in revenue in 2004—$7 billion in organic revenue growth. Profit, as measured by generally accepted accounting principles (GAAP) net earnings, grew from a loss of $928 million in 2002 to a profit of $2.5 billion in 2003 and to $3.5 billion in 2004. In 2003 and 2004 we outperformed analyst estimates for earnings per share by one penny. In 2002 the GAAP diluted loss per share was $0.31. In 2003 this grew to earnings per share of $0.83 and to $1.15 per share in 2004. We were generating between $5 billion and $6 billion in cash flow from operations per year, up from just $2.6 billion prior to the merger. We continued to fund the pension and pay dividends (with the highest yield in the industry) as we had for thirty years. By 2004, we had included all of our restructuring charges in our operating results, and we also stepped up our stock repurchases to $3.3 billion, up from just $750 million in 2003 and $670 million in 2002.

In both 2003 and 2004, HP people generated eleven patents a day, the highest rate of innovation in the company's history; and based on that track record, HP became the number three innovator in the world in 2005. Our total customer experience scores continued to improve. TBR's Customer Satisfaction Study noted, "HP has established a predictable pattern of steady as she goes and its customer loyalty position remains a sector leader. With respect to customer confidence this does not present a picture of a vendor being squeezed between two giants without a territory of its own, as implied by the technical press." Our Voice of the Workforce survey told us that our employees understood our strategy and could support our image in the marketplace. They described HP as an open, collaborative environment with strong communication.

IT IS DIFFICULT to adequately convey how much grueling work had been accomplished over the previous five and a half years. I have worked hard all my life. None of my successes came easily, but HP required a whole new level of dedication and discipline. Although not everyone could yet see it, by the end of 2004, a sustainable, successful business transformation had been achieved. It wasn't perfect, but it was perfect enough.

Such an accomplishment takes more than teamwork, although this is absolutely required. And business transformation takes big ideas to prioritize activities and align efforts. We'd begun with the big idea of the Leadership Framework to alter every aspect of an institution that had begun to atrophy. The merger was a big idea about how to achieve leadership in a rapidly changing industry. Mostly, though, business transformation is about the details—lots and lots of details.

Is our product plan competitive? Are we walking away from bad business? Are we focusing sufficient energy on the business we want to win? How should we focus management attention on cash flow more effectively? How do we improve the profitability of a product? Is our portfolio of services contracts appropriately balanced? Why is accounts receivable growing? Are we investing our R&D dollars in the right places? Are we investing enough? Is customer satisfaction improving rapidly enough? Do we have the right people in the right jobs? Are our budgets both demanding and realistic? Are our goals supported by detailed work programs that people are prepared to execute? What are employees really worried about? What are customers actually demanding? And on and on—the list of operational questions that must be addressed day in and day out goes on and on.

If transformation is required, a chief executive cannot simply delegate these operational details to others. Of course there are some details in a business that a CEO should delegate, but a chief executive cannot preside in glorious isolation or focus only on the big picture. Business is about results, not concepts, although ideas can motivate behavior and inspire action. And results are about details, not big ideas. A chief executive must strike that right balance between letting people do their jobs and constantly verifying that the details are being attended to appropriately, and then making course corrections as required. Some thought I didn't look or sound like "an operational type." Anyone who's actually delivered business results knows that operational execution is all about the substance of the executive, not the style or the personality.

A business transformation happens one product, one decision, one dollar, one person, and one day at a time. And so HP had become my life. I was consumed by the company and its requirements. It is no exaggeration to say I routinely worked twelve- or fourteen-hour days, slept little and thought always about HP. It is also impossible to overstate my deep satisfaction with what we'd accomplished as 2004 drew to a close. Once again I felt the special joy of believing in a team more than they had believed in themselves and being rewarded by seeing their pride and newfound confidence as they achieved more than they'd thought was possible. Despite all the difficulties and the external criticism, 150,000 people all over the world were on the same page. In short, we knew where we were going, and we knew how to get there. We spoke a common language and shared a common vision. Of course we still had work to do. There is always work to do, and our plans for 2005 called for continuous improvement in every aspect of our business. We had not yet achieved our full potential as a company. We'd put the detailed budgets and work plans in place to deliver that improvement.

The only clouds on the horizon were the press and the stock price. These were not insignificant, but I believed that the strong performance we would deliver over the coming year would take care of both in time. Our third quarter miss reignited all the familiar controversy about the merger. Once again, those who had originally opposed us now repeated their opinion that the merger was a bad idea and a failure. Once again, some advocated a split of the company. The press was once again personal and, in some cases, mean-spirited, but we were poised to silence our critics. The year 2005 was going to be the payoff year for all the grueling work since July of 1999.

29 | Power Politics

AFTER WE MISSED our quarter's targets in 2003, I went to the Board and expressed my growing reservations about Peter Blackmore. This wasn't a new subject, but now I said we needed to make a change. There was mounting evidence that although Peter was an excellent sales executive whom I liked tremendously, he didn't pay sufficient attention to the details of execution in his very large, complex organization. Then the Board had disagreed. Tom Perkins and Lucy Salhany were particularly adamant that we should give him another chance. I acquiesced and left him in the job for another year. It was a mistake and it was mine. The CEO is accountable for performance and, therefore, is accountable for choosing the team members. I insisted on detailed execution updates from Peter and exercised closer supervision than I'm sure he wanted, but neither could provide a satisfactory solution. When execution issues in Peter's organization cost us another quarter in 2004, I gave the Board no choice. Peter would have to leave, and Mike Winkler would replace him as the head of the Customer Solutions Group (CSG). Mike did a magnificent job of driving operational discipline and the transformation of the sales force.

I truly wish Peter could have left under different circumstances. I know his departure was painful for him and his family. It was difficult for me to face him and tell him it was time to go. It was difficult to tell him that others had to go as well. He'd earned my candor and my respect, however. We'd put him in the wrong job, and we'd left him there too long, but he was a quality executive of character who made a real contribution to the merger and the company. When we announced the significant and surprising third quarter miss, our investors naturally wanted to know what we were going to do about it. I explained in great detail what had gone wrong, the steps we would now take to fix the systems and process issues that had been uncovered, and also indicated that management changes would be made. I was pressed to name names by some analysts on our quarterly conference call, but I declined. A public hanging wasn't what I was after, but decisive action was required.

It was important to explain our course of action; while the miss was significant, it was, in fact, an isolated set of events in one organization. The rest of the company had actually performed very well. And as much as Wall Street needed to hear what our action plan was, the people of HP needed to hear it more. Building a culture of accountability and execution discipline requires real and clear consequences for failure to perform.

IN AUGUST AND SEPTEMBER of 2004, Bob Wayman and I visited with all of our largest shareholders after we had announced our quarterly results. Although disappointed in the stock's performance, they remained with us and were committed to the strategy. Several used the stock's weakness to substantially increase their holdings. Virtually all of them asked us to dramatically increase the company's purchases of HP stock. Following these visits, I informed the Board that our September meeting would be devoted to an examination of both our strategy and our operational plans. I volunteered this examination because I believed it was necessary for good Board governance. A major increase in a stock repurchase program is a signal of confidence in a company's management and strategy. The Board could not rightly make such a decision or give such a signal unless it understood the operational plans in place to deliver against the strategy and had evaluated the strategic alternatives.

Once again we enlisted the help of McKinsey & Company in evaluating our current strategy against other alternatives, including the split-up of the company. We invited both bankers and outside counsel to the meeting to provide their perspective. We provided our first views of the operational plan for 2005, which detailed goals and programs around profitable growth, lowering our cost structures, and improving our performance discipline and go-to-market effectiveness. We spent the hours from four o'clock through a late dinner in conversation. The following morning the Board had further deliberations with outside advisers as well as with other members of the management team. The Board approved a major increase in our stock repurchase program and issued a statement of confidence in the management team and support for the strategy.

Both Sam Ginn and Phil Condit had retired from the Board in January 2004. As CEOs, they understood from their own experience how large companies and their Boards operate. They knew that a CEO must balance the demands of shareholders, employees, customers and communities. They knew a CEO is responsible for business results and for the operational details required to deliver those results. They knew that a Board cannot operate a company. They knew that a small group of individuals can sometimes go off track. They provided ballast and perspective to the Board's discussions. Their presence in the boardroom was sorely missed, particularly by me. The only remaining Board members with current operational experience were Larry Babbio and Bob Knowling. They shared Sam's and Phil's views about the role of a Board and the role of a chief executive.

Dick Hackborn, Jay Keyworth and Tom Perkins (until his own retirement in January 2004, when he'd reached the mandatory retirement age of seventy-two) had formed the Technology Committee. The committee had been Tom's idea. All three loved technology and would spend hours engaged in detailed technical discussions both during and outside of committee meetings. Shane Robison, the chief technology and strategy officer, was very much like them, and he staffed the Technology Committee. All four spent a lot of time together.

Dick, Jay and Tom were technologists, not operational executives. Although they loved the minutiae of technology, they were big-picture guys; they were impatient with the details of what was necessary to actually get something done. Like many technologists, they recognized and liked their own kind, but they weren't particularly perceptive about, appreciative of, or interested in people who were different. They had strong opinions about technology and just about everything else. None of them had confidence in Ann Livermore, and I frequently found myself defending her performance. They thought Shane Robison could do almost any job, and at various times they recommended him as a replacement for Duane Zitzner as head of the Personal Systems Group, Vyomesh Joshi as head of the Imaging and Printing Group and, later, Ann Livermore as head of the Technology Systems Group. Dick, Jay and Tom liked Shane because Shane had the same interests and the same strengths as they did. They thought because they understood technology, they understood everything. Shane wasn't an operational executive either. He was, however, a great CTO and knew what he was good at, and what he wasn't good at. He did not want an operational role.

My job, as the chief executive accountable for the performance of the company, was to separate the wheat from the chaff of Dick's, Jay's and Tom's suggestions. I always listened and when we disagreed, I always explained why. Many times we did agree. In general, when they stuck to technology strategy they were insightful; they were very helpful in prioritizing our software acquisitions. When they strayed into other areas, however, they were disruptive. And they didn't know what they didn't know.

In 2004, Jay Keyworth's wife died after a long battle with cancer. Jay had nursed her with great devotion. He called and asked if I would deliver a eulogy. Of course I agreed. Afterward, his son approached me. He was worried about his father. Jay had been a nuclear physicist at Los Alamos National Laboratory. Brainy and solitary, he had relied heavily on his wife for emotional support. Now he would be alone, and his son asked if I could find ways to keep his father occupied. He was worried that Jay would drift into a depression. I returned to California and told the team working on our entry into digital entertainment that Jay would be joining many of our meetings. Jay always had an interesting point of view, and I wanted to help him through a difficult period in his life. It was a decision of the heart, not the head, and it was a mistake.

As summer turned to fall and Jay spent more time at company headquarters, he'd pop into my office more frequently. He'd always have lots of ideas about what we should be doing. Mostly he wanted me to buy things. AMD, Apple, TiVo, Veritas—his list was long and varied. He was impatient with the practical details. He argued strenuously that these acquisitions made strategic sense and that we could figure out the rest. I didn't agree at all, but Jay brought them into the Technology Committee. I spent lots of time arguing the strategic logic and stressing the real operational complexities and financial constraints. We couldn't, or shouldn't, do any of them.

Jay seemed more and more impatient with me as I rejected his many suggestions. At some point he called to tell me he'd met a woman. Later he told me he was taking her to his home in Italy and to visit with Tom Perkins at his English estate. I hoped this would make him happy and keep him occupied.

Jay was always opinionated about everything, including his fellow Board members. He had been derisive of Pattie Dunn's capabilities ever since I'd known him. He routinely complained that she didn't understand the company and relied on process as a crutch. He'd frequently encouraged me to replace her. Pattie had been the chair of the Audit Committee, and he'd always warned me that its members, including him, were growing increasingly impatient with her leadership. At one point he told me several Board members would resign if she did not relinquish the chairmanship. Pattie seemed to have some frustrations over her Barclays career. I knew she was deeply disappointed to lose the Audit chair, although she was professional about it and acknowledged that the new chair was better qualified. I felt I'd had no choice; the complaints about her leadership from the management team, our outside auditors and her fellow Board members indicated a change was required.

Jay was also dismissive of Lucy Salhany; he found her emotional and inconsistent. He wanted her replaced as well. As he spent more time at HP, he complained more and more frequently about how weak the HP Board was and urged me to quickly recruit new members.

We had been on the recruiting path for some time. The perception of a Board member's independence had changed since the introduction of Sarbanes-Oxley. It was hard to find operating executives whose own company didn't have some ongoing conflict or relationship with HP. It was also difficult to find operating executives who were prepared to spend time on a Board, given the increased duties and liabilities. While Sam Ginn had been chairman of Nominating and Governance, he'd worked directly with the headhunting firm to identify Board candidates. Many Board members had expressed concern that Sam wasn't sufficiently open about that process, so after he retired, I began to report to the Board at every meeting on the status of our recruiting efforts. We'd review the list of candidates and add or delete names after our discussion. We had succeeded in adding Bob Ryan to the Board in July. He was the CFO at Medtronic and he became the chair of the Audit Committee. Bob was unable to attend the September meeting. We were looking forward to another CEO joining the Board in the fall, but at the last minute he had concluded that his calendar wouldn't permit his sufficient attendance. (The two Board members who joined the HP Board in 2005 had been on the list as well.)

As was our process every year, the November Board meeting was reserved for a detailed discussion of the next year's operational plan. We now provided even more detail about the plans we'd talked about in September. The full executive team always participated in this session, and November of 2004 was no exception. The discussion was lively and the Board was pleased. We called our plan the Accelerated SPAR (strategic planning and review) because we were committing to a better plan than the baseline numbers that would become our threshold performance levels for compensation purposes. At this meeting the Board formally approved management's plan and authorized bonuses to be paid to the management team, including the CEO.

As was our practice, the Board went into executive session at the conclusion of the meeting. Bob Knowling was the chairman of the Nominating and Governance Committee. He had replaced Sam Ginn. Lucy Salhany had lobbied hard for this chair. She was simply not qualified to serve in this role for an $80 billion company, but I knew she was offended when I did not offer her the position. In his role as chair, Bob was responsible for leading executive sessions. He was also appropriately focused on the Board's effectiveness as a group. He had been pushing his fellow Board members to engage in a self-assessment for some time. Jay had always resisted this, both in the meetings and in private conversations. He contended that it was a waste of time, and the more Bob pushed for it, the more critical Jay became in his conversations with me. In the boardroom Jay seemed to lack respect for Bob, and Bob sometimes felt Jay was demeaning to him. Despite Jay's reluctance, however, Bob had finally succeeded in getting Board members to answer a questionnaire.

When I was asked to join the executive session, Bob said that one of the issues that had emerged from the questionnaire was inconsistent direction to the CEO. As a remedy, the Board had agreed that Bob Knowling would be designated to relay the relevant items from an executive session to the CEO. I understood this decision; we'd operated this way while Sam and Phil were on the board, and we were now returning to our standard practice. I guessed, although I did not know for certain, that Jay had resisted this.

Then Bob said a surprising thing. "Carly, some of the Board members feel we should bring Tom Perkins back onto the Board. We're having trouble recruiting another technical expert to fill in for Dick Hackborn when he chooses to retire." (Dick, though younger than Tom, had been threatening to retire for years.) "The rest of the Board agrees but we want to know what you think."

I WASN'T PREPARED for the question, and so I began thinking out loud. "Well, I don't think lack of technical expertise is our biggest problem on this Board. I think operational and big-company experience is a far greater need. Also, you may remember that we had a lot of very heated Board conversations back in 2003 about the retirement age, and we concluded that we didn't want to make exceptions. I'm not sure it will look particularly good to bring back a Board member who just retired when he's over the mandatory age limit. Tom was pretty clear when he retired that he didn't want to be asked to stay anyway. Do we even know whether he's interested?"

Now Jay jumped in. "As you know, Carly, I went to England to visit Tom on vacation. I think he really misses the Board and would love to come back." Lucy piled on. "I think he's lonely and needs something to do. I think he'd rejoin us if you asked him." Then Jay said, "Maybe he could come to our January off-site meeting to get back up to speed before we nominate him to the slate in March." We were planning a several-day, off-site Board meeting in January, such as we'd held in 2003 and in 2000.

Tom, like Jay, had lost his wife after a long battle with cancer. They had bonded over their common experience and were now close friends and confidants. I was happy for both of them. Only later did I learn that Jay had spent a lot of time telling Tom about all the ideas I'd rejected, from acquisitions to personnel moves.

I should have said no to all of it. No one else on the Board expressed any reservations, however, and I didn't think it was all that critical one way or the other. Why make a big issue of something that no one else seemed particularly concerned about?

Later, when I told him about the Board's decision, Bob Wayman was horrified. He thought I'd made a terrible mistake and that we would look foolish to the outside world. Our general counsel, Ann Baskins, felt the same way. So did our outside counsel, Larry Sonsini, when he was consulted. By then it was too late. None of them had been in the room to advise me, and Jay had rushed from the meeting to call his good friend Tom.

After the meeting, I was pleased when Jay approached me to express appreciation for Bob Knowling's role as chair. I thought that perhaps Jay would now be more supportive of Bob. "Carly, I think Bob can play an important role here in providing you with consistent feedback from our executive sessions." But Jay didn't allow Bob to play this role at all, and perhaps, in retrospect, Jay only supported the idea in November as a horse trade for Bob's agreement that Tom could return to the Board.

THROUGHOUT THE FALL of 2004 there were apparently persistent rumors circulating in the company that I would leave HP to pursue a political career. In fact, without looking for them I was offered several opportunities for meaningful and challenging public service. I did not pursue any of them; although I was tempted by some, this was exactly the wrong time to leave. We had momentum, and we needed to execute the plans that would solidify our success. Perhaps, I thought, my job will be finished in twelve months, but at a minimum we would need an agreed-upon succession plan in place before I could leave. And so I said no to all the opportunities that came my way.

I was advised by my management team to address the rumors directly during our all-employee meeting in December. And so I reminded employees that I had always told them our goal was to become the leading technology company in the world. HP's leadership would be defined by character, capability and collaboration. We would define our leadership by the numbers, but also by the positive difference we made for each other, our customers and our communities. "Every leader has a season, and some day mine will come to an end, but not yet. We still have a lot of work to do together."

Also in December, we had our semiannual meeting with Wall Street analysts and investors. At a previous meeting in June, I'd said that we were now focused on executing for leadership and growth. The strategy was in place, and we were now focused on operational programs. We'd described these programs. I'd also said that when the company executed well, we were clearly capable of earnings-per-share (EPS) growth of 20 percent or greater.

Our fourth quarter 2004 performance was strong, with record revenues in every business and the most balanced profitability across the portfolio since the merger. For the full fiscal year, despite our third quarter stumble, we'd grown revenues by 9 percent to $80 billion and generated a record $5 billion in profit from operations. And so at the December meeting we once again reiterated that the strategy was in place and that 2005 was all about execution. Given our third quarter miss, I knew there was great skepticism about both our execution abilities and the potential for 20 percent EPS growth. So we provided enormous details about all our operational programs.

I reminded our investors and analysts of what we'd told them in June about our execution priorities. I described the specific operational plans and performance programs we had in place around Accelerating Profitable Growth, Achieving Benchmark Cost Structures, Improving Performance Discipline and Accelerating Our Go-To-Market Effectiveness. These were the same programs we'd reviewed with the Board. The members of the management team who followed me presented sixty-three slides of detailed execution programs in every part of the business for over five hours. We did not talk about the size of planned layoffs specifically because we wanted to focus Wall Street on the performance of the business, not the numbers of heads we were cutting. Nevertheless, we were planning to make an additonal ten thousand to twelve thousand reductions during 2005.

At the conclusion of the meeting, I said: "We have provided first-half guidance. We don't intend to provide more than [that]. as has been our practice for the last several years. . . . We continue to use internal targets to represent the potential of this business and to drive the performance of this business. When we've talked about targets in the past, like eight to ten points of operating margin or twenty percent EPS growth, those are reasonable representations of the potential of this business, and they are reflective of the whole set of internal targets that we have to drive the performance of this business. . . . [These] are not the same as the guidance we provide." (Our guidance was always lower than our internal targets, as our investors were well aware.)

When I was asked a question about the economy in 2005 and the nature of the IT industry, I responded: "What I've said, actually since the day we announced the merger, is that IT is going through a structural transformation, not just an economic cycle. . . . [However] it is clear that the economic environment is improving. . . . [It] is a more stable, more mature industry with the growth rates that you would expect . . . two times [GDP] not five times [GDP]. . . . The economy is improving and confidence is returning.

In 2005, the economy fully recovered and HP went on to deliver over 20 percent EPS growth.

Two days prior to our January off-site meeting, Dick, Jay and Pattie came to see me. The group was odd and so was their timing. What was so urgent that they needed to see me forty-eight hours before we would have three days together? Why were they telling me they spoke "on behalf of the Board" when at our very last meeting we'd agreed that Bob Knowling would play this role when necessary? What they had to say was the oddest part of all. They began by expressing legitimate concern about the stock price, the perception of the performance of the company and the media reports. Then they gave me a precise prescription for how to reorganize the company into two units, with a president heading each. They even gave me the names of the presidents. Shane would become the president of a combined Customer Solutions Group (CSG) and Technology Solutions Group (TSG); Mike Winkler and Ann Livermore would report to him. Vyomesh Joshi would become the president of a combined Personal Systems Group (PSG) and Imaging and Printing Group (IPG). And they said the Board needed more ongoing communications with the CEO.

I asked them why they thought we should reorganize now. They said it would show "flexibility." We were under pressure in the market and in the press, and if we reorganized, we'd change the topic of conversation. It would show we were "doing something." I asked why they thought we needed more communication. In addition to our Board and committee meetings, Board members had frequent and unrestricted dialogue with any member of the management team at any time. They also had electronic access to any piece of information in the company. Pattie said she thought that we should have had a Board conference call when IBM had announced their decision to divest their PC business. I replied that it hadn't occurred to me, since they'd immediately had access to all the available information on the deal over the Board's Web site. I also expressed surprise that given the topic's supposed importance, neither Pattie nor any other Board member had asked about it during our September strategy session, which occurred just a few weeks after the deal was announced.

I assumed this meeting was a discussion. I did not believe this group could, or should, give me orders on how to execute and produce results. They became obviously offended when I didn't immediately embrace these ideas. Jay seemed particularly overwrought, so much so that I asked him straight out why he was so angry. From my perspective, their suggestions came out of left field and were half baked. Beyond that, what we needed now, what we'd just agreed to in November, was to stay the course and execute our 2005 plan. After about an hour of heated conversation, I suggested that we rearrange the upcoming Board agenda and spend the entire first day on the proposed reorganization and communications. The next day I met with my executive team and rearranged their calendars so we could accommodate this unexpected change in schedule.

The Board had always been able to find common ground with enough time for conversation. And so although the meeting irritated me, and although something about it didn't feel quite right, I arrived in San Francisco on Wednesday evening in good humor. I was immediately confronted by Jay Keyworth. "Carly, I thought we agreed to nominate Tom Perkins as a Board member right away. Ann Baskins says we can't vote on it at this meeting." Jay was agitated. "This is all just process bullshit. We can just vote him on. This is a critical meeting."

Now I defended Ann. "Jay, this Board needs to approve the company 10-K. Tom hasn't been part of the Board for a year. He can't attest to the company's performance or to the statement. He doesn't need to be voted on at this meeting. He can attend as a visitor as we agreed to in our November meeting, and we'll make sure he signs the appropriate documents for proprietary and insider information."

"That's ridiculous, Carly. He can skim the 10-K in an hour and sign it."

Once again, Jay had no patience for the basic processes of sound governance. He just wanted his buddy on the Board, although I couldn't understand the urgency. I was firm.

"No, Jay, he can't. These are serious statements that all Board members must review seriously. Bob Wayman and I are personally liable for their accuracy. No one can just skim them. It is not how this company does business."

Jay finally backed off, but he said, "Well, I'm going to bring this up with the whole Board tomorrow morning." That evening we all joined for a friendly, informal dinner, and Jay introduced his new lady friend to everyone. He seemed particularly eager to show her off to me.

The next morning we had the conversation all over again with the entire Board and Tom Perkins in attendance. I prevailed because I was adamant that we would not sacrifice our governance for an irrational urgency to return Tom to the Board. Having dispensed with this item, I asked each Board member to tell me about whatever was on their minds. Tom Perkins immediately began to play a very active role in the discussion. This was not a man coming up to speed after an extended absence. This was a man who had very strong opinions about everything from personnel to acquisitions, despite never having seen the 2005 plan that the Board had approved in November. He said we'd made a mistake in not acquiring a large software company a few months earlier. When I gave him our bankers' view that the acquisition would take half our cash and probably 20 percent off the stock price, he seemed undeterred. He was certain that Ann Livermore was unqualified to run the Technology Solutions Group. We should reorganize right away, in the way Dick, Pattie and Jay had suggested, and Shane Robison should be promoted. Jay concurred vigorously with each of Tom's suggestions.

I told them that as CEO, I was accountable for performance. Shane was not qualified to do the job. I pointed out the actual facts around Ann's performance. I reminded Tom that he'd made mistakes in his judgments about personnel before. Against my better judgment, I'd left Peter Blackmore in his job nine months longer than was wise based on Tom's guidance. I was accountable for the decision but I wasn't going to make the same mistake twice. Lucy Salhany said, "You're right, Carly. I remember you telling us you thought you needed to make a change. We talked you out of it." I was grateful for her honesty.

As the day wore on, each Board member had his or her own particular view about potential reorganizations and personnel. Despite assertions by Pattie, Jay and Dick on Monday, this Board was not, as usual, aligned in its thinking. By the end of a very long day, we had agreed on several things. One was that we would combine the Personal Systems and Imaging and Printing groups into a single unit with Vyomesh Joshi as its head. I had agreed with this part of their recommendation. It was a timely decision, and we were prepared to execute. I would spend until after midnight that evening working with several managers so we could make an announcement the following morning.

Second, because the Board had such strong and differing views about various executives' capabilities, we would ask Shane, Ann and Vyomesh to meet individually with the Board on Saturday. This had been my suggestion. I was hoping that with some extended time for conversation, the group's views on these people might begin to align. We also came, I thought, to some basic agreements about how we would evaluate various organizational alternatives over the next three to six months. Mike Winkler and I had agreed that he would be retiring in the summer when the sales force transformation would be complete. This was the logical time to consolidate TSG and CSG.

I wasn't opposed to change, and I wasn't opposed to considering their suggestions. I just didn't think one of their specific suggestions would work, and I thought it was my call. If a CEO is accountable for results, then a CEO must make the decisions necessary to deliver those results. I also didn't believe in announcements as distractions. I didn't believe you did something just to show "flexibility." Reorganizations are always disruptive, so they shouldn't be done unless the benefits outweigh the real costs of that disruption. Rearranging the deck chairs might look good on paper, but it wreaks havoc in an organization.

On Saturday, after the Board had met with the three executives, no one's views had changed much. Jay and Tom hadn't changed their minds at all about either Shane or Ann. The rest had various views about various people. Bob and Larry thought the Board should "butt out" and let the CEO make the call. We summarized all of our agreements on how to continue the personnel and organizational discussion during our next several Board meetings. I made it clear that I wasn't prepared to do something I didn't think would work, although I did think there were some good opportunities to further simplify and streamline the business over the next several quarters. I also made it clear that if we could not come to consensus about personnel and structure, ultimately I had to decide.

At the end of the meeting, Lucy said, "You know, Carly, everyone can be wrong sometimes, and this time the Board was wrong." Dick took me aside that evening and said he thought that I was absolutely right about Shane. Our evening functions were as warm and friendly as ever, and Jay's girlfriend told me how much Jay liked and admired me.

I was tired by the end of those three days. I felt as though we'd spent an enormous amount of energy on too many of the wrong things. Nonetheless, I believed that in the end, we'd had a reasoned and reasonable conversation. The Board had heard even more detail about the operational plans that were now in place and against which their organization would execute. The Board declared its substantial satisfaction with both the operational details and the anticipated results of these plans, as I conveyed to my management team in an e-mail message following the conclusion of the meeting. I was satisfied, but I remained troubled by the picture of Jay and Tom huddling together during every break in the meeting.

The following Friday afternoon I received an urgent phone call from one of our press people. The *Wall Street Journal* was going to print a detailed story the next Monday morning about our Board meeting. The reporter was talking to at least two, possibly three, Board members. Was it true we were going to reorganize? Did I have a comment?

It is hard to convey how violated I felt. Until a Board makes a decision, its deliberations are confidential. Whoever had done this had broken a bond of trust with me and every other Board member. I remembered how damaging the leak about the merger, the night before our announcement, had been. I remembered how outraged these same Board members had been when Walter had breached our confidence, and draft compensation agreements had been leaked to the media. Trust is a business imperative. No Board or management team can operate effectively without it.

I was also angry. Whoever had done this was arrogant and foolish enough to believe that their personal agenda, whatever it was, outweighed every other consideration. They had put their own interests ahead of the company's. Perhaps they thought they would put pressure on me to reorganize the company the way they wanted. Perhaps they did not care that they had also put enormous pressure on every single employee and certainly on the executives named in the article. This article would now be the subject of conversation with every customer, every partner and in every management meeting. It would be what employees gossiped about around the water cooler. It would give our competitors and our critics one more thing to point to. It did not help us perform; it distracted us from performance.

Adding to the pressure was the fact that Ann Livermore, Mike Winkler and I were heading out to the World Economic Forum in Davos, Switzerland. This is an annual conference where most of the world's business and political leaders gather, along with the world press. It was a great occasion to meet with customers and conduct business because you could see so many people in one spot in a concentrated period of just a few days. All of our calendars were chock full of important meetings there. And the *Wall Street Journal* story would hit the front page just as the conference was beginning. Quite literally, the other HP executives and I would have to explain ourselves, and our Board, to the world. When the story came out, it was quite obvious that Board members were in disagreement inside the boardroom, and so they had chosen to speak outside.

I sent an e-mail message to the Board. I informed them of the leak. I said this was completely unacceptable behavior by a Board member. I convened a conference call for Saturday morning. I was as cold as ice during the call. I said the Board could not operate in this way and I would not. Pattie was on vacation in Bali and didn't yet know what had happened. She would never ask me about that call, although later she would tell others that "everything changed" as a result of it. Jay, Dick and Tom all acknowledged that the reporter had contacted them. They all denied they had spoken with her. Jay, in particular, launched into a detailed defense of why the leak couldn't possibly have come from him. Lucy had also been contacted by the reporter, but she had called our press office immediately. She, Bob Knowling and Larry Babbio expressed shock and outrage. Was the room bugged? I assured them that I always had the rooms electronically swept by our security personnel. Could anyone have found the large sheets of easel paper I'd written on to document our agreements? I'd shredded them myself.

Larry Babbio said every Board member should immediately resign, and I should determine who would stand for reelection in March. I suggested instead that we ask the Nominating and Governance Committee to launch an investigation to be conducted by outside counsel. On rare other occasions when we'd had an ethical issue arise in the company that warranted the Board's attention, the Audit Committee had conducted an investigation with outside counsel. Because this was a matter internal to the Board, I felt the Nominating and Governance Committee should handle this one. No one argued.

Bob Knowling convened the committee by telephone ten minutes later. The members agreed that Larry Sonsini would interview each Board member. Bob requested that Larry use the interviews to conduct not only an investigation, but also an objective assessment of the Board. Beyond the leak, there was much about the Board's dynamics that was disturbing. The committee agreed. Each Board member should be asked their views of the effectiveness of the Board, the qualifications of each Board member and how we could improve our meetings and deliberations. I thought it was a great idea. We needed to know what had happened to ensure that it never happened again, but perhaps we could also accomplish something more positive and productive. I thought we could weather this storm; we had weathered so many. I didn't expect anyone to resign over this, nor did I intend to ask. I thought this could be a useful wake-up call to several Board members who were not as smart as they thought they were.

In turns out I wasn't as smart as I needed to be. Somehow, at some point during the next two weeks, certain Board members would decide to fire me.

30 | Owning My Soul

A T HOME on Sunday, February 6, 2005, I prepared for Monday's Board meeting. Ten days earlier, on our last Board call, Larry Sonsini had reported on his investigation into the leak and his assessment of the Board's dynamics. He informed us that two, possibly three, Board members had leaked confidential Board conversations. His report named only one member, because only Tom Perkins was honest enough to admit that he'd spoken to the press, although he was adamant that he had been a "second source." Although I appreciated Tom's candor, I was deeply disturbed when no one else spoke up. As the call progressed, all but one Board member asked questions or made comments.

Larry Sonsini's report had also described the Board as "dysfunctional" in important ways. I agreed with this assessment, as I knew others did as well; navigating through the thicket of personalities, ambitions and emotions had become both draining and counterproductive. A few members could take the whole Board off track by insisting on and then dominating lengthy discussions about topics that weren't germane to the agenda.

Some Board members' behavior was amateurish and immature. Some didn't do their homework. Some had fixed opinions on certain topics and no opinion at all on others. Some members were bored and distracting during important agenda items like leadership development or corporate social responsibility. This is why Bob Knowling had insisted upon, and why I supported, a Board evaluation process; we needed to acknowledge and address these real issues in an individual member's capabilities and behavior as well as in the group's dynamics.

After Larry had finished making his report, we'd turned our attention to the annual shareholders meeting, which was also our next scheduled Board meeting. Given all the recent publicity, shareholders would seek clarification from management and the Board. Were we still committed to the strategy? Were we going to reorganize, perhaps in preparation for the split-up of the company that many detractors were calling for? And so we decided to schedule a special February Board meeting to align our thinking and prepare our responses. To prevent any more press speculation about our activities, we'd chosen the Chicago airport, rather than Palo Alto headquarters, as our location.

I was mystified by the Board's recent behavior. I was suspicious of Jay's heated denials when the leak first occurred and then his complete silence on our last call. I was now appalled by the reemergence of Tom Perkins and the very active role he was clearly playing. He wasn't even a Board member yet. And I was gravely concerned by the lack of contact from any Board member since our last phone call. Larry Sonsini told me that various Board members were talking to one another. What had they talked about in those intervening ten days? Why did they feel it necessary to exclude me? Who had made accusations about me that I could not refute or defend?

For five and a half years I had dedicated enormous effort on behalf of the company and in pursuit of our agreed-upon goals. At a minimum I thought I'd earned an open conversation and some honest feedback about what was really going on. Yet I knew Dick did not give direct feedback. Tom clearly had an agenda, although I didn't understand what it was. Jay was emotional and overwrought. Lucy was insecure and could be swayed by others. Pattie seemed extraordinarily pleased to be playing a more leading role. Bob Ryan was brand-new. I could not gauge him, but he did not know his fellow Board members as well as I did.

And so I was tense and pessimistic on that Sunday. Some might wonder why I did not take it upon myself to call every single Board member and plead for my job or demand an explanation or make amends, but those ten days were filled from morning to night with all the commitments and decisions and actions that came with being a CEO. Beyond that, I didn't think it was my role to talk the Board into or out of a particular course of action; I hadn't talked the Board into hiring me and I would not talk them out of firing me if that's what they were truly contemplating. I was accountable for my own behavior and decisions. The Board would have to be accountable for theirs.

Frank kept telling me to stop worrying. He reminded me that just three weeks earlier Jay had been planning the May Board meeting on our boat. (Soon after Jay's wife died, he'd asked if he could bring his grandson to California and stay with us. Frank had entertained them for two days, and Jay had loved Frank's boat.) My husband remembered his conversation with Pattie that same evening. Pattie and her husband were both semiretired and about to leave for their Bali vacation. Frank had been fantasizing about how great life would be once I retired, and Pattie had responded, "Sorry, Frank. Encouraging Carly's retirement is against my fiduciary duty."

He could not convince me. I knew my anxiety was justified. I thought about my brief conversation with Pattie a few days earlier. I'd telephoned because to maintain secrecy her secretary had arranged the upcoming meeting. After we discussed logistics, I asked, "Pattie, is there anything I should know about this meeting? Is there anything you would advise me to do?"

"Carly, I know the leak was very unfortunate. If you could find it in your heart to go back to where we were in San Francisco, I think it would help. And I don't think you should tell anyone about this conversation."

We had talked about so much in San Francisco. We'd talked about strategy and personnel and structure. We'd agreed on many things and disagreed on some. What had I said and why? Where did we agree and where did we disagree? Given all the events of the past few weeks, there was perhaps real confusion about it. Some of our Board members tended to forget conversations from one meeting to the next. Other Board members attributed words to me that were not my own. Jay and Tom spoke to some Board members but not others. A detailed summary of our discussions was in order.

So I began to write points responsive to Pattie's advice to "go back to where we were in San Francisco," and I wrote to convey my respect for and appreciation of the Board's role. They had hired me and they could fire me. I wrote to convey my agreement that healthy debate was paramount: if I was preventing open communication in some way, I wanted to acknowledge it. I wrote to bring clarity to the table after a series of damaging and emotional events. Whatever the motivation behind those events, we could afford no miscommunication now. No Board can carry out its fiduciary duty without candor between members, care for due process, and trust that confidences will be maintained. When I finished writing, I decided to use this document as the starting point to our discussions the following morning. I did not know what various Board members were thinking, but I was determined to put the leak behind us, assume everyone had learned a lesson, and move forward on the basis of clarity and mutual respect.

There was to be no conversation the next day. When I arrived in the meeting room, the dynamics were clear. Despite his long-term disdain, I now saw Jay whispering in Pattie's ear and laughing with her at some private joke. Pattie kicked the meeting off. This in itself was strange. She was not the chair of any committee. Everyone but me seemed to know what was about to happen. She asked that the Board accept Sandy Litvack's resignation. Sandy had apparently informed his fellow Board members that he would resign rather than be a part of whatever was going to happen at this meeting. She asked the Board to vote on Tom Perkins's reelection. I abstained. I felt conflicted and unable to separate my personal misgivings about the role Tom was playing from my fiduciary duties. I didn't understand what was happening. Two others voted no. It was the first time in my tenure at HP that a decision of our Board was not unanimous. My ouster would be the second.

Larry Sonsini mentioned a meeting that had apparently taken place the night before between some Board members and a governance expert. I hadn't been made aware of it or invited to it, despite my role as chairman of the Board. It was as if I weren't in the room at all. No one would look me in the eye. And then Pattie said, "Carly, do you have anything to say?"

I was startled. This wasn't going to be a conversation; apparently the Board wanted a statement. I had made copies of the document I'd prepared the day before so now I passed them around the table. I expressed regret that a formal statement was necessary but also understood that clarity was now paramount. I began to read, hoping to be interrupted.

Here is what I said:

I serve at the pleasure of the Board. I have served in order to build a great company. I believe the Board determined that HP could be a technology leader of the 21st century, in much the same way that HP was once a leader in the 1950's, 60's, 70's and 80's. This mission of leadership was confirmed when the Board decided to undertake the complex, difficult and risky split-up of the company into HP and Agilent. This mission was reconfirmed when the Board decided to undertake the complex, difficult and risky acquisition of Compaq. Throughout this period, the pace and magnitude of change in the technology industry has been unprecedented and it continues to be so.

Given the difficulty of our mission, this company requires the best thinking of all our Board members. It is the Board's job to challenge management's thinking, assumptions and plans. We must have a healthy dialogue and debate around the Board table. Every voice must be heard, every idea examined. I am passionate and I believe this Board deserves my absolute candor. However, if I am angry or defensive or close-minded during these discussions, then I have failed. After a healthy debate, there comes a time for decision. And once a decision is made, there must be a period of execution, during which time we stay the course.

I have served because I believe deeply in this company, its people, its potential to make a positive contribution to the industry and the world, and because I believe our mission of greatness and leadership is achievable. While I appreciate the Board's decisions on my compensation, I have not served for monetary gain. I have voluntarily refused contractually guaranteed bonuses and retention payments and given up my own employment contract so that the Board could respond favorably to a shareholder vote and all the executives at HP would be treated consistently. We have set tough goals for both target and aspirational performance. Throughout this period, I have received many offers to do other things—many of which have been interesting and attractive. My first obligation is to this company and I will not leave unless it is in the company's best interests that I do so—or the Board decides it is time to do so.

ON STRATEGY

This Board has made and reconfirmed the most fundamental aspects of our strategy: that while we will compete against both Dell and IBM we must also differentiate ourselves; that we will retain a unique portfolio of imaging, computing, software and services capabilities; that we will serve the consumer, business and public sector markets. All of these decisions can be and should be revisited if the Board feels it is necessary. My personal belief is that our strategy is sound and our greater issue is execution. However, I also think the most important element of our strategy that now needs serious work is software. While our execution has sometimes been uneven in the rest of the portfolio, I think the fundamental capability exists to achieve our mission. In software, I think we now must contemplate either the acquisition of assets that will be financially difficult, perhaps almost impossible in the short term, or the aggressive and active commoditization of the software stack.

ON EXECUTION

Execution is the most important matter requiring both the Board's and management's attention. I believe we are completely aligned on the urgent requirement to accelerate execution and improve consistency. Where we have differed is around specific structural solutions. Perhaps we are driven by different assumptions and operating principles. Allow me to elaborate on my own thinking:

1) I have been operating under an assumption that the Board is vitally interested in hiring outside talent as potential successors to the CEO. In March, May and July of 2004 the Board indicated that this was a top priority. We agree that our bench strength beneath the CEO is inadequate. We have therefore been undertaking a wide search across multiple industries (see attached list of candidates we are interviewing). I believe that to bring in one or several of these candidates, we may well have to create the

right job for them. In other words, some of our structural solutions may need to be driven by a specific candidate.

2) In some cases, our acquisitions may drive structural solutions. For example, if we were to complete a major software acquisition, we would have to create a stand-alone software business, reporting to the CEO. The leader of this business might also represent a succession candidate.

3) We may have divergent views on how the business operates today. HP is less a company characterized by centralized corporate functions and decentralized businesses, and more a company of horizontal, distributed processes and vertical, line-of-sight P&L responsibilities. This is certainly not unique to HP. Virtually all large, complex companies are moving in this direction. These horizontal processes have allowed us to simultaneously drive cost and expenses down while building new capabilities. Our current operating model means that changes in processes drive real changes in behavior. In other words, process change can be as meaningful as structural change. This is why I believe changing our ASPIRE and SPAR processes, effective immediately, can have a real impact on the speed and locus of portfolio and investment decision making.

4) We agreed completely that the creation of IPSG was the right move at the right time. Reorganizations are always disruptive to the momentum of a business. Therefore considerations of timeliness and readiness are key to ensuring that the benefits outweigh the risks. IPG and PSG were ready. My own judgment is that CSG and TSG are not yet in a similar state of readiness, although they will be within a relatively short period—certainly within the fiscal year. We are in agreement that the combination of these two organizations makes sense at the right time with the right leader. We appear to have differing opinions with regard to the timing, and the leadership. In some cases we have divergent views on the capabilities of certain individuals.

5) Because day-to-day execution in our business is difficult and complex in the best of circumstances, I believe that constancy

of purpose and stability are key until we are completely prepared to make a change. Rumors of change can undermine a business.

I have laid out these thoughts on execution for the purpose of clarity, not for the purposes of bringing our conversations to a close. Sometimes what appear to be differences of opinion on a solution are actually differences of perspective on the problem or underlying assumptions.

I believe the "Accelerated SPAR" or "Operational Priorities" work that we have undertaken as a management team for FY2005 is extremely important. We now have detailed programs throughout the company around Accelerating Profitable Growth, Achieving Benchmark Cost Structures, Improving Performance Discipline and Go-To-Market Effectiveness. We will continue to review these programs and our progress with the Board on a regular basis. The impact of this work on profitability, cash flow and multiple expansion should not be underestimated.

ON CEO PERFORMANCE

At this point I am somewhat uncertain as to the process for CEO evaluation. Understanding that the Board has a great deal of information already, I thought it would be useful to provide some additional context, particularly given the recent, very negative, and in some cases, inaccurate press.

As you know, management's performance is measured against a balanced scorecard of financial performance, operational improvements, customer-driven metrics, and employee-related items. Both our target and aspirational goals for each category consistently represent real improvement and are difficult to achieve.

I've attached some facts on our financial and operational performance which have been inconsistently or under-reported by the media. With regard to employees, our Voice of the Workforce participation rate improved from 67% in 2003 to 77% in 2004. We made strong improvements in our key areas of focus from 2003. I have attached these. We also identified four areas of company-wide focus (also attached) and have rolled out action plans to address these. We just completed our pulse-survey to test our progress. 80% of our employees indicated they saw real momentum and action.

With regard to customers, I've also attached our most recent TCE results. We have made real progress and we have real work left to do.

We have also set tough goals for Total Shareholder Return—we must perform at least as well as the S&P in 2004, 2005, and 2006 in order to receive our payouts for operational cash flow performance. We have set these goals despite the fact that both HPQ and IBM have underperformed the S&P and the DJIA over a twenty-year horizon, although IBM has underperformed by a wider margin and in every year, whereas HPQ has outperformed in certain periods and been on par or below the others. I have attached multiple-year comparisons of HPQ vs. IBM, Dell, SUNW, EMC, LXK, EDS, Intel, MSFT, ORCL, CSCO, MOT, Agilent, EK, and GTW if the Board is interested.

ON BOARD COMMUNICATIONS

I am anxious to discuss and agree on any changes we believe will improve Board communications. These are the steps we've already taken, in addition to our regularly scheduled Board and committee meetings:

- Board Website
- Access to @HP portal
- Regular updates to the Board by members of management at both committee and Board meetings. Frequent contact with management outside of regular meetings, on an ad hoc basis and as desired by Board members
- Published calendar of board topics to assist in agenda planning
- Regular survey of members for desired agenda items
- All major organizational changes discussed with the Board in advance
- Ongoing talent reviews
- We've just agreed to add monthly calls.

The Board also agrees that recruiting new members is a top priority. This has been a slow and frustrating process for everyone. I've attached a list of the director prospects we've spoken to. I am eager to collaborate with the Board on how we can improve this process to achieve better results.

I finished reading, hoping to be asked a question. I was met with complete silence. And then Pattie asked me to leave the room. Having traveled two thousand miles, I was dismissed in about twenty-nine minutes.

It would be three hours before I would be asked to return to the conference room. In those hours I thought about my service on the Kellogg Board. That Board had determined that a change at the top was necessary. The CEO hadn't been ready to go, but he was well aware of the Board's deliberations and their reasoning. He was asked for his recommendation on succession, which was ultimately accepted. He was consulted about the transition. He was thanked, and his contributions were honored. There were company celebrations to commemorate his service. There was closure and an orderly passing of the baton from one generation to the next. It had been the same when John Young and Lew Platt were asked to leave. There was acknowledgment and thanks, closure and a passing of the baton.

Except in a few cases of alleged fraud or malfeasance, virtually every other CEO succession I had read or known about was handled in the same way. An orderly transition is not simply about respect for the individual; a deliberate succession process is basic to good governance because it provides calming continuity and clear direction to an organization in a time of potential turmoil.

I knew that every leader has a season, and as I sat in that hotel room I realized that my season was perhaps coming to an unexpected and abrupt end for reasons I did not understand. And yet I expected the Board to look me in the eye and tell me why.

They did not have the courage to face me. They did not thank me and they did not say good-bye. They did not explain their decision or their reasoning. They did not seek my opinion or my involvement in any aspect of the transition. When I finally received the call to rejoin the meeting, I thought about each Board member as I rode the elevator down past those twenty-four floors. I didn't know what to expect, but I assumed I would be facing them. I wasn't prepared for the empty conference room I entered.

When I opened the door and realized all but two Board members had already left, I knew I had been fired. When Bob Knowling said, "The Board has decided to make a change. I'm very sorry, Carly," I knew he had opposed my ouster. When Pattie, who had become the new chairman of the Board, said they wanted to make an announcement immediately, I realized I would not be treated like other CEOs. The meeting lasted less than three minutes. I asked for a few hours to think, and I left the room.

When I returned to my hotel room less than ten minutes after I'd left, my hands shook from the shock. Tears came to Frank's eyes. He truly had never believed this could happen.

Pattie had asked for my help in "positioning" the shocking news. She said the Board thought I should announce this as my decision. I should say I'd decided it was "time to move on." I believe the truth is always the best answer, whatever the consequences. Less than two hours after I left the room, I sent a message to the new chairman saying we should tell the truth: the Board had fired me.

When Frank and I got home, we called our families. We could not explain what had happened, we could only prepare them for what would happen next. They would see my picture over and over and read and hear terrible things about me. It would be the same all over the world. The coverage of my departure would vastly outweigh the news of the contemporaneous corporate scandals and the disgraced and indicted CEOs of Tyco, WorldCom, Enron, Adelphia and Qwest.

I was utterly devastated, but the next day the sun still came up and life went on. That day, and in the days that followed, I was more hurt than angry. I felt a curious mixture of sorrow and relief. I had worked so hard for so long; I had thought about the company constantly; I'd put everything on the line, and now suddenly it was over. I thought about my team and longed for the opportunity to gather them together and thank them and wish them well. I thought about the people of a company I had grown to love, and I ached for the chance to say good-bye and reminisce, one last time, about the remarkable journey we had taken together. I was never given the chance.

I took both solace and pride in phone calls I received from CEOs, from past and present presidents and prime ministers, from secretaries of state and secretaries-general, from powerful, prominent people all over the world. I called and thanked the Board members who had fought against my ouster and voted no. My spirits were lifted by the messages of encouragement I received from people of long ago and far away who took the trouble to track me down and tell me I'd made a difference in their lives. Yet it was the thousands of e-mail messages from the people of HP that got me through the next few weeks. They told me we'd accomplished more together than they had ever believed was possible. This, for me, is the essence of leadership.

My firing clearly changed the sentiment around the stock, which began to climb. Some investors thought the company would be split up after all. In fact, the Board had to reiterate their support for the strategy as the rumor gained strength. The Board announced that it would pay Bob Wayman a $3.5 million bonus to act as the interim CEO. He played that role for forty-five days, after which a new CEO was recruited from another company. When there was some controversy around a stock sale the new CEO had made, the board indicated that they'd identified, hired and announced my successor in ten short days.

The stock continued to climb as the organization executed the strategy and the 2005 plan we'd worked on so hard together and presented to the Board in November and January and to Wall Street in December. The company reversed the decision to combine PCs and printing, which Jay, Dick and Pattie had pushed so hard for. When Mike Winkler retired, they combined both the sales force and TSG under Ann Livermore, giving Ann the increased responsibilities that Tom and Jay had so vehemently argued against in January. Shane Robison remained chief technology officer and was not given additional duties.

I was pressed to accept another job immediately. There were many wonderful and flattering opportunities. In our society activity is frequently interpreted as significance, and I was advised by some to jump back into the fray. The wiser counsel was to take the time to rediscover life. And so I chose to pause and reflect.

As weeks became months I asked myself over and over what had happened. Were there signals I'd missed? Was there something I should have said or done that would have made the difference? Despite the earlier objections of some Board members to the idea, I had been planning to hire a consultant to work with the Board on the communications issues and "dysfunction" that clearly existed. What if I had done this sooner? Would the outcome have been the same if the two experienced CEOs, Sam Ginn and Phil Condit, had remained on the Board? Or if we'd been able to recruit more new members sooner? Did some Board members buckle under the pressure they felt because of the negative press and the stock price? Were some afraid they would lose their Board seats, either because of the leak or because of the assessment, and decide I had to go first? What if Tom Perkins hadn't returned? Was Jay, who was emotional and fancied himself my mentor, so antagonized by our open disagreements that he wanted me out at all costs? Was Tom able to persuade others in a way Jay alone could not? Having counted on my strength to complete a very difficult merger and drive the successful transformation of a company against great odds, did Board members now resent that same strength when I used it to reject their suggestions and condemn behavior like sharing Board room conversations with the *Wall Street Journal*? Or did they simply conclude they didn't need me anymore?

I thought a great deal about Jay and Tom and Dick. All three of them had historical connections with the Hewletts and Packards. Tom used to talk about his close relationship with Dave, although others seemed skeptical and rolled their eyes during these stories. Dick had served on the Hewlett Foundation Board, but had become estranged from Walter and the rest of the family when they opposed the merger. Jay had been a close friend of David Woodley Packard's until they, too, became estranged over the merger. Dick, Jay and Tom believed they were the only members of the Board who really understood how Bill and Dave had operated. In my last Board meeting they were still quoting Bill and Dave and reminiscing about how things used to be, just as they had in every other Board meeting.

I know they were bothered by the loss of ongoing contact with the families. Some of them were reunited at the official ribbon-cutting ceremony at the original garage when it was reopened after the completion of its restoration. And family members visited HP headquarters for the first time since the announcement of the merger. My firing had apparently settled a score.

All throughout 2005 I was hounded by reporters from television, magazines and newspapers to tell my side of the story. I have not spoken until now. I wanted time to reflect and for the ground to cool. I wanted to preserve my own and the company's dignity. What possible benefit could come from an argument waged in sound bites? Some Board members continued to talk to the press to explain their decision. Some said there were other meetings between Board members in January, or even in December. I do not know if this is true, but as chairman and CEO, I was never made aware of these meetings, never saw any meeting minutes and never received any feedback about what might have been discussed.

I received a letter from Pattie Dunn in which she expressed her admiration for my leadership—"you will remain a hero"—and regret that her role had been "misconstrued" by the press. She would not give me permission to publish the letter, fearing that it would be used in "a context that would reflect negatively on [her] and/or the Board." I received a letter from Tom Perkins. He granted me permission to publish it:

> I miss seeing you and I hope that you are well along in mapping out your next career move. If it should be to seek an elected office, I would be honored if you would let me participate on the fund-raising side.
>
> Probably we will never agree on what happened at HP, but I would like you to know that I, personally, think you moved the company forward in giant steps in the Compaq acquisition and in the consolidation of the two businesses. Today's HP wouldn't have the potential it clearly has, if you hadn't made those moves.

I have never heard from Dick Hackborn or Jay Keyworth.

The year 2005 did turn out to be the payoff year I'd expected. The economy continued to gather strength all over the world. As I'd predicted, Dell, IBM and Lexmark all stumbled and missed targets. HP performed magnificently and delivered the plan. I was proud of the management team and the people of HP. The company's 2005 results finally demonstrated that HP had indeed been transformed.

Life isn't always fair, and I was playing in the big leagues. Yet I realized I had no regrets. I had completed my mandate. I had made mistakes, but I had made a difference. I had given everything I had to a company and a cause I believed in. I had made tough choices, and I could live with their consequences. While I grieved for the people and the purpose I had lost, I did not grieve for the loss of my soul.

Epilogue

December 31, 2005

I T IS 11:30 A.M. I am sitting by the indoor pool at the Courtyard by Marriott hotel in West Homestead, Pennsylvania, watching our granddaughter Kara play in the swimming pool with her cousins Jacob and Jordan. Tonight she'll have a makeup party with her cousins Jennifer and Marissa. We went to Target yesterday to buy the evening's party favors. Altogether we'll be twenty-three people tonight, a loud, rambunctious group ranging in age from eighteen months to ninety-six years ringing in the New Year and celebrating just by being together.

As is my habit, I am reflecting on the year I have just lived. One year ago Frank and I had been with Carole; her husband, Greg; and Judy and Roger Hudson. As we moved around the kitchen preparing dinner, Carole had asked me, "What do you want in 2005?" I paused to think about it. A few weeks earlier, Dan Plunkett had asked me, "What's missing in your life?" I'd answered slowly, "Moments of spontaneous joy."

HP had consumed me. My entire life was programmed around it— every moment on the calendar, in advance. I did not resent it; for me HP had become, as I had told employees, "more than a job—it is a labor of love." Still, freedom and spontaneity had been sacrificed. There was always something to worry about, and a moment of joy is a moment when the soul is allowed to float, weightless. I thought about all this before I answered Carole: "I just want to be happy."

There were days after I was fired when I had to will myself not to read what was being written or watch what was being said. There were days when I had to will myself just to put one foot in front of the other: "Get out of bed, go to the gym, and definitely do not eat another piece of chocolate." Some days I succeeded, some days I failed.

There were days when I felt the weight of the world had been lifted from my shoulders. There were dark days when I replayed the boardroom scenes over and over in my mind and wondered again why I had been betrayed. There were days when I rejoiced in the simple pleasures of my new life: cooking dinner for my husband and friends, shoe shopping with my sister, arranging a bouquet of flowers. And there are days when I have that same giddy feeling I had when I quit law school: "My life is my own. I can do what I choose."

I cherish my freedom. Frank and I rented a van and drove across country and back. We spend more time with friends and family and bought an apartment in Georgetown, in Washington, D.C., to be closer to both. I enjoy doing only what I choose. I am free to say no. I know I will someday again find a cause to which I will commit all my passions. I know I will find a group of people to fall in love with again. But not yet. Not today. For now I celebrate my freedom and the contentment of a smaller, quieter life.

I love to watch the sun rise and the sun set. I take comfort in the everyday event and feel wonder knowing that it will never be the same. I love the slower, natural cadence of my life. I love to fall asleep at night and awake when I choose. I love to do something on the spur of the moment. I love to spend an hour watching the hawk or the woodpecker or the hummingbird. I love to spend a day, as I am today, in the company of children with nothing particular to do and nowhere particular to go.

I believe I have been blessed all my life. I feel blessed today—blessed to have had the opportunities and the experiences. Blessed to have met those people whose paths I've crossed. Blessed to now have financial independence beyond anything I ever imagined. Blessed to be loved by those I love. I have said the words *I am not afraid* many times in my life. I have whispered them to convince myself. I have spoken them aloud to convince others. And today I know they are finally true. My soul is my own and I am at peace.

The smell of chlorine is strong. The children's laughter echoes off the tiles. Their cannonball jumps into the pool splash water on this page. And as 2005 draws to a close, I know I have been given what I asked for. My life is filled with moments of spontaneous joy. I am happy.

Index